COMMUNITARIANISM AND CITIZENSHIP

Communitarianism and Citizenship

Edited by
EMILIOS A. CHRISTODOULIDIS

Ashgate
Aldershot • Brookfield USA • Singapore • Sydney

Published by
Ashgate Publishing Ltd
Gower House
Croft Road
Aldershot
Hants GU11 3HR
England

Ashgate Publishing Company
Old Post Road
Brookfield
Vermont 05036
USA

JF
801
. C62
1998

British Library Cataloguing in Publication Data
Communitarianism and citizenship. - (Association for legal
    and social philosophy series)
    1.Communitarianism 2.Citizenship
    I. Christodoulidis, Emilios A.
    172.1

Library of Congress Catalog Card Number: 98-74122

ISBN 1 84014 872 1

Printed and bound by Antony Rowe Ltd

Contents

About the UK Association for Legal and Social Philosophy

The UK Association for Legal and Social Philosophy (ALSP) is open to everyone interested in the interaction between theory and practice in the areas of legal, social and political thought; the interplay between these areas; and the applications and outcomes arising out of the inter-disciplinary nature of such debate. In seeking to extend debate beyond the traditional academy, it is especially concerned to include students and practitioners in its activities, as well as to promote discussion with, among and beyond full-time academics.

Membership is currently £20 (waged) or £10 (unwaged) per annum, which includes a subscription to *Res Publica: A Journal of Social and Legal Philosophy* and the Association's newsletter. For details, please write to the Treasurer, Ms P FitzGerald, 7 Adur Court, Stoney Lane, Shoreham-by-Sea, West Sussex BN43 6LY.

Introduction

EMILIOS A. CHRISTODOULIDIS

In his excellent book *The New Reckoning*, David Marquand identifies the following 'cruel paradox': '[o]ne of the reasons why social cohesion and mutual trust loom so large in the new discourse of the 1990s is that the creative destruction associated with untamed capitalism has done so much to undermine them' (1997, p. 30). The paradox becomes more acute as it becomes obvious that the very forces that unleashed the destruction of 'social cohesion and mutual trust' are the ones that have also been the most vigorous in appropriating the discourse of community in their defence. In Britain, as elsewhere, Conservatism's successful move from reactionary ideology to progressive force owes much of its success to its appropriation of the twin ideals of community and active citizenship. The appropriation is remarkable not as to its extent but in that it occurred at all, uprooting the ideals from their natural habitat in the discourse of the left and thus, as Glasman (1996) notes in a similar context, undermining the very rationality of Marxism and social democracy.

The current political fascination with community owes much of its inspiration to the rise of communitarian theory in the academy during the eighties, with the publication in the early part of the decade of MacIntyre's pivotal *After Virtue* and Sandel's *Liberalism and the Limits of Justice*. Communitarian critics of modern liberalism questioned the fundamental philosophical assumptions of liberalism. They questioned the claim of the priority of the right over the good and the picture of the freely-choosing individual it embodied, one that, according to Sandel, was both its inspiration and its undoing. They argued that we cannot justify political arrangements without reference to common purposes and ends and that we cannot understand personhood without reference to our role as citizens and as participants in a common life. Liberalism, they argued, misunderstands the constitutive ways in which social contexts inform and undergird identity and thus also the meaning of what it means to act autonomously and freely. Freedom was not something that one had to guard *from* people but something that needed to be reconceptualized as flourishing *within* social interdependence.

1

The theoretical debate has moved on since, from the 'thick' communitarian critique of 'thin' liberalism to positions that combine elements of both. A strong recent 'republican' turn in legal theory aspires to hold both communitarian ideals and democratic participation in tandem. The law, it is claimed, can indeed underpin and sustain community, promote the common good and function as a force of social and political integration. What we have here is a concept of the common good to be negotiated through participation in a polity where (liberal) rights guarantee that the process will be uncoerced, the channels of participation 'unblocked'; moreover where Aristotelian and Arendtian notions of active political participation comes back full circle to 'interpellate' the individual as citizen and thus contributes to the construction of a self-identity no longer vulnerable to the liberal misapprehension of the self as 'unencumbered'.

This reclaiming of community and citizenship from the redundant republicanisms of the past is a dominant feature not only of political and legal theory but of much current political discourse as well, where, paradoxically perhaps, both the Left and the Right have sought a coupling of community with the empowerment of citizenship. Indicatively, in 1989 Douglas Hurd wrote in *The Independent*:

> [t]he idea of active citizenship is a necessary complement to that of the enterprise culture. Public service may once have been the duty of an elite, but today it is the responsibility of all who have time and money to spare. Modern capitalism has democratized the ownership of property and we are now witnessing the democratization of responsible citizenship.

On behalf of the Labour Party, Bernard Crick pleaded for 'far more spontaneous sociability and helpfulness to neighbours and strangers – fraternity'; and Tony Blair's rhetoric of New Labour's vision of society borrows heavily from Amitai Etzioni's communitarianism.

To understand how this claiming of community and citizenship from both Left and Right is possible simultaneously, we need to appreciate how the coordinates of the political opposition have been renegotiated and challenged. And it is in the context of this challenge that we can appreciate the success that the New Right has enjoyed in appropriating the notion of empowerment from its natural constituency, an appropriation all the more effective as it is made in the name of justice. Admittedly much of the Right's community rhetoric is still couched in the language of patriotism and active citizenship understood as civic virtue along the Victorian lines of philanthropy and self-help. But in itself that would hardly have sufficed. No, to understand the success of the Right's redefinition of the terms of our political debate we must look to the emergence of a narrative that no longer sees the market as erosive to community and the self-interest of market logic as detrimental to citizenship; far from needing to shelter these ideals from free-marketers, investors, price-cutters and the rest, we were to entrust the ideals to them. And with the re-conceptualization of all that is not self-interested as irrational, 'stakeholder citizenship' was coined to capture an ideal where stakes were interests or nothing at all. From this all else follows: the elimination of ethics from the economy, the naturalization of the competition between economic freedoms and social rights as zero-sum – with a defence of freedom weighing heavily in favour of the former – the elimination of solidarity from the workplace.

While most of the contributions in this volume touch upon these subjects, not all authors share this pessimism. To give some order to the complex and multifaceted ways in which communitarian ideals articulate with conceptions of citizenship, the papers have been divided into three sections. The first concerns communitarianism and the public sphere. The focus is here on assessing the question of the compatibility of community with those of democratic choice, toleration and anti-conformism. The second section concerns questions of social citizenship and communitarianism; the focus is on social rights in the realms of exchange and work. Finally, the third section covers two quite distinct debates. The first is about the historical origins and philosophical underpinnings of communitarianism; the second visits the question of origin too, but links the meaning of community to the notions of friendship and particularity.

Philip Selznick opens the collection with a defence of the 'communitarian persuasion'. He sees communitarianism as a response to the resurgence of unfettered capitalism in the eighties, the erosion of confidence in the welfare state, 'an exaggerated concern for individual rights and a weakening concern for the common good.' And while, he stresses, the extremes to which the ideal was driven along fascist or communist paths must be resisted of course, communitarianism contains an affirmation of basic morality that orients us toward social responsibility, cooperation and reconciliation, the particularity and diversity of human experience, an understanding of belonging and freedom as interdependent. And counter-intuitively perhaps, it orients us also to oppose ideological thinking, since ideological thinking 'is at odds with the textured, nuanced, problem-solving experience of community'.

Selznick avoids definitional pitfalls that would delineate community too rigidly or remove it from people's experience of what it means to them. At the same time, however, he ensures that its conceptualization is pitched at a level where it can be meaningfully defended. A community must be a comprehensive framework, encompassing a broad range of activities; but it must also be understood as encompassing 'whole' persons, an arena where people relate not as associates but through bonds that engage them as whole persons, not role-takers.

Selznick's view is periscopic, at once showing deep knowledge and great sensitivity as he takes us through discussions of federalism, communal democracy, political liberalism and the definition of the rational. My own favourite 'antinomy' of community is his intriguing discussion of civility and piety. Civility is tied to justice and speaks fairly to a diversity of interests. Civility, says Selznick, 'strains toward a community of principle'. Piety is about love and bondedness; drawing on common history and locality, it is less rational, more personal, homed in on the uniqueness of the social bond. For Selznick, communitarianism should be judged on the success of its accommodating that tension, making it constructive, reconciling without diminishing either pole, remaining true to both ideals.

Gerard Delanty opens the second section of the volume with an overview and a critique of the current state of communitarian theory. He argues that communitarian theory taps a nostalgic myth of community – what since Tonnies' typology has come to be known as *Gemeinschaft* – that conceives of the ideal as somehow the opposite of society – *Gesellschaft*. Community has be conceived as rooted in tradition and as entailing a sense of place, proximity and a holistic fusion of culture and society. To that extent communitarianism fails to appreciate alternative expressions of community as a discourse involving trust, autonomy and solidarity. But, he argues, in order to understand the idea of community in the global era we must look beyond the communitarianism of such writers as Etzioni and Taylor. Theories of community such as those of Habermas, Maffesoli, Nancy and Cotterrell can provide us with a better insight into new expressions of community and their relationship to citizenship and reflexivity.

It is the same 'holistic fusion' of culture and society, the fixing of 'strong identities' rooted in collective memory and history, the danger of the totalizing context overwhelming that which is particular or different that is central to the question of toleration. Would communitarianism tolerate that which is incongruent or antithetical to the common good, and if yes, what would be a communitarian rationale for such protection? This is the problem that Maurizio Passerin d'Entrèves and Avner de-Shalit both address. Passerin d'Entrèves visits the debate between liberal and communitarian thinkers that is very often portrayed in terms of a simple contrast between the value of toleration and the value of community. He argues that this simplistic contrast disregards the complexity and wealth of communitarian theory. To appreciate the possibilities that communitarianism provides to recasting before answering this question, he visits four foci of critique: the liberal conception of the self, the liberal understanding of community, the nature of distributive justice and the priority of the right over the good. He seeks the answer to the question of toleration within each of these contexts and by focusing on the work of MacIntyre, Sandel, Taylor, Walzer and Unger. He argues against the standard objections to communitarian theories and concludes against the simplistic, zero-sum contrast, that it is in fact only monistic communitarian accounts that are detrimental to toleration and that communitarianism is compatible with a pluralism that 'acknowledges the legitimacy of conflict between competing visions of the good'.

Avner de-Shalit visits this debate from the point of view of a defence of nonconformism. How comfortably, he asks, does nonconformism sit with good citizenship, where what we want is a strong sense of community, where people care for and about others in a way which goes beyond their care for themselves? It seems, or so it has been argued, that community contradicts, not to mention oppresses, nonconformism. To argue his communitarian defence of nonconformism, he addresses the proposition that community contradicts nonconformism and explains why only some such arguments make sense while others should be rejected. In the context of the former, and in spite of many dominant assumptions, he goes on to argue that a certain notion of community not only lives in harmony with nonconformism, but also relies on nonconformism in order to sustain it. His normative position is this: for the communitarian argument that we are constituted by the community to be attractive what should be emphasized is not the community of chance but the community of choice. And to make sure that the former does not contradict the latter it must be compatible with free and rational agency, it must allow open criticism, critical scrutiny, and must therefore encourage nonconformism because we need the community's ideas and rationale to be always open to revisability and avoid closure. Choice, thus, to use Hirschman's typology, is more than choice over 'exit' but becomes meaningful 'voice' turning our communities rational, turning them into *topoi* of genuine deliberation (and only thus 'loyalty') rather than arbitrary closure.

In his contribution, Burkhard Schäfer assesses Kymlicka's 'multicultural citizenship' as an attempt at a truce between advocates of collective rights and liberal individualists. He argues that Kymlicka does not go far enough, and that his concessions to communitarians are not thorough enough: protections in terms of group rights are seen by him as legitimate only as external protections of minority cultures, never when they result in the oppression by a group of its own members. From a liberal perspective, Schäfer argues that a liberal *can* concede more to communitarianism and remain consistent in his defence of individual freedom. A liberal can accept internally restrictive collective rights but under a guarantee, he argues, that cannot be dispensed with: that of a concrete and effective right to leave an oppressive community. And it is precisely this right to 'exit' that turns communities dynamic and prevents them from stagnating and becoming 'community zoos' or 'museum pieces'.

Ever since its first appearance in print, T.H. Marshall's analysis of citizenship as a triad of civil, political and social rights has become something of a *sine qua non* in discussions of citizenship. The emphasis of this section is on the final category of the three, that of social rights. Social rights as described by Marshall in the 1950s entailed a right to a standard of life seen very much in terms of inclusion in a community and as the necessary last step towards the full realization of civil and political rights. At the same time though, there are even in Marshall traces of an opposition between citizenship and social class, a persistent doubt, 'a dangerous supplement'; social rights are seen sometimes as a means of extending citizenship, but sometimes merely as a means of ameliorating poverty, slowing down the erosion of social capital, alleviating some of the costs of capitalist production. In the third section of the book the papers deal with topics like these. Do corporate forms of organization force us to accept a certain disempowerment of the workers as natural? Do regimes of new public management leave any room to contest economistic fatalism and argue for some opportunities of economic empowerment through social rights? Or should we speak of a 'war' between citizenship and social class?

In one sense at least Cécile Fabre answers the last question with a qualified 'yes'. She takes issue with the 'social participatory variant' of Marshall's conception of citizenship to examine the claim that social rights ought to be ultimately justified by appealing to the concept of citizenship itself. She examines how this rather vague claim takes concrete form and argues against that version of it that allows a theory of distributive justice to rest on the concept of membership in a community, so that common membership justifies transfers of resources. For Fabre, social citizenship per se *does not* directly justify a redistribution of resources from the well-off to the poor.

From a rather different perspective Paul Havemann visits social citizenship in the 'contract State', a State that he characteristically describes as having gradually 'contracted out' from its welfarist commitments of previous decades. He explores these tendencies in the context of an increasingly globalized market where contractualism and the concomitant re-commodification of social relationships have become the dominant paradigm. The Keynesian Welfare State is abandoned in the name of a regime of new public management, undertaken in the name of consumer empowerment. He concludes by defending a vision of social citizenship as 'beyond both charity and contract' that brings with it an active commitment to social rights understood broadly to include 'economic' rights for the underprivileged, 'ecological' and 'health' rights as well as cultural rights.

Mark Bovens relates the discussion of citizenship to an analysis of complex organizations. The twentieth century, he argues, has been the century of complex organizations. And yet much political theory – here he includes many modern liberals, social democrats, and communitarians – is still operating a largely redundant vocabulary that treats as central the contrast between public and private, between government and market. From the point of view of social and political power, the antithesis between natural persons and corporate bodies, or between citizens and organizations, is nowadays at least as important as the antithesis between government and market. He argues that one of the important issues for contemporary political thinkers should be the rise and social dominance of complex organizations and the kinds of institutional arrangements for a republic in which corporate bodies dominate. What does citizenship mean in a world ruled by complex organizations? He draws an analytical distinction to explore two possible reactions: citizenship *of* complex organizations and citizenship *in* complex organizations.

Finally in this section, Elizabeth Kingdom discusses feminism's ambivalence towards communitarianism. On the one hand, communitarianism holds an attraction for feminist politics in mounting an attack on the concept of rights for its politics of individualism and in emphasizing the values of cooperative living and mutual support in the community. Yet feminists are also wary of communitarianism. For, she argues, once the moral values promoted by communitarianism are given content through its preferred institutions – the *polis*, family and church –, it is apparent that citizenship rights are 'the membership badge of communities whose norms and practices have been inimical to women's interests and hostile to feminist politics.' Kingdom is unhappy with this kind of sweeping critique of a 'thin' rights-centred liberalism. To remedy the defects, Kingdom argues for a notion of citizenship as political principle hosting multiple and changing identities and which persistently subverts existing forms of domination. She argues against wholesale rejections of rights and for the need of the refinement of 'strategic interventions' that may be couched in a selective use of the discourse of rights. Against the communitarian rejection of rights as unredeemingly individualist, she argues for an alertness to the possibilities of a rights discourse that can function as 'radical political heuristics'.

The volume's last section draws together a number of quite different papers. We have, to begin with, John Varty's enquiry into the historical origin of the modern concept of civil society in the writings of Adam Ferguson. Varty takes issue with a long tradition in political thought of counterposing society to the state. And he questions the value of this liberal and potentially 'anti-political' conception of civil society, proposing instead a republican or more strongly 'political' conception of civil society. And to do this he turns to the eighteenth century roots of this debate to seek in Ferguson's *An Essay on the History of Civil Society* an argument as to how citizens can, and must, 'contain' despotism without counterposing society against state. In the process he explains what Ferguson's concept of civil society can bring to contemporary debates, more specifically, the communitarian and republican responses to liberal political theory, as well as the continued relevance of Ferguson's republican argument that insists upon the importance of citizens' participation in maintaining liberty and preventing despotism, focuses on the limits of institutional – whether legal or political – defences of freedom, and realistically appraises the conflictual nature of community and the motivations behind people's political action.

Arto Laitinen's contribution is an interesting intervention in the debate between MacIntyre and Taylor. Both theorists, he argues, hold that conceptions of justice and right always presuppose some particular conceptions of good. They also hold that a cultural or communal context plays a central role in the justification and interpretation of goods. They both hold a teleological, hermeneutic or neo-Aristotelian position. And yet they accuse each other of grave misunderstandings of their respective positions. Taylor argues that it is possible to have a modern teleological ethics without following the Kantian path or 'premodern' MacIntyrean Aristotelianism. His is an attempt to show that one can take the teleological starting point and tailor it to modern phenomena. MacIntyre does not acknowledge such an option; he claims that Taylor's moral theorizing provides no criteria either for telling which judgments about goods are mistaken or for the choice between rival goods; his theorizing 'seems peculiarly ill-equipped to do so'. In this MacIntyre sees the double danger of emotivism and subjectivism. The multiplication of goods, he says, 'gradually frees the self from commitment to any one such set or type of life and leaves it bereft of criteria, confronting a choice of type of life from an initial standpoint in which the self seems to be very much what Sartre took it to be'. Laitinen undertakes to rescue Taylor's theory from MacIntyre's criticism. First he tries to make sense of this 'baffling' criticism of an 'ill-equipped' theory by examining Taylor's moral theory in more detail. Then he evaluates the criticism and explores how it affects our views of the possibility of modern teleological ethics.

Sandra Marshall takes issue with the way in which the communitarian critique of the liberal metaphysical self, in favour of the self as embedded, is read back into political theory. In the process very often communitarian thinking gives a foundational status to an institution – the family – which is oppressive, exclusive and inimical to freedom. But if the family model fails to provide a model of community in which to conceptualize the 'citizen self' as embedded, what structure of values will do the job? Marshall opts for an Aristotelian notion of friendship as providing the most appropriate framework. Friendship allows for a degree of distance that is absent in the family model. It is inclusive, not bounded as is the family. And what undergirds it are values of mutuality, commitment and equality, the kinds of values that are constitutive of community yet without limiting and excluding through membership-without-'exit', one might say, or preordaining and fixing what is appropriate to the community and thus pre-empting 'voice'.

Scott Veitch's 'Doing Justice to Particulars' is a fascinating enquiry not so much into community but into commonality. His analysis echoes to a significant extent Selznick's account of the difficult balance of civility and piety, with their respective emphases on universalism and particularity. Veitch's undertaking is to understand what 'the particular' is to which one must be just. He takes the cue from Derrida, for whom

> it is that which, in a sense, cannot be done justice to since the singularity (or the other or the event) can only be grasped and known by a law or language in and through which it is reclassified as other than it was. Justice [for Derrida] is the impossible but irresistible attempt to treat or address that event on its own terms.

Veitch inquires into what this means by taking the example of mercy which requires in a certain important sense a respect for the particular. Is mercy a departure from law's justice because it requires a departure from generality and a crossing of a 'particularity void'? Veitch says that to suggest that the gap – the particularity void or aporia – is the key to understanding (or failing to understand) the exercise of mercy neglects to take into account that the *justifiable* use of mercy depends less on the particular decision, but on the criteria that are used. There are different perspectives from which to see this. One comes from the point of view of the person who seeks mercy. To what are they appealing if not something: an argument, strategy, emotion, state of mind, situation, etc.? That is, there may be reasons why mercy should be granted, and the fact that we (from a descriptive perspective) cannot predict or table them in a formulaic sense does not mean that they exist as non-criteria. Likewise from the perspective of the person who grants mercy. They may not have to produce their reasons in the form we would expect of a legal judgment, say, but to suggest there are no reasons at all (that their grant of mercy is no more than whim) fails to capture the subtlety of conditions in which mercy might be thought *appropriate*. It is the argument about *appropriateness* that is the crux of Veitch's position.

The question of what is community, what sustains collective identity, what conception of citizenship secures inclusion, what empowerment, are all questions that have been addressed in various ways by the contributors to this book. And in this country, as elsewhere in Europe, where the traditional forms of social democracy are increasingly displaced by a 'modernist' centrist compromise, it is perhaps more urgent than before to reassess the terms of our political discourse. Discussing communitarianism and citizenship allows us to probe some of those limits; to argue in practical terms what the promise of 'stakeholder citizenship' might hold for us. I argued earlier that with the market-driven re-conceptualization of all that is not self-interested as irrational 'stakeholder citizenship' became a word for an ideal where stakes were interests or nothing at all. Theory will help us here to resist emptying of terms of their content, as, in this country for example, New Labour's 'third way' becomes increasingly an apologist for this appropriation of the language of justice, its defence of social democracy either in the name of an increasingly hollow defence of civil liberties or suffocated in the midst of a management speak that recasts justice as efficiency and growth. And where any reason to redistribute the fiscal dividend of growth has of course been removed *in the name of* justice, and any appeal to democratic control of production suffocated in the name of rationality, community becomes increasingly utopian the more it is asserted and confirmed, its 'topoi' eliminated, the space where it could be meaningfully anchored removed. Solidarity having been named so incessantly as to have been named away.

As is obvious from these short summaries of some of the contributions to the 'Communitarianism and Citizenship' conference in Edinburgh, debates were most varied, wide-ranging, engaging, complex and challenging. I would like to end this introduction by thanking all those that made this volume possible and that made the Edinburgh conference such a success: to Philip Selznick for his fascinating Austin lecture; to the officers of the Association for Legal and Social Philosophy: Elizabeth Kingdom, the previous president and Sandra Marshall the current president, Pat FitzGerald, the treasurer and Bob Brecher, the editor of *Res Publica*, for all their valuable help; to the team that helped organize the conference, Claudio Michelon, Emmanuel Melissaris and Burkhard Schäfer; and of course to the 60 or so participants for making it all such an interesting and rewarding occasion.

Bibliography

Glasman, M. (1996), *Unnecessary Suffering: Managing Market Utopia*, Verso: London.
Marquand, D. (1997), *The New Reckoning*, Polity Press: Oxford.

PART I
THE AUSTIN LECTURE

1 The Communitarian Persuasion

PHILIP SELZNICK

The New Communitarians

Since the early 1980s, sparked in part by the publication of Alasdair MacIntyre's *After Virtue* (1985) and Michael Sandel's critique of Rawls, in *Liberalism and the Limits of Justice* (1988), the so-called communitarian vs liberal debate has been a staple of political and social philosophy. I suppose this confrontation is partly driven by the dynamics of pedagogy and by the seductive appeal of polemical confrontations. Nevertheless, something important is going on. At stake is the creation of a public philosophy that can meet the demands of our time. We may hope it will be enriched by dialogue and chastened by self-criticism.

In the United States, the contemporary communitarian movement has had another and more compelling source. In addition to intellectual critique and self-scrutiny, communitarianism has been a response to practical issues in American society, especially a resurgence of unbridled capitalism, erosion of confidence in the welfare state, problems of family, education, drug addiction, crime, and citizenship. The intellectual and practical or policy strands are interwoven when we condemn an exaggerated concern for individual rights and a weakening concern for the common good.

The quest for a communitarian morality, to remedy the perceived defects of modernity, has been a perennial theme of post-Enlightenment thought. The reaction has taken conservative, radical, and liberal forms. In this century, for Americans, a prominent example is the social philosophy of John Dewey. Dewey was a great spokesman for what I call communitarian liberalism. He combined a spirit of liberation and of social reconstruction with a strong commitment to responsible participation in effective communities. On the other hand, more radical doctrines, especially communism and fascism, have given community a very bad name. As we try to think afresh – as we receive and revise communitarian ideas – we can never let ourselves forget these dreadful ways of justifying evil in the name of the good.

This spectre can be faced, and faced down, if we look for moral guidance to the whole experience of community. If we do so we can deal with the dangers and deficits of community, as well as the benefits and ideals. We should take account of egoism as well as altruism; and we should recognize that some forms of altruism, or of solidarity, limit the reach of community and tarnish its ideals.

Seen in its best light, the communitarian persuasion is an affirmation of basic morality. It is a way of upholding the ideal of fellowship, that is, of mutual concern and respect. More specifically, a communitarian morality looks to the enhancement of personal and social responsibility; exhibits a preference for cooperation and reconciliation in all spheres of life, including economic life; affirms the interdependence of belonging and freedom; and values the particularity and diversity of human existence. These principles presume that selfhood can be *enlarged* as a result of social experience; and they presume that selfhood is sustained by *rootedness*. The tension between this enlargement and this rootedness is the most striking feature of communitarian thought. It is a tension that brings both promise and peril.

I called the lecture on which this chapter is based 'the communitarian persuasion' as a way of stressing that this public philosophy is profoundly opposed to ideological thinking. Ideological thinking is at odds with the textured, nuanced, problem-solving experience of community. To be sure every doctrine abridges reality; every idea simplifies and selects. But ideological thinking abuses the privilege in that it fails to accommodate competing values and necessary trade-offs. It lacks a principle of self-correction.

The Encounter with Liberalism

The communitarian critique of liberalism has centred on the claim that liberal premises are overly individualistic and ahistorical, insufficiently sensitive to the social sources of selfhood and obligation; too much concerned with rights, too little concerned with duty, virtue, and responsibility; too ready to accept a thin or anaemic conception of the common good. The operative words – the words that really distinguish communitarians and liberals – are 'overly', insufficiently', 'too much', 'too little', 'too ready'. Indeed the main target of communitarian criticism is intellectual and practical excess. In contemporary liberalism, popular as well as theoretical, there is too much reliance on the power of abstractions; too much hope that some single principle will be an unerring guide to social policy; and too little appreciation for implicit limits, blurred boundaries, competing values, and unintended effects. These criticisms are communitarian in that they point to the social frameworks within which all ideals find their limits as well as their opportunities.

Consider the ideal of autonomy, or personal and political liberty. Contemporary communitarians do not reject autonomy. They certainly do not 'loathe' it, as one writer has recently suggested. Rather, they seek to revive commitment to *ordered* liberty, a notion that calls for specifying contexts, purposes, and competing values. Contextual thinking resists absolutism. It calls for discriminating and situational judgment about *kinds* of liberty and the *limits* to liberty.

Put another way, we seek a more empirical and more nuanced conception of autonomy. Genuine autonomy presumes a stabilizing centre in human life. It cannot be equated with doing as you please, driven by impulse, unconstrained by plan, purpose, or commitment. Genuinely autonomous persons have the psychic competence to make commitments, exercise self-discipline, resist distractions, and criticize their own preferences.

This conception is wholly congenial to what we may call a culture of liberty, that is, a broad appreciation for the many ways autonomy contributes to personal and social well-being. In almost every sphere of life we gain from the cultivation of personal autonomy, properly understood. A culture of liberty provides effective opportunity for growth, expression, and the pursuit of individual life-plans; for free inquiry and unburdened communication; for the chance to grow up in settings that encourage criticism and reflection.

A similar analysis must inform other criticisms of liberalism. Communitarians are not opposed to rights. No society can function without them; and claims of right have often been effective engines of moral and institutional improvement. What we resist is an excess of rights-centredness marked by the detachment of rights from responsibilities and contexts. In a rights-centred era, the idea that rights should be exercised or claimed *responsibly* tends to disappear. In the process rights become abstract, unsituated, absolute. We lose sight of the distinction between invoking rights out of a sense of duty, or to vindicate important interests, and in doing so for more narrow gains and gratifications. After all, rights are not duties; we may or may not invoke the rights we have, or think we have.

Rights-centredness may lead to exaggerated claims, as in the UN Declaration of Human Rights or the American controversy over abortion. The latter has counterposed an abstract 'right to choose' and an abstract 'right to life'. But the most egregious and least defensible example of rights-centredness is the claim to absolute rights of property, a claim that has reasserted itself in recent years. All forms of property are conflated, and conceptions of stewardship are radically attenuated. People who own shares in corporations – shares blessed with limited liability – have the decisive say in what should happen to the company, with all its stakeholders, when a merger is contemplated. On this view, property rights trump all other interests. This is offensive to a communitarian concern for the interests of the community, institution, or enterprise.

A preoccupation with rights is often justified, especially when we articulate 'basic' rights or rights that deserve constitutional protection. I believe the United States was well served by the early agitation for a Bill of Rights, embodied in the first 10 amendments to the federal constitution. In due course additional rights of personhood and citizenship were identified and affirmed. All, however, have been subject to interpretation. All have been marred, in one way or another, by the temptation to indulge in rhetorical overreaching.

The communitarian critics need not claim, and should not claim, that liberal doctrine is necessarily 'atomistic' or that it denies the social formation of selves. The concept of a social self is wholly compatible with the liberal stress on individuality and independence, that is, with the idea that people construct their own identities, choose their own associates, negotiate their own obligations. Socially formed people do make choices, including self-defining choices. Socialization produces individuality as well as conformity. The question is what kind of self we should favour, and what kind of community we should seek? What does it mean to have a moral self and a moral community?

It may be useful analytically to distinguish socially encumbered or implicated selves from those who choose their own identities and obligations. Freedom of choice is celebrated in liberal thought, as are obligations derived from consent. Contract is the preferred principle of social organization. But moral experience, encompasses constraint as well as choice. Although many obligations are indeed self-chosen, others are thrust upon us. Even if an obligation has its origin in consent, as in marriage and parenting, the element of consent becomes less salient as we encounter new and unforeseen demands. Moreover from the standpoint of morality we may be more free to fashion some of our *identities* than to decide for ourselves what *obligations* we owe to particular relatives, friends, colleagues, or institutions. On major issues of identity and obligation, moral judgment must look beyond criteria of freedom and consent. The limits of liberalism, as of so many ideologies, arise from sins of one-sidedness and overreaching, not from egregious or elementary errors, such as a failure to recognize the social formation of selves.

The Texture of Community

Let us now turn to the idea of community, which many people find troublesome and even irritating. That this should be so is not surprising. Community is one of those seminal ideas whose meaning is frustratingly elusive, often contested, routinely vulgarized. These are afflictions of ideas like democracy, morality, freedom, culture, religion, autonomy, and rationality. Each has been the subject of endless discussion; each remains opaque and ambiguous.

I have taken the view that, in dealing with these foundational ideas, we should shift debate from definition to theory. A definition should be logically weak and inclusive, a starting-point for the development of appropriate theories. Although threshold criteria must be met, the definition should allow for variations in kind and degree. We should not pack into a definition attributes that should be determined by empirical and theoretical inquiry. We should not try to solve serious intellectual and policy problems by definitional fiat.

A theory of community should rest upon a broad range of experience; it should identify recurrent elements of community, including characteristic sources of strength and weakness, stability and change. The natural history of community – the sociology of community – cannot be reduced to a single strand. Communities are marked by historicity and identity, that is, by shared experience and a sense of shared fate; but they are also rooted in the experience of *mutuality*. Mutuality creates the moral infrastructure of cooperation. It arises from all the ways people are knit together by interdependence, reciprocity, and self-interest. Mutuality invokes the special moralities of negotiation, contract, and association, notably trust, good faith, and the legitimacy of expectations. Thus mutuality finds moral imperatives in diversity as well as identity; in self-regard as well as altruism; in rivalry and competition as well as cooperation.

Any community draws much of its substance from this experience of interdependence and reciprocity. These very practical conditions account for the voluntary and rational components of community. If people do not need each other, if little or nothing is to be gained from cooperation, community is not likely to emerge or endure. To be sure the bonds of community are to a large extent emotional and non-rational. Yet rationality is by no means excluded. Participation in normal communities is hardly irrational or self-destructive. Rather, we expect communities to be settings within which people can rationally pursue their diverse interests and plan their largely independent lives. The demands of community are not counterposed to rational judgment and personal autonomy. On the contrary, a radical abridgment of these values can destroy community; and it is *loss* of community that so often leads to distracted and disorganized behaviour.

As we explore these and related themes, we see that community is a variable feature of social life. That is why the definition of community should allow for variability. A group is a community *to the extent* that it encompasses a broad range of activities and interests, *and to the extent* that participation implicates whole persons rather than segmental or specialized interests and activities. This meets two threshold criteria: community as a comprehensive framework within which ordinary life goes forward; and community as an arena within which people relate to one another as persons and not only as associates in a special-purpose enterprise.

Given these threshold criteria, we can then ask 'To what extent do we find a shared history, a sense of common identity, bonds of interdependence and reciprocity, and effective participation in the group's culture and social organization?' If we take this variability seriously we answer many of the questions raised about the name and nature of community.

It follows from what I have said that community is about structure and process as well as belief, about ways of relating as well as feelings. To understand community we must look to that structure and to the special work it does. Community has texture, and different kinds of community have different textures. With this approach we can readily distinguish communities from disciplined special-purpose organizations. We know, however, that such organizations often generate, and even require, the benefits and constraints of community. That is why I have explored the distinction between management and governance, and have stressed the significance of governance, as well as management, for effective organization.

The Federal Principle

As frameworks for the conduct of self-directed life, communities have this remarkable feature. They build upon and are nourished by other unities – persons, groups, practices, institutions. These component unities are treated as moral agents and as objects of moral concern; they characteristically claim respect and protection; they demand and are granted a variable but irreducible autonomy. Hence what we prize in community is not unity of any sort at any price but unity that preserves the integrity of the parts.

This unity is very different from the disciplined unity we associate with administrative or military hierarchies. There an ethos of efficiency and instrumentalism prevails. Subordinate units are fully deployable, manipulable, expendable. They can be modified or rearranged at will, in the light of externally determined purposes and policies. A persistent preoccupation with the integrity of the parts lends a special significance to the experience of community. To be sure, community is about integration. Effective communities are indeed well-integrated. But what kind of integration? That is the nub. A unity of unities requires integration of a special kind. It allows and fosters the self-preservation – the survival and flourishing – of its fundamental components.

There is something very familiar about all this. In 1788, writing No. 51 of *The Federalist Papers*, James Madison rejoiced that it would be practical to advance the republican cause 'by a judicious modification and mixture of the *federal principle*'. What is that principle? Is its meaning exhausted by an arrangement of national and state jurisdictions? Or should we find, in that principle, a more basic guide to freedom and order – a principle of community as well as of government.

The federal principle is another expression of what I called above the 'unity of unities'. This principle has Hebraic and Christian roots. The word 'federal' derives from the Latin *foedus* or treaty, and in biblical history the transactions of God and humanity take the form of covenants or treaties. Hence 'covenantal' theology. A covenanted people accept subordination to God, but they do so as free persons entering a sacred compact. Faith based on covenant carries a message of limited power and of authority based on consent. This tradition is an assertion of human dignity. It is a way of saying that people-in-community are responsible actors, capable of holding their own even against God, and they have an irreducible claim to respect and concern. It is this inviolability of constituent units that justifies calling the relationship to God a 'federal' union.

Federal theology was mainly developed by Protestant thinkers. As a result, the sharpest focus is on faith, commitment and the ultimate autonomy of individual persons. But the federal idea is also to be understood as a principle of social order. Thus in the thought of Althusius (1557–1638) covenant pervades social life. Society is the product of many interwoven social unions, all based on tacit or explicit agreements. These are not the covenants of feudalism, where freedom is foregone in exchange for protection. Nor do they quite match the social contract of later generations. Althusius' conception of a federated unity is more pluralist than individualist in spirit and structure. He could not accept the view expressed by his younger contemporary, Thomas Hobbes, that autonomous groups are 'lesser Commonwealths in the bowels of the greater, like wormes in the entrayles of a naturall man'. A closely related idea is the Catholic doctrine of *subsidiarity*. In what has come to be a canonical formulation Pope Pius XI said: '… it is a grave evil, and a disturbance of public order, to transfer to the larger and higher collectivity functions which can be performed and provided for by lesser and subordinate bodies'. This doctrine differs from the Protestant tradition in that consent and agreement are not so important. They do not ground the federal principle. Rather, local groups and institutions have intrinsic worth because they make indispensable contributions to human flourishing, especially that of individual persons.

What matters is well-being, not contract or covenant. The constituent units of society are to be nourished and protected, helped to grow in inner strength or to recover a failing capacity to perform their distinctive functions. They are objects of moral concern whose well-being demands self-determination. Thus the underlying model is parental. The good parent helps the child to grow, but is always aware of the child's intrinsic worth and of the vital need for independence. Thus subsidiarity cannot be equated with delegation or decentralization. Those modes of ordering are compatible with the premise that local or functional units are in principle *expendable* as well as subordinate. They can be extinguished, or radically reconstructed, if that serves the needs of a more comprehensive and higher authority. In such a regime the local units are derivative, not constitutive. The two doctrines – covenantal federalism and subsidiarity – come to much the same conclusion. Each sees major social groups as invested with moral agency and as necessary components of society. These conclusions are wholly compatible with our understanding of community as a unity of unities. They add substance to the idea by specifying what kind of integration community requires. This is not a unity without tension, nor is it a social order wholly based on shared outlooks or traditions. Pluralism is the keynote, a pluralism tempered by allegiance to more comprehensive unities of region, nation, and beyond.

The Antinomies of Community

The federal principle does not lead to easy solutions. A proper balance between the parts and the whole must reflect the genuine problems of a particular community, or kind of community, at a particular time or era. Nevertheless, despite this indeterminacy, the principle is a keystone of the theory of community. Normatively, it offers a standpoint from which to assess current institutions and practices. Descriptively, it points to basic contradictions in the experience of community. To identify such antinomies – the problems they set, the recurrent patterns they produce – is, I believe, a gateway to the integration of moral and social theory. If there are echoes here of Hegel and Marx, so be it. I do not shrink from that association.

The federal principle envisions an irrepressible tension between local and larger unities. That much is obvious. A deeper problem, however, is generated by the competing claims of historicity and principle, particularity and universalism, civility and piety. I have argued that civility and piety are different sources of moral integration and that they compete for pre-eminence as foundations of community. Civility takes autonomy and plurality for granted, and in response encourages toleration and inclusion. The most important expression of civility is the virtue we call justice, for justice speaks civilly to the diversity of interests. Civility detaches community from history and strains toward a community of principle. The natural home of civility is a comprehensive unity. Piety is less rational, more personal, more closely bound to historicity and locality. Its natural home is a community defined by local, cultural and person-centred attachments.

The animating value of civility is respect; that of piety is love. These ideals are by no means wholly antagonistic. In a well-hidden paragraph I have written:

> Respect is not love, but it strains toward love as it gains substance and subtlety. Rudimentary respect is formal, external, and rule-centred – founded in fear of disruption and lack of cooperation. The corresponding civility can be chilly indeed, as some connotations of 'being civil' suggest. An important change occurs when respect is informed by genuine appreciation for the values at stake in communication and good order ... In truly civil communication, for example, something more is required than self-restraint and taking turns. An effort must be made really to listen, that is, to understand and appreciate what someone else is saying. As we do so we move from arms-length ... to more engaged interaction. We discover and create shared meanings; the content and substance of the discussion becomes more important than the form. The outcome is often a *particular* community of discourse and a *unique* social bond. A foundation is laid for affection and commitment. In this way piety fleshes out the bare bones of civility.

Here indeed is the greatest challenge to communitarian thought and communitarian policy – how to reconcile the competing claims of universalism and particularism. I have no knockdown answer – the topic requires all our best efforts – but the following applications of the federal principle point the way.

First, we can uphold the autonomy and defend the vitality of particular groups, institutions and communities. As in the larger realm of ethics and justice, the moral primacy of the particular must be respected. Thus if we ask what 'moral equality' means, or what is a 'human' right, we cannot answer by appealing to postulates and arguments alone. We must focus on the lived experience of degradation, lost opportunity or arbitrary judgment. Only then can we know whether a universalist principle of justice has been properly formulated, or makes sense in the context.

Second, we can respect diversity without allowing its claims to override those of humanity and justice. There can be no set rule for striking such a balance, because too much depends on history and circumstance. But we can do much to spell out what respect for diversity does and does not entail. We can draw on universalist ideals for guidance in reconstructing parochial experience. We can reject the extremes of radical multiculturalism, which would fragment society, and of cultural imperialism, which is indifferent or hostile to local sources of identity and authenticity

Third, we can recognize that particular attachments are not only compatible with but can also preserve and strengthen more comprehensive unities. If people feel that their cultural origins and distinctive identities are respected, they can more readily give their loyalty to a larger 'community of communities'. Indeed loyalty to a larger whole can reinforce local life, as in traditional small-town America, or among many religious communities, by providing compelling rituals, symbols and beliefs.

In short, each perspective must accept an ordinance of self-denial. Advocates of 'fundamental' rights need to limit their claims, especially enforceable claims, to matters that are truly vital to the lives of citizens and the integrity of institutions. At the same time, defenders of particularism must accept the premise that parochial experience is not an unqualified good. Other goods, including the virtues of universalism, have their own part to play in the construction of communities.

Communal Democracy

At this point I turn to the special theme of the conference: communitarianism and citizenship. I believe the connections to what I have said above are not obscure, nor are they far to seek. There is a remarkable concurrence among communitarian thinkers that democracy is something more than majoritarian decision, and that it must allow for constraints on speech and association as well as legislation. The constraints are suggested by the idea of *deliberative democracy*. An ideal of deliberative democracy has far-reaching consequences for constitutional interpretation and institutional design. If deliberation is taken seriously, as a guiding principle, it is bound to check populist impulses. Deliberation requires orderly process and attention to multiple values, informing contexts and unintended effects. Therefore deliberative democracy limits government by referendum, resists the influence of pollsters and restrains the manipulation of opinion by disinformation, deception and appeals to prejudice or raw emotion. In these ways, self-government is held accountable to its own internal morality. Deliberative democracy makes sense of the question of how the will of the people is to be governed.

Deliberative democracy runs counter to the conception of free speech held by those many American liberals who are tempted to treat that freedom as an absolute. As a result, variations in kinds of speech and in the appropriateness of constitutional protection are ignored or rejected. In the United States a watershed of sorts was reached when freedom of *speech* became freedom of *expression*, thus widening the category of protected utterance and detaching it from contexts of deliberative democracy, institutional integrity, or even personal well-being – indeed from context of any kind. But contexts are decisive. It is the context that tells us what liberty means and what limits must be accepted. Without attention to context we cannot make sensible rules about the role of money in political campaigns or about the true justification for academic freedom.

Oddly, it is a more conservative, more cautious, more community-centred liberalism that, in theory at least, places the most severe constraints on deliberative democracy. I have in mind the views expressed by John Rawls, especially in *Political Liberalism* (1993) and in the essays that preceded publication of that book. Rawls argues for a political morality of exquisite self-denial. A political community is best served by limiting the reach of collective judgment. Politics and government must be divorced from what he calls 'comprehensive' doctrines, which are religious or philosophical conceptions of goodness and virtue. Such ideologies purport to identify basic truths about humanity and society, truths that extend beyond the requirements of political theory as Rawls understands it. Thus Christianity is a comprehensive doctrine,; so are utilitarianism, pragmatism, and, as he puts it, the comprehensive liberalisms of Kant and Mill. At another point Rawls says the liberal state can no more act to advance human excellence than it can act to advance Catholicism, Protestantism, or any other religion.

Rawls takes for granted that comprehensive doctrines are necessarily divisive, and grievously so, because they put ultimate values in play. The paradigm fear is religious or ideological warfare, and the use of government to promote conformity. A democratic system governed by principles of respect must protect politics from these dangers. Therefore politics must be separated from all 'perfectionist' moralities, including those we believe are good and true. The quest must be for common ground, which he says can be found in an 'overlapping consensus' among 'reasonable' doctrines. The criterion of reasonableness is political self-restraint, dictated by norms of civility and respect.

We can heartily agree that government should be largely neutral as to what constitutes the good life for individuals and groups. Within broad limits, on these matters, there should be self-determination. We can also agree that democratic *constitutions* should leave ample room for future collective judgment as to what goods should be sought, what virtues should be encouraged, what wickedness should be restrained.

In fact Rawls is hazy about the difference between the morality of constitution-making and that of ordinary political decision. However that may be, a proper understanding of government neutrality leaves plenty of room for collective judgment as to what the community should aspire to as well as what it should guard against. These aspirations are inevitably contested, sometimes very vigorously. However it is a parody of democracy to say that its institutions are mainly geared to managing diversity, and that the main evil to be considered is moral coercion; that is, the burden of accepting, as legitimate, conclusions that offend one's own convictions. We cannot and should not expect a fully shared conception of the common good; we must always presume plurality and dissensus. Nevertheless, democracy is above all a way of exercising collective will. It does so by solving problems and bringing people together, not mainly by keeping them from one another's throats.

An important issue, which resonates strongly with communitarian concerns, is what weight we should give to local demands for cultural self-determination. How much power should a local majority have to invent or embrace a moral code, and to demand conformity? On questions of moral ordering, what are the rights of political minorities? To answer these questions we must remember that majorities do not usually speak for the community as a whole, that is, for everyone that matters. On questions of cultural identity, significant minorities should not be shut out by a mechanical or unresponsive majority. So long as they meet a threshold standard of morality, minorities should share in the process of cultural self-determination. This principle reflects a communitarian commitment to the people as a whole and therefore to the protection and integration of minorities. Majoritarian democracy finds little support in communitarian doctrine.

But majorities should be respected as well. How much so depends on the size of the majority and the extent to which fundamental rights are threatened. If a broad majority makes moderate claims, for example with respect to restricting pornography or endorsing religion, some deference to those claims seems appropriate. Although minorities should not be asked to endure palpable harms, they should be willing to suffer – on some matters, at some times – a sense of exclusion and apartness.

Always in the background of the issues I have just mentioned is that major antinomy of community – the competition between universalism and particularism. The universalist impulse disparages groups and favours the rights of individuals. The ideal is a nation or super-nation whose chief constituents are individuals, not states or local communities. At stake is the locus of citizenship and of meaningful participation in political life. We cannot escape contextual judgments about the limits of localism and the dangers of centralization. Each carries a virus of oppression; each can sap the vitality of community; each must be checked by a countervailing principle; neither is self-limiting.

The Sovereignty of Reason

I close with a brief coda on the sovereignty of reason. The communitarian persuasion does not entail a flight from reason into the warm, unreflective embrace of particularity and historicity. As I see it, there can be no retreat from the Enlightenment quest for a critical morality invested with ultimate authority over our minds, if not our hearts. The conclusions of such a morality stem from our best effort to study the vicissitudes and contexts of moral experience; to do so in a scientific spirit and with the aim of applying collective intelligence to moral issues. It follows that every purported moral truth is subject to inquiry and open to correction.

Having said that we must also say that the conclusions of critical *morality may either confirm or amend* the norms of conventional or received morality. Critical morality should not be understood as wholly different from or counterposed to conventional morality. Indeed the interplay of the two is what matters most and is (or should be) a chief preoccupation of moral inquiry.

The sovereignty of reason is wholly compatible with recognizing the moral worth of particularity, historicity, and non-rational attachments. Although universalism appeals to abstract thought and rational principles, it does not encompass all the findings of a science of morality. Such findings point just as clearly to the benefits of particularism. When they do so they purport to be 'universal', in that they are based on knowledge of all human communities and speak to the problems of all. However such generalizations are not necessarily 'universalist'. They may refer to different virtues, different obligations, and different foundations of morality. Each morality – universalist and particularist – finds support in our studies of communal history and well-being. Each competes for attention and adherence. Neither leaves the stage.

A commitment to the *sovereignty* of reason requires a reconstruction of the *meaning* of reason. We cannot identify reason with rationalism, or with rationality as that is often understood, or with abstract thought or long chains of reasoning, or with simplified models of conduct or cognition. In *The Moral Commonwealth* I discussed, with some presumption, what I called the 'five pillars of reason': order (including intellectual order), principle, experience, prudence, and dialogue. No doubt some better formulation is available or can be stated. My point is: moderate claims and enlarge horizons. Thus understood, reason shows that we must expand the concept of reason to avoid the mistakes of rationalism. Reason and reflection, properly understood, are inductive as well as deductive, empirical as well as theoretical. Thus a genuinely empirical critical morality will readily recognize, without idealizing, the tacit knowledge in custom and social practice. Moreover reason brings to bear an array of intellectual virtues, not only rigour in thought but prudence and openness to dialogue as well. Reason anchors and restrains the rational pursuit of proximate and specific goals or of raw self-interest. Reason criticizes preferences and moderates choice by bringing to bear knowledge of multiple values and of constraining contexts, available opportunities and unintended effects. In these ways, reason identifies the moral framework of thought and action. As it does so it demands empirical inquiry and earnest self-scrutiny, especially in the assessment of means and ends.

From Socrates to Freud, I have said, reason has been understood as a distinctive achievement, a complex of virtues, a form of moral competence, whose office is to discipline impulse, liberate thought, moderate claims and enlarge horizons. Thus understood, reason lights the way to moral and communal well-being. Thus understood, reason redeems the lives of intellectuals and scholars. Thus understood, our jobs are safe.

Bibliography

MacIntyre, A. (1985), *After Virtue: a study in moral history*, 2nd edn, Gerald Duckworth and Co.: London.

Rawls, J. (1993), *Political Liberalism*, Columbia University Press: New York.

Sandel, M. (1982), *Liberalism and the Limits of Justice*, Cambridge University Press: Cambridge.

PART II

2 Reinventing Community and Citizenship in the Global Era: A Critique of the Communitarian Concept of Community

GERARD DELANTY

My concern in this paper is to attempt to place the concept of community on a new foundation beyond communitarianism. The idea of community is central to a theory of citizenship, for citizenship implies in the most general sense membership of a political community. But the problem is that community has been tied to a particular discourse – the discourse of communitarianism – which reduces citizenship too much to an organic notion of cultural community. In other words, the discourses of citizenship and communit,y while being mutually bound up with each other, can involve a certain tension. In my view this tension is likely to increase when it comes to discussing issues such as post-national citizenship, in the sense of citizenship beyond the nation-state. How can the idea of community be made relevant to post-national citizenship?

A major challenge for citizenship theory is to explore ways in which deter-ritorialized forms of citizenship can be linked to an appropriate kind of global community. While citizenship, like community, has mostly been territorially specific, there is an increasing concern today with post-national citizenship as a response to the limits of nationality, both in the context of human rights and as a response to the problems of migrants, global democracy and European integration (Soysal, 1994; Held, 1995; Jacobsen, 1997). One of the problems, of course, is giving a deeper, substantive dimension to such kinds of citizenship. Many discussions on post-national citizenship tend to sidestep this question and fail to see that the more citizenship is globalized the more formalized it becomes. This is where the question of community arises since the idea of community gives the deeper level of a substantive dimension to citizenship.

33

This is so because citizenship is about membership of a political community as much as it is about rights and responsibilities. The idea of membership of a political community suggests the salience of identity and participation (Delanty, 1997b). But the question of community, which suggests proximity, unity and place, is a complex one and can undermine as much as support citizenship.

This tension derives from the sense in which community is commonly perceived: national communities and the power of tradition. In general, an understanding of community as the antithesis of society has prevailed. A crucial challenge today is to overcome this dualism of community versus society, tradition versus modernity. This is particularly urgent since we are witnessing today the return of community in the context of postmodern political culture: in order to understand the implications of this development we shall have to rethink radically our understanding of community in order to resist the fragmentation of the social.

From a theoretical point of view, I believe Jürgen Habermas' (1996) critique of communitarianism and his advocation of a post-national citizenship and 'constitutional patriotism' provides an important alternative to communitarian thinking, such as Amitai Etzioni's (1995) approach, while at the same time acknowledging the importance of community. However, Habermas' model needs to be supplemented by a theory of community that appreciates the uniqueness of contemporary developments which point towards the disembedding and globalization of community around a new cultural 'imaginary' (Castoriadis, 1987). In this context, I shall draw from Michel Maffesoli's (1996) concept of 'emotional communities' and Jean-Luc Nancy's (1991) theory of the 'inoperative community'. A further theoretical perspective is suggested by Cotterrell's (1995) theory of the legal community and the more postmodern approaches of William Corlett (1993) and Maurice Blanchot (1988) who argue for a conception of community beyond unity and identity. These approaches provide us with a means of seeing how community today can be seen as what Benedict Anderson (1991) terms an 'imaginary community' which is always incomplete.

What is Community?

In sociological theory community has had a long history but one largely associated with a particular ideological world view, namely a conservative functionalism. The classic work is Ferdinand Tönnies (1963), *Gemeinschaft und Gesellschaft*, published in 1887. In this work, community and society are pitted against each other to the detriment of the latter: 'community' signifies the organic and cohesive world of traditional society while 'society' refers to the fragmented world of modernity with its rationalized, intellectualized and individualized structures. Communities are culturally integrated totalities while society is essentially defined by its parts. Tönnies largely regretted the passing of community – the world of the village and the rural community – and the arrival of society – the world of the city – believing that community could supply the individual with greater moral resources. The idea of community thus suggests a strong sense of place, proximity and totality, while society suggests fragmentation, alienation and distance.

This myth of community was also perpetuated by Durkheim for whom society is essentially a community based on common cultural values. Modernity is defined by the movement from mechanical forms of integration, characterized by ascriptive values and an immediate identification of the individual with the collectivity, to organic forms of integration, which are characterized by contractual relations and require cooperation between groups. Lacking the disenchantment with modernity that was central to Tönnies' nostalgia for community as a lost totality, Durkheim nevertheless saw the recovery of a sense of community which could be compatible with the requirements of an individualized era as the challenge for modern society. In his view society was always oscillating between integration and anomic, mechanical forms of integration and the more functionalized organic forms. Durkheim, of course, was no romantic but a postivistically-inclined liberal, and had no difficulty in accepting the burden of modernity and its individualized and differentiated social organization which was potentially liberating. He believed that occupational groups and a democratic political culture could provide a foundation for community as proximity and totality.

Like many of the sociological classics, Durkheim's vision of society was dominated by the transition from tradition to modernity as an epochal movement. While he reconciled himself to society, his vision of a functionalized social order bore the imprint of a fascination with community as an ontological reality and as a symbolic order. Both Spencer and Weber, too, were preoccupied with the advent of modernity and the passing of traditional society. While Weber was more ambivalent than Spencer and Durkheim on the historical process of modernity and did not see many opportunities for the recovery of community, he was also centrally concerned with understanding the transition from traditional society to modernity. His pessimistic vision of modernity did not see much room for community. It may be suggested Weber looked to charisma as an alternative to the loss of community under the conditions of modernity.

The penchant for community in sociological discourse was enhanced by the rise of anthropology, which perpetuated the myth of primitive society as being a holistic fusion of culture and society around a symbolic order. The early anthropologists called primitive societies 'cultures', preferring to reserve the word 'society' for their own allegedly superior scientific society. In fact, community has been traditionally understood as precisely the fusion of culture and society – the identification of the cognitive and normative order with social institutions. Primitive societies are supposed to be totalities in which cultural values and social practices are intertwined and can be understood by reference to the category of the symbolic. Communities are supposed to be symbolic orders with a strong sense of group boundaries. This is furthermore underlined by the idea of proximity and a sense of place which characterizes primitive societies. At a time when anthropology and sociology were not differentiated into separate disciplines, sociology – in particular the functionalist tradition – inherited this powerful myth of community as a lost totality rooted in place and proximity. The result was that sociology tended to be distrustful of modernity, which it viewed as a having brought about a rupture with totality. It was not only conservative functionalists who adopted this position. The myth of community as a holistic fusion of culture and society was also behind liberal and Marxist interpretations of modernity (Nisbet, 1953 and 1967). The Chicago School, too, was very much preoccupied with the idea of a tension between community and society. The studies of the Chicago School on the impact of industrialism and urban modernization on traditional communities greatly contributed to the myth of community. Parson's (1966, pp. 10–1) functionalism, too, was guided by the belief that modernity was ultimately regulated by the moral order of what he called the 'societal community'. The search for community in the form of the utopian communist society at the end of history was also central to Marxism. Few philosophies have been more successful in advocating a notion of community than Marxism, which conceived the communist society of the future as a perfect fusion of culture and society.

The myth of community has endured throughout the 20th century as a counterforce to society. This was particularly prevalent in conservative sociology, which contrasted 'mass society' (which had weak symbolic resources and loose boundaries) and the more cohesive world of community. The vision of a recovery of totality has been a very powerful idea and ideal and has inspired many sociological and philosophical theories, as well as political ideologies (Cohen, 1985). It may be said that the 20th century has witnessed the triumph of the spirit of community over the spirit of society. The ideologies of modernity – socialism, liberalism, conservatism, nationalism, fascism, anarchism, kibbutz democracy, even democracy itself – have all been inspired by the quest for community. Indeed, it may be suggested that the quest for community has been inspired precisely because of the failure of the social. While society has been associated with the negative aspects of modernity – rationalization, individualization, industrialism – community has been more successful in expressing the emotional demands and needs of solidarity, trust, and autonomy. These characteristics may be said to be the defining components of community. Community implies: (1) solidarity in the sense of a feeling of togetherness, a feeling of collectivity and mutual attachments; (2) trust as opposed to the secrecy and distance that characterized life in the social; and (3) autonomy, in that community involves the recognition of the value of the person as a social being.

In my view this definition of community is more satisfactory than the ideas of totality, proximity and place with which the idea of community has also been associated. Totality suggests too much the fusion of culture and society, proximity too much personal relations and place imposes too many restrictions on non-geographical communities. Trust, solidarity and autonomy are the most fundamental dimensions to community and are characterized by a certain emotional dimension which can be exploited by authoritarian and populist movements. I shall argue that trust, autonomy and solidarity do not have to be understood from the perspective of the symbolic.

Society, on the other hand, has been defined by reference to structural and institutional processes. The values of solidarity, trust and autonomy have not been central to the definition of the social. This is perhaps why the social has been seen in communitarian-inspired interpretations of modernity as fundamentally untrustworthy, divisive and dehumanizing. The decline and corruption of community into the social has been central to sociological theory in the 20th century. One of the challenges today is to overcome this dualism. I am not suggesting that community is to be rejected but that the false dichotomy of community and society must be overcome. Community is an important concept for an understanding of society and many of the problems with it derive from a framework of historical time in which the two concepts are located.

In many ways the distinction between society and community parallels the distinction between structure and agency. Community implies a stronger sense of the autonomy of agency while society entails the alienation of agency by objectified and ossified societal structures. Thus the task of radical sociology was to infuse the social with a sense of agency. I shall argue against this distinction between structure and agency, society and community, and I shall propose that the social be reinterpreted from the perspective of community. In this regard it is helpful to recall a point made by Raymond Williams (1976, pp. 65–6): the polarity between society and community was a product of the 19th century and overshadowed the Enlightenment polarity of state and civil society. In other words, in the 18th century the idea of society as civil society was seen in much the same terms as community is today imagined – as immediate and embodying direct relationships – while the state was seen as the realm of organized relations. Today we are faced with a different situation: we are faced with the spectre of the return of community as a societal and global imaginary.

The Contemporary Rediscovery of Community

There is much to indicate that there has been a revival in the idea of community. The communitarian debate has been important in the perpetuation of the myth of community. Communitarianism is a diffuse category and can mean many different things, but in general it is associated with a particularly North American obsession with community as an antidote to the liberal emphasis on the individual as a member of civil society (Avineri and de-Shalit, 1992). Communitarians can be divided into three categories: liberal communitarians such as Walzer (1993), Taylor (1990), Sandel (1982) and Selznick (1992); conservative communitarians such as MacIntyre (1981); and neo-republicans such as Arendt (1958). The first group emphasizes community as a social entity and can be contrasted with the more conservative position of MacIntyre, for whom community is defined by tradition and moral virtues. For MacIntyre the project of the Enlightenment failed because it was unable to provide a moral foundation for the self released from tradition. These varieties of communitarianism can be related to the more radical neo-republican communitarianism which tends to stress the political dimension of community. The intellectual hero of the communitarians is Aristotle, whose vision of the fabled *polis* is the model of community. In modern times Rousseau and Kant provided the intellectual basis for the Enlightenment concept of the social contract and the republican order of civil society. Thus for modern neo-republicans the self-legislating republic is an essentially political community.

The communitarian position entails a strong association between community and tradition and presupposes a view of community as a culturally cohesive totality. This fascination with community as a moral voice is not specific to communitarian philosophical circles but is also reflected in a certain tradition in sociology and political theory. Works such as those of Amitai Etzioni, Robert Nisbet, Christopher Lasch, Richard Sennett and Daniel Bell all display the enduring appeal for community as a haven from society. The idea of community has now become part of our social language and is used to describe various kinds of commonalities, from residential communities to work-related communities and from care-related communities to ethnic communities. It is used to refer to community policing, community planning, communities of communities (such as supracommunities of the United States, the European community, the international community), local and national communities.

The aim of this paper is to assess the importance of community and to ask whether community can be interpreted in a way that can make the concept appropriate to the cultural and social challenges of postmodernity and globalization. What, then, is the problem with community? I believe the myth of community in communitarian discourse is open to many objections. Rather than take up the well-rehearsed liberal critique of communitarianism (Mulhall and Swift, 1996), I wish to take the slightly different route suggested by Habermas (1996) and Frazer and Lacey (1993) in order to arrive at a reassessment of the idea of community. This will entail transcending the liberal-communitarian debate. At this juncture it is important to say that my aim is to rescue the idea of community from the political philosophy of communitarianism. It is for this reason that my position is more Habermasian than liberal, for it is Habermas' aim to transcend both liberalism and communitarianism. In other words, I believe, with Habermas, that the liberal critique of communitarianism is valid, as is the communitarian critique of liberalism, and therefore both are invalid. However, my position differs from Habermas, who does not sufficiently link his discursive alternative to the idea of community. As Gerd Baumann (1991) has demonstrated in his analysis of multi-ethnic communities, I believe the idea of community can accommodate a notion of contestation and must not be anchored in cultural consensus or a symbolic order. This is also evident in the case of movement activists, as Lichternman (1996) demonstrates in his study of community and commitment.

Community, then, is important even though interpretations of it may differ. Before outlining my theoretical conception of community below and explaining why I think Habermas' critique is inadequate, more needs to be said about the contemporary salience of community. The revival of community in sociological theory and political philosophy cannot be divorced from the return of community in the global political culture in the world. Indeed, it may be that community is becoming the universal ideology of our time and is usurping the idea of the social. The idea of community, after all, is more central to the social movements of the late 20th century than is society. The appeal to community was central to Bill Clinton's election campaign of 1992 and Tony Blair's election campaign of 1995 was very much articulated in terms of a neo-republican idea of community. The rhetoric of New Labour favours terms such as 'community' and 'nation' more than 'society'. If liberal individualism was the ideology of the 1980s, community is the ideology of the 1990s. Zygmunt Bauman (1991, p. 246) remarks that postmodernity is also the 'age of community'. While in the older sociological accounts community was associated with the rural communities of the past, it may be the case that community today is the result of the postmodernization of culture (Lash, 1994). This is something communitarian philosophy is incapable of understanding. The identity politics of nationalism, religious revivalism, neo-fascism, new age travellers and the whole range of media cultures, such as the idea of 'virtual communities', all revolve around the idea of community. Indeed the very idea of the 'global village' is based on the idea of community. The idea of community penetrates the identity politics of many social movements, as for instance the idea of 'gay communities'. Nor must the greatest myth of community – the European community – be forgotten. We might quite well ask why Europe is considered a community and not a society. Indeed, since the publication of the well-known volume edited by Karl Deutsch (1957) *Political Community and the North Atlantic Area*, the idea of community has been central to international relations. There is perhaps a certain suggestion that the idea of society is the realm of the nation-state, while community can refer to something more transcendent and elusive.

In recent times few books have been more influential in setting the terms of debate for community than Amitai Etzioni's (1995) *The Spirit of Community*. Against liberalism and radical individualism, Etzioni argues for the need to recover a sense of community. Though he explicitly says he is not advocating a nostalgic return to the past, it is significant that he constantly uses the term a 'return' to community or a 'recovery' of community, thus making the assumption that community was a thing of the past and the present is all the poorer for letting it pass. The idea of community is expressed very much in terms of personal proximity. Community entails voice, a 'moral voice' and social responsibility rests on personal responsibility. A concern with responsibility articulates a core idea of Etzioni's communitarianism, as is clear from the title and manifesto of his quarterly, *The Responsive Community*. Etzioni's conception of responsive community is rooted in 'social virtues' and 'basic settled values' (1995, p. 25). The family and the school are the typical institutions which can cultivate the kind of citizenship required by responsive community.

While Etzioni recognizes that complex societies and cities with many different cultural traditions cannot easily form the basis of community, his model is ultimately based on the idea of the traditional community. He grants that modern economic structures make the return to the past impossible and that traditional communities were too homogeneous and have been too constraining and authoritarian (1995, p. 122). The city, not the village, is his concern. Thus the sociologically correct response to the typical liberal critique is that:

> communities are best viewed as if they were Chinese nesting boxes, in which less encompassing communities (families, neighbourhoods) are nestled within more encompassing ones (local villages and towns), which in turn are situated within still more encompassing communities, the national and cross-national ones (such as the budding European Community). Moreover, there is room for non-geographic communities that crisscross the others, such as professional or work-based communities (1995, p. 32).

Yet, his definition of community as a moral voice rooted in social virtues and personal responsibility does not square with his view of community as being also highly differentiated. His conception of community is ultimately a reappropriation of the traditional idea of community as a cohesive unity. If he were to take seriously the differentiated nature of society, he would come to a different understanding of community.

In order to understand contemporary developments which point towards the revival of community in the world today, we must part company from the sociological and philosophical myth of community in communitarian discourse. This myth is fundamentally incapable of understanding the real significance of community today: the appeal of community cannot be explained by reference to the quest for a lost totality, a moral order or a traditional order. We need to ask whether 'community beyond tradition' (Morris, 1996) or what Willaim Corlett (1993) calls 'community without unity' can be possible. The political philosophy of communitarianism is also incapable of understanding the discourse of community since the terms of its debates have been almost entirely shaped by two issues: the related problems of accommodating difference and individualism. In my estimation there is little point in rehearsing the well-known liberal critique of communitarianism, since most advocates of communitarianism – including Etzioni, with the possible exception of the conservative version proposed by MacIntyre (1981) – have answered the charge of majoritarianism and intolerance of dissent. Thus communitarianism is in fact liberal communitarianism (Miller and Walzer, 1995). Instead, I am arguing that communitarianism is unable to deal with the formation of new discourses of community which cannot be explained by reference to the conventional terms of reference. In short, the problem of community today is not a question of accommodating tolerance of cultural differences, the theme of much of communitarian political philosophy.

What the new discourses of community have in common is not the hankering after a lost totality or a concern with difference or individualism, but a search for a new cultural imaginary. The postmodernized communities of the global era are highly fragmented, contested and far from holistic collectivities; they are characterized more by aesthetic codes than by a moral voice. I shall outline this in more detail later. It will suffice here to remark that new cultural imaginaries suggest that social responsibility cannot be reduced to the sense of personal moral responsibility and that globalization involves the emergence of new kinds of proximity that cannot be reduced to a sense of place (Castells, 1996). The only adequate kind of community is one that can accommodate itself with reflexivity and an awareness of its incompleteness (Blanchot, 1988).

Beyond Communitarianism: New Theories of Community

A useful entry into new conceptions of community is to consider Habermas' critique of communitarianism. For Habermas, communitarianism emphasizes the existing community too much and reduces politics to the ethical. He rejects Taylor's (1990) model of political community on the grounds that it is too holistic and does not see how community, insofar as it is to be a foundation for citizenship, involves the transcendence of particular cultural traditions. His concept of discursive democracy has the merits of incorporating the strengths of the liberal and communitarian perspectives while rejecting their disadvantages. Discursive democracy resides not in the ethical substance of a particular community, nor in universal human rights or compromised interests as in liberalism, but in the rules of discourse and forms of argumentation whose normative content derives from the structures of linguistic communication which can always in principle be redeemed. Discursive democracy is rooted in the public sphere, which provides it with an informal institutional reality in civil society. Habermas is centrally concerned with the social conditions of critical debate in society and how such public discourse can shape democracy which involves a relationship to legal institutionalization. Law is rooted in democracy which in turn is rooted in public debate. Habermas is less concerned with actual participation in decision-making than in the necessity to have decision-making mediated by communication. In his model communication is essentially about contestation.

Habermas also breaks from communitarianism in another crucial respect: he strongly defends the possibility of a post-national society whose collective identity is defined by reference to the normative principles of the constitution rather than by reference to a cultural tradition, territory or loyalty to the state. Only what he calls a 'patriotism of the constitution' can guarantee a minimal collective identity today (Habermas, 1994 and 1996). This idea may be generalized from the specifically German context in which he developed the idea to all modern societies and is especially pertinent to such transnational polities as the European Union (Delanty, 1995, 1996 and 1997b).

While Habermas has established the basis of a non-communitarian theory of community, his own alternative runs the risk of being too decontextualized. We need to see how community actually operates in the sense of real and lived communities. Habermas speaks from the perspective of the observer, a position he insists is available to everybody. In other words, cultural traditions are not so constraining as to prevent people from critically reflecting on their otherwise taken-for-granted assumptions. But, in general, community is a problem for Habermas for whom the discourse ethic is modelled on face-to-face dialogue (Delanty, 1997a). Operating largely within the same paradigm of critical hermeneutics, Karl-Otto Apel (1980) argues for a concept of community as being central to a discursive concept of ethics, politics and science. The idea of community refers to the very process of communication itself as a self-transcending community of those engaged in critical reflection. Apel's emphasis on community as communication points to a new and non-communitarian notion of community. Though Apel does not attempt to develop his concept of community, I would argue that one way it differs from the conventional sociological and philosophical accounts is that community is essentially a transcendental and cognitive concept. The existing literature over-emphasizes the symbolic nature of community as a cultural category (Cohen, 1985), to the neglect of the possibility that community might express a deeper level of the cognitive (Strydom, forthcoming 1999). In order to develop this possibility, I shall examine some new accounts of community which I think point to a deeper sense of community as a cognitive order or the basis of the cultural model of society.

An alternative conception of community is suggested by Michel Maffesoli's (1996) *The Time of the Tribes*. Under the conditions of postmodern complexity, according to Maffesoli, the age of the masses is giving way to new social relationships and as a result we have entered the age of the 'tribes'. The idea of the tribe suggests for Maffesoli an 'emotional community' which is defined by an affectual and aesthetic aura. Community means the experience of everyday life which, according to Maffesoli, involves the constant flow of images and situations. Unlike the communities of the past, which were spatial and fixed, emotional community is unstable and open, a product of the fragmentation of the social and the disintegration of mass culture. People are increasingly finding themselves in temporary networks, or 'tribes', organized around lifestyles and images. Maffesoli sees community extrapolating a sense of 'sociability' from the 'social'. Community still involves proximity but this is something temporary and has no fixed purpose; it is characterized by 'fluidity, occasional gatherings and dispersal' (1996, p. 76). Community serves to 'reenchant' the world and to provide a sense of solidarity that comes with proximity. But the new proximity is located in urban-metropolitan spaces and is an expression of what he calls the vitality and creativity of action. For Maffesoli (1996, p. 104) this all amounts to the end of modernity:

> [w]hile modernity has been obsessed with politics, it may be equally true that postmodernity is possessed by the idea of clan, a phenomenon which is not without its effect on the relationship to the Other and, more specifically, to the stranger.

Community is then something radically open and unconstraining.

Two ideas stand out in the new conceptions of community: the contrast with the social and the idea of community existing in a 'non-place'. Community is an expression of fragmentation of society and is forever in tension with it but cannot exist without it at the same time. This is evident in Maffesoli's work and, for instance, Jacques Rancière's (1995) *On the Shores of the Political*. Community is the province of equality while society remains in thrall to inequality: '[a] Community of equals can never become coextensive with a society of the unequal, but nor can either exist without the other' (1995, p. 84). Marc Augé (1995) also writes about the increased salience of 'non-places' in the age of what he calls 'supermodernity'. Non-places differ from places in that our experience of them is fragmentary and transitory. Supermodernity involves the production of more and more spaces through which we travel (supermarkets and other non-places of consumption, transit lounges, leisure spaces, holiday resorts, cashpoints, the spatial images of TV and virtual realities of cyberspace). Supermodernity and its manifold of space is also characterized by the increased production of meaning that comes with ever more possibilities for agency to interpret its surroundings. It may be argued that community is increasingly being located in a world dominated by such non-places and the kind of aesthetic hermeneutics it involves for its participants. These hermeneutics have little to do with the symbolic order or a sense of proximity based on exclusion. Indeed the 'other' is not central to their definition. The kind of community that is suggested by writers such as Maffesoli is something more aesthetic and emotional and refers ultimately to the wider cognitive order of society.

A work of significance on the idea of community is Jean-Luc Nancy's (1991) *The Inoperative Community*. Nancy defends the idea of community as relevant not only to modern but also to postmodern society. Community is the basis of human experience and the identity of the self as a social being. However, his notion of identity is more that of non-identity: the experience of otherness as an absence. His approach is far from that of communitarianism in that he does not hanker after a lost community and insists that community is always based on the individual and the experience of the 'other': '[c]ommunity is what takes place always through others and for others' (Nancy, 1991, p. 15). Stressing finitude or present time as the key to community, Nancy opposes the attempt to locate community in the past or as a project for the future. Community cannot be reduced to an organic concept of social relations or to a place; it is something that always negates itself and is constituted in the differential relations of human beings. The 'inoperative community' is the tendency of community to undermine or 'interrupt' itself in the self-assertion of its members and in the struggle to define community: community is itself the experience of the loss of community. This seems to be his central message in this very obscure book. Nancy's idea of community is not unlike that of Maurice Blanchot (1988) in *The Unavowable Community*: community as an incomplete project. Yet for all his attempt to render community compatible with postmodernity (in the sense of the experience of difference) Nancy ultimately retreats into a kind of communitarianism for his conception of community, which is very much influenced by Heideggerian hermeneutics and a postmodernized and secularized Christianity, reflecting a concern with community as ontological in the sense of the expression of a human essence.

An example of a postmodern approach to community that avoids the dangers of essentialism and recognizes the political nature of community is

William Corlett's (1993) *Community without Unity*. Corlett aims to apply the deconstructionist philosophy of Derrida to community, arguing that difference is the essence of community. Community, he argues, must be understood as something more than the problem of collective unity versus individualism; it is the mutual appreciation of differences and does not require a holistic notion of culture, for there is always an excess of meaning which cannot be reduced to a particular moments.

Roger Cotterrell's (1995) *Law's Community* is also a major contribution to the idea of community. The essential characteristic of community for Cotterrell is mutual interpersonal trust, for without trust a society cannot function. Trust is an important dimension to social cohesion and is increasingly becoming a major theme in social, legal and political theory (Misztal, 1996). Cotterrell argues that geographical proximity is not an essential characteristic of community; he also rejects the communitarian emphasis on shared values. In his view, communities can be very varied in size and character. Drawing from Luhmann, Cotterrell elucidates how social complexity makes proximity impossible and ultimately shifts the burden of trust from culture onto law. Thus, law is placed in the foreground in the contemporary conceptualization of community. Community also has a connection with communication and it is this which makes trust possible. Trust does not exist in a vacuum outside social interaction. Since social interaction is essentially communicative, we must view trust as a process of social communication. In Cotterrell's view this entails the need for a regulatory structure that fosters and supports relations of mutual trust in society. He argues (1995, p. 332) that this will involve collective participation and public altruism (the provision of the necessary material and cultural resources):

> Collective Participation – the opportunity and freedom for all members to be involved fully and actively in determining the nature and projects of the community as a whole – is a means of stabilizing and reinforcing mutual trust through the continuous ongoing negotiation of its consequences and it conditions of existence.

My conclusion so far is that recent literature on the idea of community points to a notion of community as a cognitive structure rooted in processes of communication, law and democracy. Postmodern conceptions emphasize community in various ways as the experience of difference, whereas legal theorists stress issues such as trust. Others, such as Habermas and Apel, speak of community in terms of the reflexivity of communication. These approaches make the traditional notion of community as a symbolic order redundant, for they allows us to see community as a contested cultural imaginary. In order to develop this understanding of community, I shall extend the idea of the cognitive into a theory of the cultural imaginary and relate this to the new idea of community as a postmodern and globalized discourse.

Community as a Cultural Imaginary

Following Cornelius Castoriadis (1987), the 'imaginary' refers to the ability of a society to imagine itself; it is the cultural model of society in its cognitive, normative and aesthetic dimensions. The idea of community being advocated here sees community as part of the cultural dimension of society in its capacity to reflect upon itself. As Maffesoli (1996, p. 118) argues, the 'imaginary is increasingly granted a role in structuring society'. Benedict Anderson (1991) has stressed the importance of community as an imaginary in the making of the nation-state. With the creation of large-scale nations organized around a state, community had to be reinvented around an imaginary community. The nation became the focus of this imaginary community, its cultural codes being greatly aided by print cultures. Thus physical proximity was replaced by an imaginary proximity in the creation of a wider national community. In the global age we are witnessing an extension of this imaginary community. If print cultures facilitated the rise of the national community, the computer age and cybersociety may be accompanying the rise of a new kind of community compatible with transnational governance and postmodern fragmentation.

The emergence of what I would prefer to call a neo-communitarian cultural imaginary must be seen in the context of the deterritorializing and globalizing of community. The new discourses of community are not those of the traditional peasant communities about which the founding fathers of sociology wrote: community is decentred and is thereby open to new interpretations. Nor is it a moral order based on cultural consensus, or a moral voice, as the communitarian philosophers would have it. The return of community today is a response to the failure of society to provide a basis for the three core components of community: solidarity, trust and autonomy. To appreciate this we do not need a notion of the holistic fusion of culture and society around a symbolic order. In fact the contrary is the case: community today is a product of the uncoupling of culture and society. Culture is separating from society whose institutional complexes are unable to constrain cultural value systems. Anthony Giddens (1994) refers to this as a process of disembedding by which tradition loses its force and agency transformed by reflexivity becomes emancipated. However, I would argue the reflexivity brought about by late modernity cannot be explained by agency's emancipating itself from structures, as Beck and Giddens (Beck et al., 1994) believe, but by the formation of new cultural systems of meaning (Delanty, 1998).

The contemporary discourse of community, then, must be located in this new cultural context, which provides a basis for a cultural imaginary built around the idea of community. The attraction of community is that it offers a focus for the reappropriation of the cultural symbols of identity and ideology. Under the conditions of globalization, community can be taken out of its existing context and given new meaning. Thus many groups appeal in one way or the other to community. It is no coincidence that the idea of community has particular appeal to global cultures, such as the deterrorialized discourses of academia, the European Union, migrants and technology cultures such as those of the cybersociety (Jones, 1995; Meyrowitz, 1986). In the past community was shaped by the symbolic practices of tradition and custom; today it is shaped by a variety of forces of which the most important are the global processes of technology, knowledge and images (Castells, 1996). It must be noted that these have the characteristic of being strikingly non-communicative; they are primarily nonverbal and products of the postmodernization of culture. In disembedding community from its traditional sediment of morality and cultural consensus, the danger facing a postmodernized community is that it will fail to provide a basis for trust, solidarity and autonomy, the core components of community. This is the problem with cyberspace communities. In surmounting space and time, computer-mediated communication is primarily conceptual and deverbalized.

The nation-state and the national society failed to provide community with a firm foundation; the question, then, is whether the deterritorialization and globalization of community will be able to solve the problem of community – adaptation to the increasing conditions of complexity in the social environment. At this point the final dimension to community can be introduced: communication. Both community and communication are mutually implied in each other's definition. A community involves the flow of communication. Without a notion of communication, the ideas of solidarity, trust and autonomy would be meaningless, or at least would be reduced to the symbolic. The problem of community can thus be seen to be the problem of adapting flows of communication to the societal context. Thus we can see how, with the change in the wider societal environment towards greater globalization – in particular in communications systems – on the one side, and on the other social fragmentation, community returns to provide fragmented societies with a cultural imaginary capable of compensating for the loss of the social and at the same to provide the new globalized systems of communication with a basis in the life-world. But the reception of the new discourse of community is problematic for two reasons.

The first, as already suggested, is that the postmodernization of community runs the risk of emptying community of its relationship to communication and, second, there is the risk that community will degenerate into an authoritarian neo-communitarianism. In the first case the discourse of community loses its connection with communication and the core components of trust, solidarity and autonomy. Postmodern community – such as the European Union – is neither a *demos* nor an *ethnos*, but a globalized and deterritorialized cultural imaginary which runs the risks of reducing communication to incoherence. In the second case, as the examples of nationalism and neo-fascism attest, the idea of community reduces political community to cultural community and, moreover, involves an aesthetization of community. In both cases the idea of community is seen as the antithesis of the idea of society. In this sense, community and society are still two fundamentally opposed discourses.

In order to bring these domains closer together, and thereby overcome the false dichotomy of community and society, we need to see how they require each other. While community involves relationships of trust, autonomy and solidarity, an important dimension to the social is the sphere of institutionalized action. Taking up some themes in the theory of citizenship, I should like to claim that community and the social are linked by virtue of requirements of the ethic of responsibility to find an institutional foothold. Democracy and the institutions of civil society such as the public sphere are the means by which the spirit of community and the idea of the social are linked. However, in order for this to be a realistic prospect today in the global era, the ethic of responsibility must be modified to accommodate collective responsibility and the role of collective actors. We must therefore modify our concept of community accordingly.

Conclusion: Towards a Reflexive Community

My contention is that the idea of community is important and the challenge is to rescue community from either of the two tendencies – postmodernized incoherence or neo-communitarian authoritarianism – and to relink it to the idea of society and citizenship. The idea of community is relevant to postmodern society and is capable of articulating a cultural imaginary appropriate to our global age, but it is important for it to be related to processes of communication and the social life-world. The tremendous popularity of nationalism and various kinds of populist neo-communitarianism is precisely that they have been able to monopolize the discourse of community. In short, then, I am suggesting that the idea of community must be linked to the idea of the social and not seen as its antithesis. The social must not be fused with the idea of community – for this would only be to prolong the myth of total communities – but it must be mediated with it in the institutionalizing of spaces for trust, solidarity and autonomy. Community, in other words, could become the reflective dimension of society, as Scott Lash (1994, p. 162) has also argued. I believe that the idea of discursive democracy is the most appropriate means of conceiving of this. A reflexive community is a discursive community. Only in this way can we rescue the discourse of community from either its absorption into meaningless semiotic global communities or the dangers of the symbolic as represented in authoritarian neo-communitarianism. The aesthetic and emotional dimension to community may have a role to play in this, insofar as it is capable of articulating a new sensibility.

Bibliography

Anderson, B. (1991), *Imagined Communities*, revised edn, Verso: London.

Apel, K.-O. (1980), 'The a priori of the Communication Community and the Foundation of Ethics: The Problem of a Rational Foundation of Ethics in the Scientific Age' in *The Transformation of Philosophy*, Routledge & Kegan Paul: London.

Arendt, H. (1958), *The Human Condition*, Chicago University Press: Chicago.

Aristotle (1962), *The Politics*, Penguin: Harmondsworth.

Augé, M. (1995), *Non-Places: Introduction to an Anthropology of Supermodernity*, Verso: London.

Avineri, S. and de-Shalit, A. (eds) (1992), *Communitarianism*, Oxford University Press: Oxford.

Baumann, G. (1991), *Contested Cultures: Discourses of Identity in a Multi-Ethnic London*, Cambridge University Press: Cambridge.

Bauman, Z. (1991), *Modernity and Ambivalence*, Polity Press: Cambridge.

Beck, U. (1992), *The Risk Society*, Sage London.

Beck, U., Giddens, A. and Lash, S. (1994), *Reflexive Modernization: Politics Tradition and Aesthetics in the Modern Social Order*, Polity Press: Cambridge.

Blanchot, M. (1988), *The Unavowable Community*, Station Hill Press: Barrytown, New York.

Castells, M. (1996), *The Rise of the Network Society,* Blackwell: Oxford.

Castoriadis, C. (1987), *The Imaginary Institution of Society*, Polity Press: Cambridge.

Cohen, A. (1985), *The Symbolic Construction of Community*, Tavistock: London.

Corlett, W. (1993), *Community Without Unity: A Politics of Derridian Extravagance*, Duke University Press: Durham.

Cotterrell, R. (1995), *Law's Community*, Clarendon: Oxford.

Delanty, G. (1995), *Inventing Europe: Idea, Identity, Reality*, Macmillan Press: London.

Delanty, G. (1996), 'Habermas and Post-National Identity: Theoretical Perspectives on the Conflict in Northern Ireland', *Irish Political Studies* 11, pp. 20–32.

Delanty, G. (1997a), 'Habermas and Occidental Rationalism', *Sociological Theory*, 15, 1, pp. 30–59.

Delanty, G. (1997b), 'Models of Democracy: Defining European and Identity and Citizenship', *Citizenship Studies*, 1, 3, pp. 285–303.

Delanty, G. (1998), *Conceptions of Modernity: Understanding Social Change*, Polity Press: Cambridge.

Deutsch, K. et al. (1957), *Political Community in the North Atlantic Area*, Princeton University Press: Princeton.

Durkheim, E. (1960), *The Division of Labour in Society*, Free Press: Glencoe, Ill.

Etzioni, A. (1995), *The Spirit of Community*, Fontana Press: London.

Frazer, E. and Lacey, N. (1993), *The Politics of Community: A Feminist Critique of the Liberal-Communitarian Debate*, Harvester Wheatsheaf: Hemel Hempstead.

Giddens, A. (1994), 'Living in a Post-Traditional Society' in Beck et al., op. cit.

Habermas, J. (1994), 'Struggles for Recognition in the Democratic Constitutional State' in Gutmann, A., *Multiculturalism: Examining the Politics of Recognition*, Princeton University Press: Princeton.

Habermas, J. (1996), *Between Facts and Norms: Contributions to a Discourse theory of Law and Democracy*, Polity Press: Cambridge.

Held, D. (1995), *Democracy and the Global Order: From the Modern State to Cosmopolitan Governance*, Polity Press: Cambridge.

Jacobsen, D. (1997), *Rights Across Borders: Immigrants and the Decline of Citizenship*, Johns Hopkins University Press: Baltimore.

Jones, S. (ed.) (1995), *CyberSociety: Computer Mediated Communication and Community*, Sage: London.

Kant, I. (1995), 'What is Enlightenment?' in Kramnick, I. (ed.), T*he Portable Enlightenment Reader*, Penguin: Harmondsworth.

Lasch, C. (1991), *The True and Only Heaven*, Norton: New York.

Lash, S. (1994), 'Reflexivity and its Doubles: Structures, Aesthetics, Community' in Beck et al., op. cit.

Lichternman, P. (1996), *The Search for Political Community: American Activists Reinventing Commitment*, Cambridge University Press: Cambridge.

MacIntyre, A. (1981), *After Virtue: a study in moral history*, Gerald Duckworth & Co.: London.

Maffesoli, M. (1996), *The Time of the Tribes: The Decline of Individualism in Mass Society*, Sage: London.

Meyrowitz, J. (1986), *No Sense of Place: The Impact of Electronic Media on Social Behaviour*, Oxford University Press: Oxford.

Miller, D. and Walzer, M. (eds) (1995), *Pluralism, Justice and Equality*, Oxford University Press: Oxford.

Misztal, B. (1996), *Trust in Modern Society*, Polity Press: Cambridge.

Morris, P. (1996), 'Community Beyond Tradition' in Heelas, P., Lash, S. and Morris P., *Detraditionalization*, Blackwell: Oxford.

Mulhall, S. and Swift, A. (1996), *Liberals and Communitarians*, 2nd edn, Blackwell: Oxford.

Nancy, J.-L. (1991), *The Inoperative Community*, Minnesota University Press: Minneapolis.

Nisbet, R. (1953), *The Quest for Community*, Oxford University Press: Oxford.

Nisbet, R. (1967), *The Sociological Tradition*, Heinemann: London.

Parson, T. (1966), *Societies: Evolutionary and Comparative Perspectives*, Prentice-Hall: Englewood, NJ.

Rancière, J. (1995), *On the Shores of the Political*, Verso: London.

Rousseau, J. (1968), *The Social Contract*, Penguin: Harmondsworth.

Sandel, M. (1982), *Liberalism and the Limits of Justice*, Cambridge University Press: Cambridge.

Selznick, P. (1992), *The Moral Commonwealth: Social Theory and the Promise of Community*, University of California Press: Berkeley and Los Angeles, Ca.

Soysal, Y. N. (1994), *Limits of Citizenship: Migrants and Postnational Membership in Europe*, University of Chicago Press: Chicago.

Strydom, P. (fortchoming 1999), 'Hermenuitic Culturalism and its Doubles: A Key Problem in the Reflexive Modernization Debate', *European Journal of Social Theory*, 2. 1.

Taylor, C. (1990), *Sources of the Self*, Cambridge University Press: Cambridge.

Tönnies, F. (1963), *Community and Society*, Harper and Row: New York.

Walzer, M. (1983), *Spheres of Justice*, Basic Books: New York.

Williams, R. (1976), 'Community' in *Keywords*, Fontana: London.

3 Communitarianism and the Practice of Toleration

MAURIZIO PASSERIN D'ENTRÈVES

I

The aim of this paper is to explore a question that has recently become a topic of concern for sociologists, political scientists and philosophers, and for all of us as citizens; one which has an immediate and pressing political relevance. It concerns, in fact, one of the very preconditions of civil coexistence, namely, the ability on the part of individuals and groups belonging to different cultures and traditions to tolerate and respect one another. I should like to address this question by focusing first on the debate between liberal and communitarian thinkers, a debate that could be characterized at first sight in terms of a contrast between the value of tolerance and that of community. From the standpoint of this debate, the question that I want to examine may be formulated as follows: does an appeal to community negate the value of tolerance? Is community, in a strong and constitutive sense, inimical to pluralism and the acceptance of difference? The most common or intuitive reply to such questions would probably be affirmative: tolerance and community are inimical notions, which stand opposed on the spectrum of political values and represent what the language of symbolic logic would call a disjunction. According to this view, community is a term associated with strong identities, fixed by custom and tradition and rooted in history and/or collective memory. Tolerance, on the other hand, suggests more flexible identities, less rooted in history and collective memory and more open to the acceptance of difference, of plurality and of alternative lifestyles. The practice of tolerance seems to flourish best in a context characterized by modes of behaviour and cultural lifestyles that do not require unconditional support or identification and that may be constantly modified by means of rational reflection and critical evaluation.

In the modern age it would seem, therefore, that those who uphold the principle of tolerance have little in common with those who uphold the principle of community. How is it possible to defend tolerance if one is a bearer of an identity rooted in history and fixed by tradition, afraid of being assimilated or displaced by other identities? Conversely, how is it possible to defend the value of tolerance if cultural differences and different lifestyles are all endowed with equal dignity and value, to the point where all differences tend to disappear?

In what follows I should like to soften this picture of a necessary conflict between tolerance and community and to modify certain assumptions which are usually associated with these two principles. In order to do so I shall examine a recent and influential critique of liberal theory that has been advanced by a number of communitarian theorists, such as Alasdair MacIntyre, Michael Sandel, Charles Taylor, Michael Walzer and Roberto Mangabeira Unger. This critique has focused on two important liberal traditions in moral and political theory, namely, utilitarianism and Kantianism. Communitarian thinkers have criticized the conception of rationality and the understanding of human agency articulated by these two traditions, since they claim that utilitarianism reduces rationality to the instrumental calculation of costs and benefits and views the agent has a maximizer of utility, while Kantianism conceives rationality in purely formal and procedural terms and considers the agent in abstraction from any concrete historical, social or political context. In opposition to utilitarianism communitarian thinkers have advocated a more substantive conception of rationality that emphasizes the role of reflection, deliberation and rational evaluation, while in opposition to Kantianism they have formulated a view of human agency that situates it in a concrete moral and political context and that stresses the constitutive role that communal aims and attachments assume for a situated self.

We may identify four central issues around which the communitarian critique of liberal moral and political theory has focused: the liberal conception of the self, the liberal understanding of community, the nature and scope of distributive justice and the priority of the right over the good. It is my belief that the critique of the liberal conception of the self may be of great help in addressing the question of tolerance. I am convinced, on the other hand, that certain versions of community advanced by communitarian thinkers are in profound contrast with the principle of tolerance and the recognition and positive acknowledgement of value-pluralism. Let us then examine the four issues around which communitarian theorists have articulated their critique of liberal moral and political theory.

Conception of the Self

The critique of the liberal conception of the self has been formulated most forcefully by Taylor, Sandel and MacIntyre. Taylor has argued that much of contemporary liberal theory is based on an atomistic conception of the person and on a view of human agency which focuses almost exclusively on the will and on freedom of choice. Against the atomistic conception, expressed most clearly in the writings of Robert Nozick, Taylor has articulated and defended a relational and intersubjective conception of the self that stresses the social, cultural, historical and linguistic constitution of personal identity. Against the voluntaristic conception of human agency, he has formulated a cognitive conception that emphasizes the role of critical reflection, self-interpretation and rational evaluation (Taylor, 1985). Sandel has advanced a number of similar arguments, stressing the constitutive role of community in the formation of personal identity, showing the inadequacy of the disembodied and unencumbered conception of the self that underlies Rawls' theory of justice, and highlighting the cognitive dimensions of reflection and deliberation for a theory of human agency (Sandel, 1982). MacIntyre, for his part, has defended a teleological conception of human nature and a contextualist view of human agency. According to the teleological conception, moral conduct is characterized not by the conscientious adherence to rules and principles (deontology), but by the exercise of the virtues which aims at the realization of the good. Such good may be attained through what MacIntyre calls the 'narrative unity' of a human life. According to the contextualist view of human agency, no agent can properly locate, interpret and evaluate his or her actions except within the boundaries of a moral tradition or those of a moral community. For MacIntyre the great fault of the Enlightenment project of providing a rational foundation to morality and politics has been to reject both the teleological conception of human nature and the contexualist understanding of human agency, because in so doing it has left the agent with no criteria on which to adjudicate between competing values and without a moral context within which his or her actions could be rendered meaningful and coherent (MacIntyre, 1981 and 1988).

Conception of Community

The major advocate of a strong conception of community is MacIntyre, who has argued that the moral life and its attendant virtues can only flourish within local forms of community united around a shared conception of the good.

One of the principal drawbacks of modern liberal theory, according to MacIntyre, is the absence of an adequate theory of community as constitutive of moral character and as the locus of moral practice. Both Kantian and utilitarian moral theories fail in this respect, the former because of its abstract and formal conception of community, the latter because it views community in purely instrumental terms (MacIntyre, 1981). Another strong advocate of community is Sandel, who has argued that community should be understood in a constitutive sense. He has distinguished between an instrumental, a sentimental and a constitutive conception of community, and has argued that only the third provides the basis for a politics centred on friendship, self-knowledge and the cultivation of moral character (Sandel, 1982). Walzer, for his part, has stressed the way in which community not only shapes moral character, but is constitutive of our various conceptions of justice. According to him, the just distribution of social goods depends on the shared understandings that members have of these goods, and these understandings depend, in turn, on the nature of the community that members inhabit. For Walzer, membership in a community is itself the most important good, since it shapes our understandings of social goods and determines our various conceptions of justice (Walzer, 1983). Another important defender of community is Unger, who has formulated two distinct conceptions of community. The first, centred around the notion of 'organic groups', aims at overcoming the antinomies of liberal thought, such as the opposition between reason and emotion, fact and value and individual and community. The theory of organic groups overcomes these antinomies by reconciling the particular and the universal within the context of an open and egalitarian community (Unger, 1975). The second formulation centres around the idea of 'formative contexts' and attempts to overcome the strict opposition between autonomy and dependence and between piecemeal and revolutionary change. By revising the formative contexts and making them open to institutional change such oppositions can be overcome and new forms of democratic community can be established (Unger, 1987).

Nature and Scope of Distributive Justice

The question of justice has been at the centre of recent communitarian critiques. Walzer, Taylor and Sandel have argued that the liberal conception of justice, especially the version articulated by Rawls, is deficient in several respects. Walzer has maintained that there can be no single principle of distributive justice applicable to all social goods, but rather that different social goods ought to be distributed for different reasons and according to different criteria, which are derived from the different understandings that members have of the social goods themselves. Since for Walzer the most important good is membership of a political community, distributive principles must be specified in the light of a background conception of the nature and purpose of community and of the social goods that are attained through it (Walzer, 1983). Taylor, on the other hand, has argued that modern liberal democratic societies operate on the basis of different and at times mutually exclusive principles of distributive justice, like rights, desert, need, membership and contribution, and that we should therefore abandon the search for a single principle of distribution. Distributive arrangements should instead be based upon and evaluated by independent and mutually irreducible principles of distributive justice (Taylor, 1985). Both Taylor and Walzer argue, moreover, that the search for a single overarching principle of distributive justice, applicable to different goods and across different spheres, appears plausible to contemporary liberals only because they start from the perspective of the autonomous self as bearer of rights, and proceed to frame the issue of distributive justice in terms of the conflicting rights-claims of sovereign individuals. If the framework adopted starts instead from a social conception of the individual and from the acknowledgment of the primacy of community, then it is possible to argue that principles of justice must be pluralistic in form (Walzer, 1983), and that different principles of distributive justice articulate different conceptions of the good and different understandings of the value of human association (Taylor, 1985). Sandel, for his part, has challenged the primacy of justice over the claims of community and has argued in favour of an understanding of politics that stresses the values of friendship, mutual knowledge and the attainment of the common good. In his view, Rawls' claim for the priority of justice over the common good can only be sustained if the parallel claim for the priority of the self over its ends is valid, and Sandel maintains that this conception of the person is incoherent because it fails to account for the constitutive role of our communal aims and attachments. By formulating an alternative conception of the person that takes into account these constitutive aims and attachments, Sandel claims that we may be governed by the common good rather than by the principles of right and justice would still have a limited application, but they would no longer have primacy over the values of community or the requirements of the common good (Sandel, 1982 and 1984a).

Priority of the Right Over the Good

One of the central claims of Rawls' theory of justice is that a just society does not seek to promote any specific conception of the good, but provides instead a neutral framework of basic rights and liberties within which individuals can pursue their own values and life-plans, consistent with a similar liberty for others. A just society must therefore be governed by principles that do not presuppose any particular conception of the good. What justifies these principles is that they conform to the concept of right, a moral category which is prior to the good and independent of it. The right is prior to the good, then, in the sense (1) that individual rights cannot be sacrificed for the sake of welfare or the general good; (2) that the principles of justice that specify these rights cannot be premised on any particular conception of the good, but must be independently derived from the concept of right (Rawls, 1971). This strict priority of the right over the good has been questioned by Sandel, Taylor and MacIntyre. Sandel has argued that the priority of the right over the good rests upon a conception of the self as always prior to its ends, values and attachments, a conception that he finds implausible because we cannot conceive ourselves as wholly detached from our communal ends and values. To acknowledge the constitutive dimension of our communal ends means to challenge the strict priority of the right over the good, and to question the neutrality of the principles of justice with respect to different conceptions of the good (Sandel, 1982 and 1984b). Taylor, on the other hand, has maintained that every conception of the right and of justice presupposes a conception of the human good and of the good of political association. In his view, Rawls' claim of the priority of right cannot be sustained, since it is itself premised on a prior conception of the human good (the exercise of free moral agency) and of the good of political association (securing the conditions for the full development and exercise of our moral powers) (Taylor, 1985). MacIntyre, for his part, has argued that there can be no neutral justification of principles of justice, since every conception of justice is located within a particular tradition and articulates its specific conception of the good. The good is thus always prior to the right, and the question for him is whether the conception of the good articulated by the liberal democratic tradition can be shown to be rationally superior to others (MacIntyre, 1981 and 1988).

II

In the light of this critique of liberal moral and political theory, I should like to examine its implications with respect to the question of tolerance. As I mentioned earlier, I believe that the conception of the person advanced by communitarian theorists, in particular Taylor and Sandel, may provide many elements in favour of the principle of tolerance.

Charles Taylor, in his essay 'What is Human Agency' (1985) has suggested a distinction between a conception of the agent as 'simple weigher' of preferences and desires, and a conception of the agent as 'strong evaluator' of his or her choices with respect to given preferences and desires.[1] The distinction between simple weigher and strong evaluator corresponds to the distinction between the voluntaristic and the cognitive conception of the person. In the cognitive conception, corresponding to that of the strong evaluator, the stress is laid not so much on the freedom of choice of the agent, but on his or her capacity for critical reflection, self-interpretation and rational evaluation. The agent who evaluates her preferences and desires employs a qualitative language based on distinctions of worth or value, and by means of this language (and a corresponding cognitive attitude) is able to decide whether they are worth pursuing. The agent who judges her preferences and desires critically and reflectively goes deeper than the simple weigher, because she examines her motivations in depth. As Taylor puts it (1985, pp. 25–6):

> [A] strong evaluator, by which we mean a subject who strongly evaluates desires, goes deeper, because he characterizes his motivations at greater depth. To characterize one desire or inclination as worthier, or nobler, or more integrated than others, is to speak of it in terms of the kind of quality of life which it expresses and sustains .... Whereas for the simple weigher what is at stake is the desirability of different consummations, those defined by his *de facto* desires, for the strong evaluator reflection also examines the different possible modes of being the agent. Motivations or desires do not only count in virtue of the attraction of the consummations but also in virtue of the kind of life and kind of subject that these desires properly belong to.

It follows, therefore, that

> whereas a reflection about what we feel like more, which is all a simple weigher can do in assessing motivations, keeps us as it were at the periphery; a reflection on the kind of beings we are takes us to the centre of our existence as agents. Strong evaluation is not just a condition of articulacy about preferences, but

also about the quality of life, the kind of beings we are or want to be. It is in this sense deeper.

This capacity to examine in depth one's motivations and desires seems to me to be an important element in favour of the principle of tolerance. I would argue, in fact, that among the factors responsible for intolerance and prejudice vis-à-vis other individuals and groups and other traditions and cultures, one of the most common is the lack of self-reflection about one's identity. The numerous instances of hostility against people of a different ethnic, religious, cultural or racial background are often the product of insecurity about one's identity; an insecure identity, I would argue, will always appear threatened when confronted with different cultures and lifestyles. In this respect, the lack of self-reflection upon one's identity, the absence of a rational evaluation of one's motives, beliefs and desires, tends to produce fear and hostility towards those groups that appear to be different. Through a simple and well-known psychological mechanism we tend to project upon these groups all those elements or our identity that have been repressed or left unexamined. I would argue, therefore, that the cognitive conception of human agency formulated by Taylor – that is, of a subject that critically evaluates his or her beliefs and desires, that reflects upon his or her needs and motives and that judges the worth of his or her preferences – is a conception that works in favour of the recognition and extension of the principle of tolerance, insofar as it articulates the conditions for the establishment of post-conventional identities based on autonomy, reflexivity and the acknowledgement of difference.

I should like now to examine the conception of the person advanced by Sandel. This conception is greatly indebted to the one put forward by Charles Taylor, in particular to the distinction between a voluntaristic and a cognitive conception of agency. Sandel, for his part, has stressed the constitutive role of community in the formation of personal identity and the importance of communal loyalties and attachments for the definition of our public identity. In his view, one of the principle flaws of Rawls' theory of justice is to conceive the subject as always prior to his ends, that is, as a being who is individuated in advance of his values and aims. This conception, Sandel argues (1982, p. 179),

> fails plausibly to account for certain indispensable aspects of our moral experience. For [such conception] insists that we view ourselves as independent selves, independent in the sense that our identity is never tied to our aims and attachments. Given our moral power to form, to revise, and rationally to pursue a conception of the good, the continuity of our identity is unproblematically

assured. No transformation of my aims and attachments could call into question the person I am, for no such allegiances, however deeply held, could possibly engage my identity to begin with. But we cannot regard ourselves as independent in this way without great cost to those loyalties and convictions whose moral force consists partly in the fact that living by them is inseparable from understanding ourselves as the particular persons we are – as members of this family or community or nation or people, as bearers of this history, as sons and daughters of that revolution, as citizens of this republic …. To imagine a person incapable of constitutive attachments such as these is not to conceive an ideally free and rational agent, but to imagine a person wholly without character, without moral depth.

Sandel has also argued that this conception of the person does not acknowledge the role of reflection and deliberation on the values and ends which are constitutive of one's identity. Rawls' voluntaristic conception presupposes an antecedently individuated self, a self whose identity is established prior to its ends and whose choices are determined by contingent preferences. The adoption of an end does not presuppose a reflection upon one's identity, and cannot therefore provide reasons for our moral choices. Sandel's argument is that only by adopting a cognitive conception of the person – a conception that stresses the role of reflection and deliberation on the ends and values constitutive of one's identity – is it possible to provide a rational justification of our actions and moral choices.

Now, at first sight, this critique of Rawls' conception of the person would seem problematic for those who want to defend the value of tolerance. The appeal to communities constitutive of one's identity – the family, the nation, the people or its history – has often been associated with forms of intolerance, tribalism, closure and social exclusion. But to interpret Sandel's appeal to community in this way would be misleading. His aim is not to defend a conception of the self as totally determined by its membership or identification with a particular community. He wants to avoid the pitfall of either radically situating the self in a communal context or abstracting it entirely from particular loyalties and attachments. His conception of the self acknowledges the partially constitutive role of community in the formation of personal identity, but stresses at the same time the role of self-reflection, rational deliberation and critical evaluation of the ends and values of the community (or, rather, of the various communities we belong to as members of a modern and differentiated society). The identity of the subject is thus not fixed in advance by communal values and attachments, but is shaped and transformed by critical reflection and self-interpretation. Such conception maybe called that of a *reflexively situated self*, since the self is open to growth and transformation with respect to its identity and is able to evaluate critically its loyalties, values and attachments. As Sandel puts is (1982, p. 172, emphasis added):

> [W]e cannot be wholly unencumbered subjects of possession, individuated in advance and given prior to our ends, but must be subjects constituted in part by our central aspirations and attachments, *always open, indeed vulnerable, to growth and transformation in the light of revised self-understandings.*

I would argue that if we start from this reflexive conception of the self, many of the objections levelled against communitarian theories lose their force. Intolerance and prejudice are not attitudes that characterize those who critically evaluate the ends and values of their communities and are open to self-reflection and self-evaluation. Intolerance, on the contrary, is the response that normally arises in situations characterized by anomie, by social dislocation, by the lack of valid cultural models and by the absence of a public context of argumentation and debate. It is, in this sense, the product of situations in which individuals lack the normative resources for the formation of autonomous and reflexive identities. Sandel himself has offered an argument along these lines in the introduction to *Liberalism and Its Critics*, where he makes the following observations (1984a, p. 7):

> Liberals often argue that a politics of the common good, and the moral particularity it affirms, open the way to prejudice and intolerance. The modern nation-state is not the Athenian polis, they point out; the scale and diversity of modern life have rendered the Aristotelian political ethic nostalgic at best and dangerous at worst. Any attempt to govern by a vision of the good is likely to lead to a slippery slope of totalitarian temptations. Communitarians reply that intolerance flourishes most where forms of life are dislocated, roots unsettled, traditions undone. In our day, the totalitarian impulse has sprung less from the convictions of confidently situated selves than from the confusions of atomized, dislocated, frustrated selves, at sea in a world where common meanings have lost their force. As Hannah Arendt has written: 'What makes mass society so difficult to bear is not the number of people involved [...] but the fact that the world between them has lost its power to gather them together, to relate and to separate them.' Insofar as our public life has withered, our sense of common involvement diminished, to that extent we lie vulnerable to the mass politics of totalitarian solutions.

III

I should like now the examine the various conceptions of community that have been advanced by communitarian thinkers. For the purpose of my argument I shall focus on those of MacIntyre, Sandel and Unger.

MacIntyre, in my view, offers a conception of community which is radically hostile to the principle of tolerance. His conception of community is based upon a strong rejection of pluralism, in particular the value-pluralism of modern liberal-democratic societies. For MacIntyre, the main problem of modernity is the lack of an authentic moral consensus on the values and norms that should govern our public life. The condition of moral philosophy and of political debate in general, he argues, betrays this fact clearly enough: we find ourselves surrounded by arguments which proceed from premises to conclusions in a perfectly consistent manner, but whose premises are simply undebatable. For example, those who uphold an egalitarian position in economic and social matters argue that income should be more equally distributed on the basis of need, while believers in the (natural or acquired) right to private property object that it is unjust to take away from anyone what has been lawfully acquired by their own efforts. To each party the other seems to be begging the question of where to begin the argument, since their premises are so radically opposed as to appear incommensurable, and neither has the hope of convincing the other of the rightness or legitimacy of his starting point. This lack of normative consensus, according to MacIntyre, is one of the consequences of our liberal-pluralist culture. As he writes (1981, p. 229):

> [O]ur pluralist culture possesses no method of weighing, no rational criterion for deciding between claims based on legitimate entitlement against claims based on need [...] these two types of claim are indeed, as I suggested, incommensurable, and the metaphor of 'weighing' moral claims is not just inappropriate but misleading.

For MacIntyre, the only solution to this condition of conflict and anomie is to revive the ancient and medieval conception of morality of Aristotle and St Thomas Aquinas, i.e. to revive the idea of the virtues and the teleological conception of human nature that predated modernity, since he believes that only on its basis we can reconstitute a genuine moral consensus on the values and norms that should govern our social and political life. I would argue that this proposal, together with the idea of constructing local forms of community integrated around a shared conception of the good, does not leave much space for tolerance, since it does not acknowledge the legitimacy of conflict and the existence of a genuine pluralism of values in the moral and political spheres of contemporary society.

The conception of community articulated by Sandel is not open to this type of objection, because it recognizes the existence of a plurality of conceptions of the good and the possibility of conflict between alternative conceptions that may occur both within a community and between different communities. Sandel has traced a distinction between three conceptions of community, which he calls respectively instrumental, sentimental and constitutive.[2] In defending this last conception he has not argued in favour of a strong moral consensus on the lines suggested by MacIntyre; rather, he has stressed the conflict that may arise between different values and different moral or political identities and the need to operate a choice among conflicting values and identities by exercising our capacities for judgment, for rational deliberation and critical self-evaluation. In a passage in *Liberalism and the Limits of Justice*, in which he examines Rawls' arguments in defence of the difference principle, Sandel has in fact made the following argument (1982, p. 146, emphases original):

> Rawls seems generally to assume that once the rights of the individual are dealt with, an unspecified social claim predominates without any account of a determinate community or wider subject of possession being required ... [But] there is no such this as '*the* society as a whole' or '*the* more general society,' taken in the abstract, no single 'ultimate' community whose pre-eminence just goes without argument or further description. Each of us moves in an indefinite number of communities, some more inclusive than others, each making different claims on our allegiance, and there is no saying in advance which is *the* society or community whose purposes should govern the disposition of any particular set of our attributes and endowments.

It seems clear from this passage that Sandel acknowledges the existence of a plurality of conceptions of the good and the conflict that may arise between them. We are not members of a single community or of communities whose purpose is to attain a shared conception of the good. Insofar as we are members of modern societies, i.e. of societies which have attained an institutional differentiation of value-spheres, of social roles and of action-domains, we belong to a plurality of communities with different and at times conflicting visions of the good. Within each of these communities we may also find that we are pursuing not one but different goals, and these may not always be in harmony with each other. It follows, therefore, that the problem of conflict between different goals, values and identities, both in the case of membership in a single community and membership in a plurality of communities, must be acknowledged and addressed constructively, rather than avoided or ignored by appealing to a pre-modern conception of the unity of values. Sandel, in my view, has addressed this problem in a manner that is neither reductive (such as: conflict may exist, but can always be overcome by employing game-theoretic or rational choice strategies), nor monistic (such as: genuine conflict does not exist, and if it does, it can always be overcome by appealing to a higher or supreme value). Like Taylor, Sandel has emphasized the importance of judgment, or self-reflection and self-interpretation for the justification of our moral choices and of public discussion and unconstrained argumentation for the justification of our political or collective decisions (Sandel, 1984b, 1984c and 1988).

I should like now to consider briefly the two conceptions of community formulated by Unger. Both conceptions, in my view, are compatible with the acceptance of the principle of tolerance. The first conception, centred around the notion of organic groups, aims at overcoming the antinomies of liberal thought, such as the opposition of reason and emotion, fact and value and individual and community. The theory of organic groups overcomes these antinomies by reconciling the particular and the universal within the context of an open and egalitarian community based on ties of solidarity. This conception maintains the distinction between self and society and emphasizes the open character of community in respect of new members and of alternative communities. Such conception seems therefore compatible with the recognition of the value of tolerance. The second conception, characterized by the notion of formative contexts, attempts to overcome the tension between autonomy and dependence and the opposition between reformist and revolutionary programmes of social change. According to Unger, these oppositions can be overcome by constructing democratic forms of community which empower individuals and groups and enable them to revise their formative contexts. Unger maintains that this conception of community does not presuppose value-consensus or value-integration. Community is valued because of its ability to provide people with

> a zone of heightened mutual vulnerability in which they can free themselves, partly, from the experience of a flat and insoluble conflict between self-assertion and attachment to others .... *Politics* argues that a conception of community that gives pride of place to heightened mutual vulnerability and to the partial reconciliation of self-affirmation and attachment can be justified more

persuasively, and corresponds to more inclusive and radical concerns, than views of community that emphasize shared values or conflict-free harmony (1987, pp. 43–4, emphasis original).

This conception seems therefore to present no obstacles to the affirmation and recognition of the principle of tolerance.[3]

IV

My final remarks address the question what has divided liberals most strongly from their communitarian critics, namely, that of the priority of the right over the good. As we saw previously, liberals such as Rawls and Ronald Dworkin want to uphold this priority as well as the neutrality of the principles of justice with respect to different conceptions of the good. A just society, they claim, does not seek to promote any specific conception of the good, but provided instead a neutral framework of basic rights and liberties within which individuals can pursue their own values and life-plans, consistent with a similar liberty for others. Communitarian thinkers, on the other hand, have maintained that there cannot be a neutral justification of principles of justice, since every conception of justice is located within a particular tradition and articulates its specific conception of the good. The right cannot therefore be prior to the good and cannot be established independently of the ends, values and understandings of a particular community (such community need not be local in character and may indeed coincide with the modern nation-state).

I do not want to enter into the merit of this particular debate, which has seen one of the principle contenders, namely Rawls, progressively modify his position to the point of accepting many of the communitarian arguments (cf. Rawls, 1971, 1980, 1985, 1987, 1988 and 1993). I am interested, rather, in examining the consequences that the communitarian thesis may have with respect to the question of tolerance. I would argue that the priority of the good over the right has negative consequences only in those cases where it is joined to a *monistic* conception of the good. Of the authors I have examined, only MacIntyre explicitly defends a monistic conception of the good, while Taylor, Sandel, Walzer and Unger defend a pluralistic conception, acknowledge the legitimacy of conflict between alternative visions of the good and argue in favour of democratic procedures of conflict-resolution based on tolerance, mutual respect and unconstrained political debate.

Notes

1   This distinction is indebted to the one put forth by Harry Frankfurt, between 'first-order desires' and 'second-order desires'. Cf. Frankfurt (1971). According to Frankfurt (p. 6) 'human beings are not alone in having desires and motives, or in making choices. They share these things with members of certain other species, some of which even appear to engage in deliberation and to make decisions based on prior thought. It seems to be peculiarly characteristic of humans, however, that they are able to form ... second-order desires'. In other words, it is a characteristic of human beings to be able to evaluate one's desires, to discriminate between those that are worth pursuing and those that are not. This is the reason why 'no animal other than man ... appears to have the capacity for reflective self-evaluation that is manifested in the formation of second-order desires' (p. 7).

2   The instrumental conception characterizes most versions of utilitarianism and libertarian theories of politics (e.g. Nozick and Hayek). The sentimental conception is the one attributed to Rawls and refers to the sentiments of solidarity and fraternity that may arise between individuals whose identity is already defined prior to the establishment of social ties. The constitutive conception is the one defended by Sandel and refers to the partially constitutive role of community in the formation of personal and public identity.

3   I shall not examine Walzer's conception of community because it has always been joined to a defence of the principles of tolerance, pluralism and the separation of institutional spheres and respect for different conceptions of the good (see 1983, chs 1, 2 and 13 and 1984).

Bibliography

Barry, B. (1989), Theories of Justice, Harvester Wheatsheaf: Hemel Hempstead.

Barry, B. (1995), Justice as Impartiality, Clarendon Press: Oxford.

Baynes, K. (1988), 'The Liberal/Communitarian Controversy and Communicative Ethics', Philosophy and Social Criticism, Vol. 14, Nos 3–4, pp. 293–313.

Baynes, K. (1990), 'The Liberal/Communitarian Controversy and Communicative Ethics' in Rasmussen, q.v.

Beiner, R. (1992), What's the Matter with Liberalism?, University of California Press: Berkeley, Ca.

Bell, D. (1993), Communitarianism and its Critics, Clarendon Press: Oxford.

Bellah, R. et al. (1985), Habits of the Heart, University of California Press: Berkeley, Ca.

Benhabib, S. (1982), 'The methodological illusions of modern political theory: the case of Rawls and Habermas', Neue Hefte fuer Philosophie, No. 21, Spring, pp. 47–74.

Benhabib, S. (1989), 'Autonomy, Modernity, and Community' in Honneth, A., McCarthy, T., Offe, C. and Wellmer, A. (Hrsg), Zwischenbetrachtungen Im Prozess der Aufklaerung, Suhrkamp Verlag: Frankfurt.

Benhabib, S. (1992), Situating the Self, Polity Press: Cambridge.

Berry, C. (1989), The Idea of a Democratic Community, Harvester Wheatsheaf: Hemel Hempstead.

Buchanan, A. (1989), 'Assessing the Communitarian Critique of Liberalism', Ethics, Vol. 99, No. 4 (July), pp. 852–82.

Chapman, J. and Shapiro, I. (eds) (1993), Democratic Community: NOMOS XXXV, New York University Press: New York.

Damico, A.J. (ed.) (1986), Liberals on Liberalism, Rowman and Littlefield: Totowa, NJ.

Delaney, C.F. (ed.) 91994), The Liberalism-Communitarianism Debate, Rowman and Littlefield: Lanham, Md.

Doppelt, G. (1988), 'Beyond Liberalism and Communitarianism', Philosophy and Social Criticism, Vol. 14, Nos 3–4, pp. 271–92.

Doppelt, G. (1990), 'Beyond Liberalism and Communitarianism' in Rasmussen, q.v.

Douglass, R.B. et al. (eds) (1990), Liberalism and the Good, Routledge: New York.

Dworkin, R. (1977), Taking Rights Seriously, Harvard University Press: Cambridge, Mass.

Dworkin, R. (1985), A Matter of Principle, Harvard University Press: Cambridge, Mass.

Dworkin, R. (1986), Law's Empire, Harvard University Press: Cambridge, Mass.

Dworkin, R. (1989), 'Liberal Community', California Law Review, Vol. 77, No. 3 (May), pp. 479–504.

Frankfurt, H. (1971), 'Freedom of Will and the Concept of a Person', Journal of Philosophy, Vol. 67, No. 1 (January), pp. 5–20.

Frazer, E. and Lacey, N. (1993), The Politics of Community, Harvester Wheatsheaf: Hemel Hempstead.

Galston, W. (1991), Liberal Purposes, Cambridge University Press: Cambridge.

Goodin, R. and Reeve, A. (eds) (1989), Liberal Neutrality, Routledge: London.

Gutmann, A. (1985), 'Communitarian Critics of Liberalism', Philosophy and Public Affairs, Vol. 14, No. 3 (Summer), pp. 308–22.

Johnston, D. (1994), The Idea of a Liberal Theory, Princeton University Press: Princeton, NJ.

Jordan, B. (1989), The Common Good, Basil Blackwell: Oxford.

Kymlicka, W. (1989), Liberalism, Community, and Culture, Clarendon Press: Oxford.

Larmore, C. (1987), Patterns of Moral Complexity, Cambridge University Press: Cambridge.

Macedo, S. (1990), Liberal Virtues, Clarendon Press: Oxford.

MacIntyre, A. (1981), After Virtue, 2nd end 1984, University of Notre Dame Press: Notre Dame.

MacIntyre, A. (1984), Is Patriotism a Virtue?, the Lindley Lecture, University of Kansas.

MacIntyre, A. (1988), Whose Justice? Which Rationality?, University of Notre Dame Press: Notre Dame.

Mendus, S. (1989), Toleration and the Limits of Liberalism, Macmillan: London.

Milligan, D. and Watts Miller, W. (eds) (1992), Liberalism, Citizenship and Autonomy, Avebury: Aldershot.

Moon, J.D. (1993), Constructing Community, Princeton University Press: Princeton.

Moore, M. (1993), Foundations of Liberalism, Clarendon Press: Oxford.

Nozick, R. (1974), Anarchy, State, and Utopia, Basic Books: New York.

Oldfield, A. (1990), Citizenship and Community, Routledge: London.

Phillips, D. (1993), Looking Backward: A Critical Appraisal of Communitarian Thought, Princeton University Press: Princeton.

Rasmussen, D. (ed.) (1990), Universalism vs. Communitarianism, MIT Press: Cambridge.

Rawls, J. (1971), A Theory of Justice, Harvard University Press: Cambridge, Mass.

Rawls, J. (1980), 'Kantian Constructivism in Moral Theory', The Journal of Philosophy, Vol. 77, No. 9 (September), pp. 515–72.

Rawls, J. (1985), 'Justice as Fairness: Political not Metaphysical', Philosophy and Public Affairs, Vol. 14, No. 3 (Summer), pp. 223–51.

Rawls, J. (1987), 'The Idea of an Overlapping Consensus', Oxford Journal of Legal Studies, Vol. 7, No. 1 (Spring), pp. 1–25.

Rawls, J. (1988), 'The Priority of Right and Ideas of the Good', Philosophy and Public Affairs, Vol. 17, No. 4 (Fall), pp. 251–76.

Rawls, J. (1989), 'The Domain of the Political and Overlapping Consensus', New York University Law Review, Vol. 64, No. 2 (May), pp. 233–55.

Rawls, J. (1993), Political Liberalism, Columbia University Press: New York.

Reynold, C.H. and Norman, R.V. (eds) (1988), Community in America, University of California Press: Berkeley, Ca.

Rosenblum, N. (ed.), Liberalism and the Moral Life, Harvard University Press: Cambridge, Mass.

Sandel, M. (1982), Liberalism and the Limits of Justice, Cambridge University Press: Cambridge.

Sandel, M. (ed.) (1984a), Liberalism and its Critics, New York University Press: New York.

Sandel, M. (1984b), 'The Procedural Republic and the Unencumbered Self', Political Theory, Vol. 12, No. 1 (February), pp. 81–96.

Sandel, M. (1984c), 'Morality and the Liberal Ideal', The New Republic, 7 May, pp. 15–7.

Sandel, M. (1988), 'Democrats and Community', The New Republic, 22 February, pp. 20–3.

Selznick, P. (1992), The Moral Commonwealth, University of California Press: Berkeley, Ca.

Stern, P. (1991), 'Citizenship, Community and Pluralism: The Current Dispute on Distributive Justice', Praxis International, Vol. 11, No. 3 (October), pp. 261–97.

Sullivan, W. (1982), Reconstructing Public Philosophy, University of California Press: Berkeley, Ca.

Taylor, C. (1985), Human Agency and Language (Philosophical Papers, Vol. 1), Philosophy and the Human Sciences (Philosophical Papers, Vol. 2), Cambridge University Press: Cambridge.

Taylor, C. (1989), Sources of the Self, Cambridge University Press: Cambridge.

Unger, R.M. (1975), Knowledge and Politics, Free Press: New York.

Unger, R.M. (1987), Politics: A Work in Constructive Social Theory (3 vols), Cambridge University Press: Cambridge.

Waldron, J. (1993), Liberal Rights, Cambridge University Press: Cambridge.

Wallach, J. (1987), 'Liberals, Communitarians, and the Tasks of Political Theory', Political Theory, Vol. 15, No. 4 (November), pp. 581–611.

Walzer, M. (1981), 'Philosophy and Democracy', Political Theory, Vol. 9, No. 3 (August), pp. 379–99.

Walzer, M. (1983), Spheres of Justice, Basic Books: New York.

Walzer, M. (1984), 'Liberalism and the Art of Separation', Political Theory, Vol. 12, No. 3 (August), pp. 315–30.

Walzer, M. (1987), Interpretation and Social Criticism, Harvard University Press: Cambridge.

Walzer, M. (1990a), 'The Communitarian Critique of Liberalism', Political Theory, Vol. 18, No. 1 (February), pp. 6–23.

Walzer, M. (1990b), 'Two Kinds of Universalism', Nation and Universe: The Tanner Lectures on Human Values, Vol. 11, University of Utah Press: Salt Lake City.

Walzer, M. (1994), Thick and Thin: Moral Argument at Home and Abroad, University of Notre Dame Press: Notre Dame.

4　Nonconformism and Community[1]

AVNER DE-SHALIT

Introduction

The problem I want to address is this: if, on the one hand, we want to see good *citizens* around us, what we tend to look for are people who think originally, who search for new solutions to old problems, dare to ask questions and seek ways to protect the individual against the majority or the government; in short it seems that we look for nonconformists. If, on the other hand, we want good *citizenship*, then what we want is a strong sense of community, where people care for and about others in a way which goes beyond their care for themselves. Moreover, often citizenship reflects a 'conception of the purpose of the political community' (McLean, 1996). If this is so, then we are looking for – indeed assuming – community. I'll take these two assumptions, namely that the search for the good citizen implies a search for the nonconformist and that good citizenship implies community, for granted, given that both enjoy wide acceptance. They form part of our 'common sense' thinking about citizens and citizenship.[2] However, I want to address a certain problem which these assumptions give rise to: it seems, or so it has been argued, that community contradicts, not to mention oppresses, nonconformism. If this is true, how can we square the circle? How can we encourage nonconformism (good citizens) and community (good citizenship) at one and the same time? In fact, this is the social expression of a problem which may sound more familiar to you: how can we both be loyal to our values and achieve progress at the same time? Since progress derives from a process of critical reflection, is it impossible for a society to progress when its members are expected to be loyal?

I proceed to answer this question as follows: I start with the proposition that community contradicts nonconformism. I then explain why several such arguments make sense while others should be rejected. Finally, but perhaps most importantly, I claim that a certain notion of community not only lives in harmony with nonconformism, but also relies on nonconformism in order to sustain it.[3] If I am right, then the two positions mentioned above can be held simultaneously.

Before I go on I want to make clear what I mean by nonconformism. Nonconformism is quite often discussed in the context of private matters such as one's sexual habits or one's tastes in food or literature. I would tend to call such people 'eccentric'. But I refer to 'intellectual' nonconformism, where a person holds views and puts forward ideas and reasoning which are nonconformist. In what way? It seems to me that one crucial component of nonconformism must be that a person's views, ideas, reasoning, or acts are unexpected. Society expects people to act and react and hold views according to its experience and knowledge about prevalence and frequency. That is to say that if 95 per cent of people react by doing or believing in X when you present them with circumstances C, then we expect any individual faced with the same circumstances (C) to do X as well. In cases where about five per cent of people deviate from the norm, this is likely to be a symptom of being a minority. The question of when it becomes nonconformism is a function of its rarity. If only one person in a million holds a particular belief this person is *likely to be* a nonconformist. However, there must be an additional component, namely that this person puts forward reasoning and justifications for her holding this rather than that view or for doing this rather than that, a reason which must not derive only from her belonging to a different group or subgroup. The latter is the difference between being 'strange', or a stranger, and being 'nonconformist'.

Indeed, the rarity criterion is not enough. For example, a person who retreats from society is not necessarily a nonconformist. Thus nonconformism is also distinguished from dissidence. Nonconformism must involve deciding to remain with the conformists and challenging the basic beliefs, concepts or methodological assumptions of the conformists. Even if they have the opportunity to leave the community, they prefer to stay and put forward their claims. In Hirschman's (1970) terms, they 'voice' rather than 'exit'. If it is in music, for instance, nonconformists challenge the common rules of harmony.[4] If it is in philosophy, the nonconformists challenge the basic questions and paradigms[3] which most philosophers use. In that sense the conformists cannot stay indifferent to the nonconformists; there is something in what the latter do and say that forces the conformists to redefine their positions and to rethink their arguments.[5]

Last but not least, I do not claim that nonconformism is intrinsically good. It may be, but arguing so is beyond my aim here. Rather, I would like to claim that nonconformism does not contradict community and that indeed it is instrumentally good for a community.

Community vs Nonconformism

There are three claims about possible tensions between community and nonconformism: the traditionalist, the psychological, and the liberal. The first two (traditionalist and psychological) claim that community cannot or should not tolerate nonconformism; the third (liberal) claims that nonconformism within community is incoherent. Let me now examine these claims one by one.

The first group starts with the *claim from tradition*.[6] The more conservative notion of community as the search for roots implies that tradition plays a crucial role in the constitution of one's personality or 'self' and is therefore inconsistent with nonconformism.[7] If nonconformism is about renewal through criticism, community in the sense of searching for one's roots is about preservation and fighting renewal. The self is to be protected from radical change. This claim is therefore right. If you accept that community derives from tradition, as a conceptual claim, nonconformism cannot exist within community since it contradicts tradition. Even such a moderate traditionalist as Edmund Burke could not tolerate nonconformism, but rather expected people who wanted to change to do so within the existing framework of values, norms and institutions. Any other way of change was seen as dangerous.

However, such a model of community can be rejected not only on the basis of its being incompatible with free and autonomous citizens, but also from the point of view of morality. On the one hand it asserts that the community constitutes the self. On the other it allows no way of exit. There is no real exchange between the self and the community and there is no moral choice. If the results of the game are already known – once one is born into a community, one's moral principles are given – there is no genuine political role for the community and for personal morality. So I see no point in relating to this theory of community as a moral theory. This is nothing more than a theory of moral determinism. But if it is, what point is there in asserting that the community constitutes the self?[8]

So we move to the second claim in this group: the *psychological claim*. The self, it is argued, starts from an independent position, but in its search for wholeness it tries to identify with its social context. At the same time, nonconformism seems to suggest that one's moral identity at least is totally independent of the context. Thus how can the notion of community support nonconformism? To put this differently, community may imply something about the good citizen as well: the good citizen is not the original, but rather the one who finds a way to 'belong' (and thus conforms). Conformity in this model is the opposite of psychological alienation, and the role of community is to help people find a 'place', a 'home', and thereby overcome alienation.

I think that if you accept this version of communitarianism you do indeed oppose nonconformism, at least to a certain point. In fact, Michael Walzer (1970, ch. 1) puts forward an even stronger claim, namely that there is no nonconformism which is not related to the search for conformity within a community. In his book *Obligations*, he examines the question of the obligation to obey the law (which is conforming to the norms of the community). Refusing to obey the law, argues Walzer, is never done in the name of one's private norms, but in the name of loyalty to and conformity with the values of a certain sub-community.

Empirically Walzer may be right. Even John Locke, who cannot be 'accused' of being a communitarian, thought that people would disobey the ruler only when they could do so in and as a group. However, Walzer's assertion is also interesting from the theoretical standpoint. He assumes that this psychological alienation is actually impossible. Every appearance of nonconformism, then, becomes an identification with the norms of a sub-community vis-à-vis the norms of the larger community. For example, an artist who detaches herself from a community and is very critical of it, actually does so in the name of the values of a sub-community of artists. Nonconformism collapses into conformity with the sub-community. The bottom line is that if one accepts this model of community, there is no place for nonconformism as we have defined it, i.e. an individualistic, heroic position.

The third claim is that nonconformism necessitates limiting community, which is the *liberal claim*. For its flourishing, nonconformism needs a sort of release from social responsibility. In cases when the conflict between responsibility to one's community and nonconformism is inevitable, the balance should be in favour of nonconformism and the release from responsibility to one's community. The claim is that a nonconformist cannot be a nonconformist and loyal to her community simultaneously: loyalty to one's community weakens and undermines one's nonconformism. Notice that this is both a conceptual claim (about incoherence) and a normative claim (that nonconformism should have priority).

Think, for example, about the community of academics. Suppose a scientist develops an innovative theory, which is a departure from 'common knowledge'. The idea of an academic community implies that she has a social responsibility towards her colleagues to re-check and re-examine her theory before it can be published, and the more innovative the theory is, the stronger these obligations are, because such theories might cause an 'earthquake' in the community. Indeed, as Thomas Kuhn argues (1962, p. 135, quoted in Rescher, 1993, p. 39), the scientific community is constituted on the basis of such consensual commitments. For example, it took the ideas and theories which led to the 'New Deal' (which refined accepted opinion on economic growth) quite a long time to be published and advanced, in part because the nonconformist economists held a sense of responsibility, towards their fellow economists, who in turn had an impact on politics. Even though – perhaps because – the new theories rendered previous theories invalid, the reform economists had to consider the effect of their findings on the credibility of the community of economists. What if now everybody realised that the community of economists had been wrong all these years?

Another example is the silencing of the theory and theorists who eventually developed an immunisation to polio. Their claim was that the whole approach to the issue, which was based on vivisection, was mistaken because the illness in animals was different from the one in human beings. But this meant questioning the system and conventional medical research and had far-reaching implications for their fellow scientists. It took many years and many sick children before their theory gained legitimacy. During those years nonconformism was seen to have lost and community won. Research on animals showed that the virus attacked only nerve cells. Only in 1949, after examining cultures of human tissue as opposed to tissues taken from monkeys, did scientists find that the virus attacked other cells as well. This was the breakthrough to finding the polio immunisation (Enders, Weller and Rubbins, 1949).

This leads me to the most common argument for nonconformism – more or less the argument put forward by J.S. Mill in his *On Liberty*. Mill asks why we as a society need these 'trouble makers' who put our beliefs under critical scrutiny and raise doubts about our institutions. Mill's answer is that whenever we hold a certain belief we may be wrong, partly wrong, or right. If we are wrong it is clear why we need nonconformists who doubt our beliefs: we do not want to hold false beliefs. The same goes for the most common case, in which we are partly right and partly wrong. It's better if the wrong part of our beliefs is pointed out and corrected. But why do we want our beliefs to be doubted if they are right? Mill puts forward quite a simple, but nevertheless an attractive, explanation: even when we know we are right, we must know *why* we believe in what we believe. In other words, any belief which is not questioned soon becomes a prejudice and thereby loses its moral status. To this one could add that the mechanism of questioning a belief is a useful device for reducing mistakes, experiment biases and so on. But this is a less dramatic claim than Mill's, because all it says is that allowing nonconformists to doubt our beliefs is a way of preventing ourselves from falling into particular errors rather than assuring truth. In the last part of this paper I shall return to this claim and explain why I find it attractive in our context.

However, Mill's defence of nonconformism is problematic. Notice, that for Mill the philosophical inquiry is often a search for the truth. It is part of a package of individualism, intellectualism and progress that will be combined in a way as to enable society to improve itself, basing its institutions on scientific information. But if truth is the goal, why should we go out of our way to allow particular information or beliefs, which we know are true, to be questioned? To put this bluntly and perhaps controversially: if truth is the goal, who cares why and how we came to believe in this?[9]

There is, perhaps, a second way to interpret Mill's quest for nonconformism. Mill wants to maximise society's happiness (rather than come closer to finding the truth). This would overcome the difficulty I have just raised, but it would still seem problematic, since by this Mill is justifying nonconformism for the sake of the most conformist idea of his time, namely the maximisation of happiness. Indeed utilitarians assumed that 'everyone' sought to maximise happiness. If this is what *everyone* sought, why assume that nonconformists do so as well?

However, I think that there is a better explanation for Mill's insistence on having nonconformists around us. The reason is that nonconformists are engaged in the debate about social and moral beliefs. These beliefs constitute our identities: our 'self'. Now, when we say that this or that *idea* constitutes our 'self', we actually mean that the way this idea relates to other ideas is what constitutes our 'self'. We therefore mean that the *rationale* for this idea is a crucial part of it. When, for example, Mr Smith says he is a moral person because he is a socialist, or a humanist, or a good Christian, or an animal welfarist, he actually means that what makes him a moral person is not simply the set of values of socialism, Christianity, or whatever, but rather the set of arguments which defends his moral position and the fact that he is convinced by these (rather than opposing) arguments. It is the fact that every morning Mr Smith so-to-speak wakes up and weighs his positions against other positions and decides to be a socialist, Christian, or whatever. Being moral, then, is not only *doing* A rather than B, but also being able to understand why A is better than B and hence (being able to explain) choosing A. This choice must be according to the arguments supplied. Thus, inevitably, we need people to question our beliefs so that we become engaged in debate about them, even if they are true beliefs. Thus nonconformism is to be welcomed because it helps us define our identities. This leads me to the final part of my paper in which I describe the conception of community which supports, in fact relies on, nonconformism. To do this I now depart from the liberal claim and move to the republican model of community.

The model of community which does allow nonconformism to flourish is the republican model. I want to emphasise immediately that by the 'republican' model of community I mean something quite narrow. I do not mean the sort of argument which seeks to revive the glorious past or recreate conditions in which this past may be resurrected. Rather I mean the theory of citizenship and participatory democracy as the essence of community. The latter, then, becomes a political concept; a framework within which political and moral discourse is taking place.[10]

But before explaining how the republican model of community allows and encourages nonconformism, I would like to raise two possible arguments according to which even the republican model of community tends to inhibit nonconformism. One is that even community as participatory democracy may imply limiting nonconformism. Although on the face of it participatory democracy implies freedom of expression and encouraging public criticism, it may also lead to pressure to conform. In a less communitarian society the nonconformist is left alone to her own thoughts and acts, either because being politically involved is not necessarily a virtue or because others express indifference. However, the more participatory the community is, the more likely it is that the majority will put pressure on the nonconformists to conform, even if this is done with good intention and without meaning to oppress. In other words, if people are encouraged to participate, more will do so. Hence more conformists, who would otherwise remain indifferent and inactive, now join the political discourse and put additional pressure on the nonconformists. On the surface, at least, republican communitarianism therefore appears to oppose or limit nonconformism.

But this position seems odd. There is no reason why a community that encourages participation will not also guarantee by law or other means (e.g. book subsidies) that nonconformists are able to put forward their ideas without pressure to conform. The fact that everybody participates does not automatically imply that the majority's way of participating should involve continuous pressure on the nonconformists to conform, and there are legal and institutional ways of preventing this. Moreover, the assumption that if the majority puts pressure on the nonconformist to conform it is likely to succeed is mistaken. We may be misled to assume so because we sometimes tend to see a link between being free (in the sense of the space one has for oneself) and being nonconformist, but this is not necessarily true. Freedom is not a necessary condition for being nonconformist. There have been nonconformists in every totalitarian society.

There is, however, a second argument why the republican model of community may restrict nonconformism. The community has its own goals and ideas as to what constitutes the good. Fostering virtuous citizens means inculcating these rather than other values and therefore any community will seek to educate, organise and empower its members. The individuals, the citizens, will be 'educated, organised and empowered' (Fowler, 1991, p. 1). Notice that the individual's behaviour is described in the passive. This does not necessarily mean that the citizen is passive; rather that her activity is within a given framework. In fact, the more seriously a community takes itself, i.e. takes upon itself to organise, educate, empower, the more likely it is to encroach on spheres which are thought to be private, from the economy to the family and religious beliefs. This attitude leaves very little, in any, space for nonconformism. Contrary to this, I want to suggest that if you follow a modified version of the republican model of community, there is no reason to reject nonconformism.

There are many ways to understand the concept of community (see Hillery, quoted in Fowler, p. 164, fn 10). However, the most important argument put forward by communitarians is that the community 'constitutes' the self: one's notion of what and who one is is derived from the community. At this point the different models of community vary in the way they interpret the verb to 'derive'. But it seems to me that the only way one can argue that the self is indeed constituted by the community is if the derivation of values is accompanied by rational and critical reflection. I begin my defence of this position by refuting a counter-position and thereby reaching a positive defence.

To begin, then, communitarians have not always acknowledged that critical reflection is a necessary condition for the assertion that the self is constituted by the community to make sense. Indeed, community is often thought to be in contrast to many liberal values that have to do with critical reflection, such as freedom, equality and nonconformism. I think that there are two reasons for the mistaken belief that community cannot allow critical reflection of its own values. The first is that there are and have been communities that have not been engaged in such a process. In these cases, members have a sense of obligation that supersedes any new information which might question the reasons for these obligations. An example is the Jewish ultra-orthodox community of Jerusalem. Scientific achievements and discoveries have not affected their basic beliefs – e.g. the belief that the world was created 5,757 years ago. In the eyes of this community, loyalty and commitment take precedence over the existence of new facts; if the member leaves the community – for instance, by marrying an 'outsider' – the community will practice seven days of mourning as if that person had died. Thus, reflection does not constitute a necessary part of what every community is in the anthropological sense. This, however, does not worry me, because I am interested in a normative requirement which is the only interpretation of community that will fit the case of rational persons.

The second reason for the mistaken belief that community cannot allow critical reflection of its own values is that when we associate community, quite rightly, with communication between the members, many people then make a false move: they think that in order to communicate we should share beliefs and values, either because these beliefs allow communication or because we have to understand each other and this can be achieved only when we share values.[11]

This, however, is absolutely unnecessary. Why should we *share* values in order to communicate? Political and moral communication is not about how to agree but how to live together. The main point, then, is not to share values by agreeing on ideas but rather to be able to interpret each other's ideas, that is to make good sense of what the other has claimed and wants. Communicating properly should not require commonality of beliefs, but rather a certain degree of coordination:[12] debating the same beliefs or values (and interpreting them in a common way) on the basis of a common background (e.g. language in its broad sense). In fact, agreement often closes down communication. It is disagreement which opens it up, by raising questions. So communication within community should not assume shared beliefs as a precondition. Hence nonconformism can flourish in a communitarian framework of communication.

Other communitarian theorists, however, claim that shared beliefs are not a matter of better communication, but rather given norms to which the members of the community try to measure up, thereby gaining self-respect (Walzer, 1983, p. 278). If this is right, nonconformists can never gain self-respect unless they conform to the shared beliefs. Hence, nonconformism within community is incoherent. But the idea of shared beliefs is paradoxical: it does not make sense. The claim is that these shared beliefs constitute shared understanding. If there are norms or beliefs that constitute all members (hence they are shared) it is not necessary that they be *understood* in the same way. Indeed, if they constitute all members they are very likely to be *understood* differently by different members. These norms are a product of a debate about them. If so, we cannot have shared 'understanding'; rather, we have shared 'debating'. Moreover, any *belief* which is considered an idea (constituting the self), encompasses two elements: the declarative and the argumentative. The latter is the rationale, the explanation and defence of the former. If they are separated the declarative element loses its status as an idea and collapses into a groundless, and hence superstitious, belief. Now, no rational person wants to be constituted by a superstitious belief. Hence 'constituting' beliefs imply reasoning, hence different interpretations.

Once again my claim should be distinguished from a much weaker claim, namely that a community that seeks to be completely homogeneous in thought cannot prosper.[13] I argue that such a community is also conceptually impossible. Let me explain this again: many communitarians think that the community constitutes the self inasmuch as the declarative elements of its 'beliefs' seem *intuitive*. I claim that the community constitutes the self inasmuch as the arguments supporting the declarations seem *reasonable*. If Smith claims that he is *constituted* by the community, and that in that sense he is 'Scottish', 'nationalist' or 'demands his cultural autonomy', he cannot seriously claim so unless he has examined Scottish culture, found it appealing, and decided that self-governance or some sort of autonomy would make him better-off. There is, then, a process of weighing the *arguments* that form part of the 'Scottish' values, ideas, etc. In order to claim the above, Smith has to be *convinced* – not only feel – that he is part of this community.

So it is the argument, rather than the declaration, and its test is whether it is reasonable, namely whether we accept it after a critical, rational reflection, rather than whether we accept it intuitively. But if this is true, then the deliberation about the rationale and the argument is extremely important. Without the collective process of a critical assessment of our values how can one reach the point in which he or she evaluates his or her values and is able to detach himself or herself from them? It is only by being challenged by other opinions, put forward by other members of the community, that one can reassess one's beliefs. Therefore a group of people completely homogenous in thought cannot form a 'community': it lacks the mechanism and processes of critical reflection that help people become genuinely constituted by their community.

A practical question, with normative consequences, may be raised here. How can one decide upon whether a certain argument contributes to the debate about the idea of the good or whether it does not? Is it not a matter of prejudice ideas or a certain attitude one has towards the person who is putting forward this or that argument? And if we do have a certain principle according to which we know which argument contributes and which one does not – e.g. 'only arguments put forward by members of the community' – are we not put back in the position in which the community rejects not only the nonconformist argument but also the person who puts it forward?

On the face of it this is a difficult question, but it seems to me that the answer is very simple. In fact everything contributes, expect for very limited and well-defined cases. The reason that everything contributes is that this is *potentially* true: one may not be aware of the fact that a certain idea or argument will contribute in the future. Sometimes ideas are kept 'frozen', either in purpose or because they have 'disappeared' until they are found and become very meaningful to the deliberation. This is often true about pieces of art or certain works of composers that are forgotten for decades or found in places previously unknown (of course, I relate here to a piece of art as a text which puts forward an idea), such as some of Marx's early works, which were found only after his death. But this is also true with regard to cases in which one's ideas seem to one's contemporaries irrelevant or unimportant, and only after several years or decades are thought to be exciting, illuminating, etc. (e.g. most of Mozart's works). Thus my answer is that everything is relevant. However, there are limits.

The first limit is that the idea should be put forward with good intention. Ideas that are meant to manipulate and deceive others are irrelevant because they do not contribute to a *rational* deliberation, but rather are meant to make individuals be constituted by false beliefs, which is what this model tries to prevent. Second, 'everything' should be *reasonable*, in the sense that these ideas should not contradict all or almost all the community's ideas. For example, it may be considered irrelevant if the abolition of all East Asia's traditional values and the adoption of a liberal-democratic regime is advocated. However, suggesting a non-liberal democracy without abolishing traditional values there is relevant indeed (Bell, 1977). And third, it goes without saying that ideas that imply harming others physically are to be rejected legally and are therefore not relevant. Thus, one should be open to new ideas and challenges and evaluate one's beliefs according to them.

Communitarianism, then, should be about the process of collective reflection rather than about the beliefs themselves. In other words, I am claiming that in order for the communitarian argument that we are constituted by the community to make sense, we must emphasize not the sharing of beliefs but rather the process in which one's self is transformed, hence constituted.[14]

What should be emphasized is not the community of chance (e.g. the one to which we are born) but the community of choice. This act of choice is so meaningful precisely because one is defined by one's obligations and commitments. As David Miller argues (1988, p. 650), 'to divest oneself of such commitments would be, in one important sense, to change one's identity'. But since these relationships within community constitute one's identity, they must be compatible with free and rational agency. If this is true, they must allow not only simple deliberation, but *open* criticism, *critical* scrutiny, and must therefore encourage nonconformism because we need the community's ideas and rationale for them to be challenged in the most provocative and sophisticated manner. Only then can we know that the rationale or the argumentative element of this or that belief can be accepted and is meaningful.

At this point a counter-argument may be raised. Perhaps all I am suggesting is that we extend the 'borders' of community to include nonconformists of one sort, but leave outside nonconformists of another, namely those who don't belong to our community. In reply I want to refer again to the definition of nonconformism. It is that the nonconformist prefers to stay in the community, rather than leave it. Outsiders cannot be 'nonconformists', however critical they are of the community's ideas.[15] Thus I am not arguing that we should extend the borders of the community.[16] Rather, it is that the community takes seriously all its members, including the nonconformists. This is nonconformism within community and communitarianism which not only respects nonconformism, but is dependent on the existence of it. Good citizenship, then, should imply good citizens as well.

Notes

1   A shorter version of this paper was presented at the annual meeting of the Association of Legal and Social Philosophy, Edinburgh, April 1997. I would like to thank the participants – in particular Mark Bevir – for their fruitful comments. While writing this paper I benefited from the comments of Daniel Attas and Gayil Talshir.

2   Many liberals accept that citizenship is related to community. Ronald Dworkin, for example, argues that liberals can accept the idea of a 'political' community (see his 'Liberal community' in Avineri and de-Shalit, 1992).

3   I have claimed that this is the only reasonable notion of community which can be accepted by liberals and must be accepted by communitarians. See ch. 5 of my *The Environment Between Theory and Practice* (forthcoming, 1998)

4   I should make it clear that not every musical genius is also a nonconformist. J.S. Bach was no doubt a genius, but his works are far from being nonconformist.

5   I also want to distinguish nonconformism from being 'abnormal', especially when the latter refers to prolonged (as opposed to mundane, minor) psychological problems. Nonconformists do what they do and think what they think voluntarily and can control their behaviour and thoughts. They may not want to believe in X or do Y, but they are capable of doing so and are aware of their thoughts and acts. I emphasise this because there were periods in history in which nonconformists were interpreted as mad or as having some psychic illness (e.g. women fighting for their rights in the 18th and 19th centuries, or Abraham, the first believer in an abstract God). See Swaan, 1990, especially pp. 142–9.

6   Indeed, community has always been a term used by the most conformist of institutions, i.e. religion.

7   This is to be distinguished from a much weaker claim, such as made by Philip Selznick, that 'historicity' makes the bonds of community stronger (see 1992, p. 362). Here tradition is the only component of community.

8   Notice that I am not claiming against moral determinism, but rather against presenting moral determinism as (the essence of) community, or as a communitarian theory. Community assumes an exchange, deliberation, questioning – as I shall explain below.

9   It remains to be considered what constitutes the truth of a belief. If it is that a consensus regulating the belief's truth has been reached, this will emphasise the potential tension between community and nonconformism. If, however, it is that a consensus regarding the belief's truth would be reached in ideal circumstances (everybody is rational, etc.), this would allow some place for both community and nonconformism, yet it is still problematic, especially since science and philosophy are not necessarily matters of consensus. This is not the place to discuss these problems. The reader may refer to Nicholas Rescher's most interesting book *Pluralism*, 1993, pp. 56–9.

10   For this reason a party (or perhaps the 'old fashion' party) can be a model for this community, or to be more precise, the framework, the institution, in which community exists.

11   This, by the way, often leads to an argument based on moral relativism: the reason an American cannot understand an Indian who believes in the caste system or who justifies burning the widow with the body of her late husband is that the two persons, the American and the Indian, do not share the same values. My following argument answers, I believe, this claim as well.

12   I am following Rescher's description of the scientific research.

13   For example, Philip Selznick writes (1992, p. 368): 'Nor will a community prosper if it tried to be completely homogeneous in thought and action. This was understood by Aristotle, who in his Politics criticised Plato for assuming "that the greater the unity of the state the better"'.

14   One may also decide after reflection not to change one's beliefs. In this case the self is not actually transformed.

15   A good example may be two persons who write about the Holocaust. The first is an historian who claims that the Germans were not responsible for the Holocaust and raises this argument in academic conferences. He then expects criticism and is ready to consider this critique. He also uses the same language (including data and sources) that the community of historians do. The other is an historian who publishes a book in which he denies the Holocaust. He claims that those historians who have been doing research about the Holocaust are not partly wrong about the reasons for this tragedy, but rather are a gang of crooks who are part of a Jewish conspiracy. By this he sets aside everything that constitutes a community of historians, e.g. academic integrity, responsibility, reliance on documents, value-free research

and so on. Thus he exists the community of historians, and there is no reason why this community should consider his claims at all. This, by the way, points to the very interesting possibility that a certain person will be a nonconformist in circumstances (or community) X, but totally irrelevant in community (or circumstances) Y, and, furthermore, a regular conformist in community (or circumstances) Z. I am thankful to Avigail Eisenberg for this point.

16 In any case, I do not think that a community has 'borders' in any geographical or temporal sense. See my *Why Posterity Matters*, 1995.

Bibliography

Bell D. (1977), 'A communitarian critique of authoritarianism: the case of Singapore', *Political Theory*, 21, pp. 3–33.

de-Shalit, A. (1995), *Why Posterity Matters*, Routledge: London.

de-Shalit, A. (1998, forthcoming), *The Environment Between Theory and Practice*.

Dworkin, R. (1992), 'Liberal Community' in Avineri, S. and de-Shalit, A. (eds), *Communitarianism and Individualism*, Oxford: Oxford University Press.

Enders J., Weller, T.H. and Rubbins, F.C. (1949), 'Cultivation of the Lansing strain of poliomyelitic virus in cultures of various human embryonic tissue', *Science*, Vol. 109, pp. 85–96

Fowler, R. (1991), *The Dance with Community: The contemporary debate in American political thought*, University Press of Kansas.

Hirschman, A.O. (1970), *Exist, Voice and Loyalty*, Boston: Harvard University Press.

Kuhn T. (1962), *The Structure of Scientific Revolution*, Chicago: Chicago University Press.

McLean I. (1996), *Concise Dictionary of Politics*, Oxford: Oxford University Press

Miller, D. (1988)., 'The ethical significance of nationality', *Ethics*, 98, p. 650.

Rescher, N. (1993), *Pluralism*, Oxford: Clarendon Press.

Selznick, P. (1992), *The Moral Commonwealth; Social Theory in the Promise of Community*, Berkeley: California University Press.

Swaan, A. de (1990), *The Management of Normality*, London: Routledge.

Walzer, M. (1970), *Obligations*, Boston: Harvard University Press.

Walzer M. (1983), *Spheres of Justice*, New York: Basic Books.

5 Community Zoos, Theme Park Cultures and the Right to Leave them All

BURKHARD SCHÄFER

Introduction

This paper is the somewhat illegitimate offspring of a larger research programme into the semantics of collective expression in law. What, if anything, do expressions such as 'conspiracy', 'company', 'community', 'nation' or 'legal culture' refer to? Is it possible to make a rational choice between a theory which employs this kind of term and an ontologically less promiscuous one? What if such a choice is not based directly on the a priori rejection or acceptance of collective terms?

From this arguably very abstract background, it follows that my analysis is in considerable danger of displaying all the negative features of liberal theorising which Philip Selznick has described so convincingly in the first chapter of this book: remoteness from practical problems, sweeping generalizations and disregard for the particular. A danger which is further enhanced by the fact that it is indeed written from a liberal perspective.

I hope nevertheless to show that very general questions about the logic of collective expressions can help us better to understand the debate between liberalism and communitarianism, to assess the relative claims, and to find possible points of agreement between them. And even more, I hope to show how this kind of consideration can act as a heuristic to make concrete proposals for legislation.

As example and object of my investigation, I have chosen Will Kymlicka's influential work on multicultural citizenship. In the second part, we will see how his claim of having established a compromise between communitarianism and liberal thought can be assessed in the light of the above. I will argue that rather than presenting a true compromise, his theory is in large part a verbally-enriched version of liberalism. Communitarian vocabulary remains a mere surface phenomenon, always reducible to longer, less elegant 'individualistic' formulations. Can liberals make more concessions? In the third part, I will discuss some *normative* constraints which these concessions must fulfil in order to be acceptable for a liberal, while falling short of straightforward reduction. This will involve some liberal 'soul searching', and, I am afraid, some rather personal remarks about 'degenerative symptoms' in the communitarian discourse. The communitarians among my readers might, however, bear in mind that it is written in order to argue for more concessions for their views than Kymlicka offers.

In the final part, I will give an example of how the discussion translates in concrete legislative proposals to regulate the status of minorities within a liberal mainstream society.

Political Liberalism and Explanatory Liberalism[1]

In his influential book on multicultural citizenship, Will Kymlicka describes a disease, its symptoms and a cure for the liberal discourse on rights.[2] The disease is the *theoretical* purity of liberal theories. The bearer of interests – and with this, the bearer of rights – is always the individual and only the individual. Groups, communities or other collectives do not appear among the theoretical vocabulary. The symptoms are the *practical* failure of liberals to give answers to some of the most urgent questions of modern societies. The claims of minority groups for protective rights are a social fact. They dominate discussions on equal opportunities, affirmative action, the protection of cultural inheritance and the preservation of minority languages. They preserve cultural diversity and protect the identity of its members against the unifying tendencies of the global Nintendo-culture. They have caused only recently a most terrible war in Europe, when the different ethnic and religious groups in the former Yugoslavia tried to annihilate each other. They still cause bloodshed in Ireland, Turkey, Indonesia and hundreds of other places around the globe.

To all these pressing questions liberals have, strictly speaking, no answer. Not the wrong answer, but none at all. The very idea that individuals are constituted by their membership in different cultures and groups, essentially segregated, is anathema for the universalist ideals of the classical liberal. It violates their core commitment to equality and personal freedom as well as the theoretical priority of the individual versus the collective. *The* Kurds cannot have rights, because they, as Platonic entity different from the individual Kurd, do not exist. The question for the rights of groups is as meaningless as that of the baldness of the present king of France. On the other hand, liberals will probably have relatively clear intuitions about some of these questions. For instance, prohibitions by the state preventing the speaking of one's original language or the wearing of one's traditional clothes will probably not find the approval of the liberal. And when the reflexive equilibrium between moral intuitions and expressive power of one's ethical theory is so disturbed, a remedy for the situation becomes necessary. Kymlicka makes roughly the following proposal: we add notions for collective entities to our theoretical vocabulary, but restrict heavily the attribution of rights to these new entities. In particular, minority groups can be bearers of a certain kind of right only. A typical example would be the right to send a guaranteed number of representatives to the legislative organs of the larger state (Kymlicka, 1995, p. 6).

The distinguishing feature of these 'acceptable' group rights is that they protect the group externally. They regulate the relation between the group and the larger state. Ruled out from the outset are 'internally restrictive' rights. An example of these would be to allow minority groups to exclude some of its members, e.g. women, from education or other resources on religious grounds. Kymlicka argues, convincingly I think, that rights of the first kind should pose no serious problem for the liberal. He also at least implies that rights of the second kind always do. It is this last point which I will be questioning later on.

What is the theoretical status of this new liberalism, with its increased expressive powers? Or, formulated differently, is the use of collective expressions enough to establish a theory of group rights? Sure enough, we use permanently in our everyday language expressions for collective or similarly-structured entities. We speak of the beauty of a forest, the wickedness of a conspiracy, the aggressiveness of a state, or the British view on landmines. We speak of molecules, species and natural kinds. How seriously do we have to take this ordinary person's metaphysics? The use of expressions of this kind has never prevented philosophers, or scientists, from attempting to eliminate them from serious theories. Those, for instance, who developed a special interest in physics often maintained (and maintain) that what there really is is nothing but the entities mentioned in physical theories; very small packets of energy – according to the best explanations presently available, at least. There are higher levels of descriptions, for sure. Some of the more complex concentrations of energy become atoms and molecules, and this gives rise to the language of chemistry. These again organize in complex groups and structures, trees, elephants, and you and me. Suddenly we use the explanatory, even richer, language of biology or even psychology. Humans organize themselves in even more complex forms, families, clubs unions and nations. And almost unexpectedly, we need such diverse theories as sociology, economics or mass-psychology. But this does not mean that we have to take the objects of the higher levels 'really' seriously. These different levels of description and the terms typical of each level correspond to an increase in complexity and size of the objects to which they refer. The bigger, complex objects on the comparatively high level of biology are mode of or constituted by the more simple objects on the lower level of physics; the very complex objects of economics are composed of the smaller, less complex objects of the lower level of biology, i.e. humans. Because the different levels of interrelated in that way, it was always tempting to treat the explanations and concepts of the higher level as mere abbreviations of the concepts used at the lower level. Ideally, it would have been great to explain the behaviour of the complex objects by the properties of their constituents alone. Political or ethical theories seldom attempt to go far down on the explanatory hierarchy, but often develop a special interest in individual human beings as theoretical atoms. Aarnio's treatment of the community of heirs is an example in point. He wants to show that expressions such as 'the community of heirs owns the property of the deceased' can always be replaced by the expression 'A, B and C are all and the only heirs of D and they own D's property' (Aarnio, 1971).[3] Whenever we can distribute in such a way properties of a higher level object to its lower level constituents, I will speak of strict reduction. In that case, the higher level explanations are more definitorial extensions of the lower level explanations and can be replaced without loss of meaning.

The core theory of Kymlicka's solution seems to be based on such a strict reductionism. Take the example of externally protective rights. What they describe is not so much the balancing between individual and collective as an individual faced with two collectives as possible addressees for her claims. It describes a shoot-out between two suspect collective entities, the larger state and the minority group. And the individual remains the measure for who wins in this shoot-out. Externally protective rights are acceptable because they distribute advantages (more rights) to the individuals in the group. Equally, internally restrictive rights are measured only against their distribution; they are deemed unacceptable because at least one individual is distributively disadvantaged by them. The group as independent entity does not enter the equation of value maximization. Sentences which mention groups can therefore always be replaced by longer, clumsier formulations about individuals only.

And this again means that the truce between liberalism and

communitarianism remains a surface phenomenon. The same words are used, but for different entities. The communitarian will read our hierarchy 'upside down', with the explanatory priority on the collective. Collectives constitute individuals, not the other way round. Selznick's warning against definitions and his plea for theories shows here its full justification.

I think however that there are compelling reasons for the liberal to go further than proposed by Kymlicka, without ever reaching the other extreme. His solution has both practical and theoretical shortcomings which can be solved.

I have termed the middle way between strict reductionism and group Platonism[4] 'explanatory liberalism', borrowing this term from Wilkerson (1995). Wilkerson has also described brilliantly some of the theoretical problems of the reductionist approach. The biggest problem of the philosophical commitment to reductionism is that it almost never works in scientific practice. To quote one of his examples, economics describes patterns of economic change – say, the development of unemployment. But while these changes can be intelligible on the level of the whole economy, they never fit totally to variations even in the next lower level of, e.g., multinational companies. And for the single worker, the rate of unemployment is always 100 per cent or zero (ibid., p. 13). His conclusion is the context-dependency of explanation and description. The point of theories is to make sense of what is going on around us. This requires different kinds of explanations, at different levels, and the acceptance of different kinds of irreducible entities. But ethical theories must match the explanatory power of the theories about the reality they intend to evaluate. If the best of our economic theories require collectives – e.g. unions and companies – then so does the ethical evaluation of companies and unions.

This theoretical problem corresponds to a more pragmatic question. I doubt that any right can have the property of being 'external' or 'internal', independent of the context and the question asked. Later on, I will show how the right to speak a minority language can display both features. Given the sometimes bizarre preferences of individuals (and as liberals, we should respect these) we can almost certainly always construct a context in which an externally protective right turns into something internally restrictive.

This insight in epistemological problems is matched by facts about the semantic of collective expressions. There are totally innocent properties of collectives which fail the test of strict distribution. I have only a few Italian friends, but 'being few' is not a property of any of them. Students can be asked to assemble in the examination room, but we do not punish a single one of them for her failure to assemble. There are more interesting examples for our discussion. If, for instance, we take Kripke's private language argument seriously, then even one of Kymlicka's prime examples, minority languages, becomes a problem. A strictly distributive reading of the idea that groups have the right to speak a certain language would mean that we should be able to reformulate it without mentioning the group at all. In this case, the single *individual* and the individual alone would have the right to speak a minority language. But this expression on its own does not make much sense, which becomes obvious if we think of a situation where I'm the only speaker left. The best we could say is that individuals have the right to participate in a group which speaks a certain language, which nevertheless means that we have to refer to groups as irreducible entities.

There are now methods to deal especially with this semantical kind of problem. I cannot go into the technical detail here, and refer the reader to Lesniewski's and Goodman's seminal works on nominalistic ontologies for plural expressions.[5] The idea is roughly this: collectives are neither independent Platonic entities nor are they mere distributive collections of individuals. Rather, they are cumulative wholes, complete *Gestalten* in the terminology of psychology. This means that they have properties which are not distributed over their members and hence – using Leibniz – identity,[6] irreducibly different from their constituents. Nevertheless, wholes remain constituted by their parts and only by them. In that regard, our theory stays in the nominalistic camp and the solution proposed remains in the liberal tradition. I call this analysis weak reduction: it is reductionist, since the collectives are meta-theoretically interpreted as compose of their atomic elements and dependent on them; it is weak, because the resulting cumulative collectives are different enough from their parts to make their replacement in the object-theories impossible.

The solution which I am going to elaborate in what follows mixed explanatory liberalism with weak reductionism. Collectives do not necessarily distribute rights to their members, neither external nor internal entitlements. Therefore, they are distinct from mere sets of individuals. However, they remain constituted by individuals. This fact guarantees that arguments about the individuals affected remain *relevant*. Rather than using insights about the constituted nature of collectives directly to rule out internally restrictive rights by definition, we accept the possibility that groups can be legitimate bearers of these rights. However, it remains a legitimate task to develop arguments which determine the scope of these rights for each concrete application. And the fact that individuals constitute collectives means that liberal arguments about the effect of group rights on every individual remain relevant.

Community Zoos

How far can liberals go in accepting internally restrictive minority rights? This depends largely on an understanding of the fears of the liberal towards the communitarian challenge. In the following, I will try to articulate a very personal worry with any temptation to write a blank cheque for the rights of minorities of which I am not a member. The following will be nothing else but an *ad hominem* argument. But this has a certain theoretical necessity. Of course, I hope to convince you, the reader, of my position. However, this seems to entail a belief in the universality of arguments outside any cultural frame of reference. This might already prejudice the discussion towards the liberal position. Maybe any philosophical argument worth contemplating is either *ad hominem* or *a petitio principii*. For this paper, I have chosen the first option by indicating clearly where I stop arguing and start appealing.

While I was writing these lines, the second Earth Summit was taking place in Washington. The USA, and most of all Australia, had just announced that they saw no possibility in reducing their CO_2 emission, and hence the environmental threat largely produced by the industrial developed world. But they might be prepared to help the Third World reduce theirs. This, while considerably less than that of the West, has a higher rate of increase, a sign that their economies have still to catch up.[7] Additionally, the Western nations are very determined to prevent the destruction of the South American rainforest. We recall that the destruction of forests in eighteenth century Britain was a prerequisite for her industrial development, first in order to build the ships which ruled the waves, later as a source of energy for the emerging industry. A hundred years later, the USA followed suit with *their* forests, equally driven by the needs of a developing economy.

There can be two readings of this, and I will concentrate in what follows on the nastier of the two: after having destroyed our own natural environment, we are looking for new ways to spend all the money we earned in the process. And what better way to do so than a nice holiday far away from our pollution-haunted cities? And were do we find unspoilt nature? Obviously, in the less-industrially developed world. So please stop trying to reach the same levels of luxury and living standards which we already enjoy. This threatens our holiday resorts, where we pitch our tents for one week a year to experience unspoilt nature ... before returning to our electrically air-conditioned homes for the rest of the year, when the weather in the holiday resorts is less agreeable, leaving the 'natives' behind to experience even more of it.[8] They want the same exceptionally high standards of living? Then let us tell them that we have *learned from experience* that sacrificing the environment for economic growth is not worthwhile. *We* made that mistake, but *they* really shouldn't. And after all, money does not guarantee happiness, does it? And to add insult to injury, we can even claim that it is in the best interests of the inhabitant of these reserve lands, forever 'in harmony with nature'. The occasional starvation? Terrible, of course, but at least ecologically sound. What we create here are zoos, dead museum pieces fixed at a level of development, which we associate vaguely with the state of nature or our own youth.

Why this lengthy excursion into a seemingly unrelated topic? Because I fear that the same pattern can be found in some of the discussions on minority or generally group rights. Again, we have allegedly learned from our experience; this time that too many rights might endanger a community. And we can't force minorities to make the same mistake to share that freedom, can we? But let's face it. You, my dear reader, are under a minimal threat of being married against your will by your parents, or undergoing painful or dangerous interference with your bodily integrity on cultural grounds, or obeying a restrictive code of behaviour which excludes you from developing your own informed option. You and I, as members of the (Western) academic community, are amongst people with the greatest possibilities of enhancing our individual development, from constitutionally-protected freedom of research to sabbatical leave. And if we were really to face one of the dangers mentioned above, then we would have a fair chance of leaving our community. Because of our training and experience, we have clearly an above-average chance to flee. A simple look at the job advertisements in this week's *Higher* will show you that the academic market comes as close to free movement of work, even outside Europe, as you could wish for. Under the Nazi regime, academics faced the least difficulty in escaping. Popper, Carnap, Einstein and Treitel are testimony to this – the untrained and uneducated often had to stay. And my department here in Edinburgh did not only welcome me (a German), a Pole and a Greek, but even people from England. We pay for this freedom with de-rootedness. And as a result, we long not only for the occasional holiday in an unspoilt natural environment, we also occasionally miss an unspoilt cultural environment. The romantic landscape should ideally be inhabited by happy natives dancing in traditional costumes. This drives the masses into Irish theme pubs, and the academic to conferences *à la recherche du temps perdu*. Here we can demand the preservation of idealized images of cultural minorities, to which we do not belong, but which we might visit, if only in our minds – or for one hour in the evening and a pint. The 'holiday organizer' will guarantee that we do not see too much of the darker side of these minority cultures. And when we have to pay for our own individual freedom by the occasional *angst* of rejection by equally independent partners, then we find comfort in the idea of 'functioning' communities where everybody lives happily ever after. This is all too human and understandable. But can we ask others to pay the price for this new cosiness which communitarianism promises? It is one thing to enjoy the umpteenth return of 'happy times', but quite another to create a timeless 1960 Orange Country society for *others* to live in. We must not enjoy the freedom and potential for our individual development and require others to contribute to the maintenance of static museum pieces of cultures – the community zoos – either for their own sake, or, even more, for the sake of the communities in question.

After all this, I can now formulate, in hypothetical form, two interrelated reasons to explain my thesis that internally restrictive rights for cultural minorities are morally indefensible.

1   Without the need to buy Rawls' theory of justice wholesale, it seems to be a requirement of sound ethical theories not to create duties for others which cannot possible apply to oneself. This is the 'negative' side of the 'view from nowhere'. If accepted, it would explain why liberals have fewer problems with, say, expropriation of property for the common good than with allowing religious minorities to require their female members not to leave the house without their spouse.[9] Both acts are 'anti-individualistic', but while you and I might be subjected to the first, the second will definitively never apply to us.

2   Internally restrictive rules are sometimes said to be necessary to preserve a culture or a community. In this form this is wrong. They might be necessary to preserve a culture in a historically contingent state of affairs, frozen in time. They create not authentic communities, which necessarily develop and change, but theme park cultures. And if we see a value in this, we must be honest with our reasons for it. Do we want to protect a culture *from* us for the sake of this culture and its members, or do we not really want to create a community zoo *for* us, the visitors?

To be totally sure about one point, I do *not* claim that any of these points is really the motivation for anybody who advocates internally restrictive rights for minority groups, neither consciously nor subconsciously. Nor do I accuse the participants in the environmental debate of this hidden agenda. The picture is, hopefully, wrong. We might be able to learn from our mistakes and to communicate this in a way which allows others, by their own choosing, to avoid them. It might be right to preserve the environment of other people, even if we can't do it for our own. There might be a value in preserving minority cultures from the unifying tendencies of the 'Macdonaldocracy', even if this means restricting some of the choices of their members. I painted an intentionally bleak picture of possible degenerative developments of this specific form of rights talk, to increase the awareness of its dangers and to give the hidden fears of the liberal a name. The purpose of the whole enterprise is to get a clear picture of what we want to avoid. If we see that clearly, we might be in a position to accept even some internally restrictive rights, if we make sure that this does not lead us to one of the problems described. The goal is, if we remember, to open a dialogue between communitarians and liberals which goes farther than what Kymlicka has to offer.

In the final part, I want to offer some safeguards in the form of comprehension principles[10] which should avoid the problems discussed so far.

Groups – Internal and External

So far we have set the framework for a truce between liberals and communitarians. Three requirements emerge from the discussion so far which set the framework for any true compromise between the two schools of thought.

1   We want to guarantee a non-distributive reading of groups rights. That means that the right of a group need not be 'distributed' over its individual members.

2   We want nevertheless some protection for the individual against internally restrictive group rights.

3   The 'costs' of granting internally restrictive rights for minority groups which are deemed necessary for the survival of a group should not be borne entirely by the individuals affected. The mainstream culture which grants these rights must shoulder some of the costs.

Requirement 1) guarantees that the status of groups, ontologically and ethically, is taken seriously. To achieve it, we cannot rule out *by definition* internally restrictive rights. This would automatically result in a reductionist approach, where group talk can always be replaced by talk about individuals. This however does not mean that we do not reject most or even all actually proposed rights of this sort. But if we do so, then we must do it on grounds of arguments independent of the principal debate between the two camps and ideally acceptable to both. 2) introduces the liberal element. The precise formulation of this constraint will largely dictate whether the resulting theory is a communitarian compromise to the liberal camp or vice versa. Later on, I will propose safeguards which root the result firmly in the liberal approach. 3) guarantees that we avoid the problems outlined in the third part. Group rights do not come free; political correctness has its price.

To motivate my own proposal, I want to introduce two examples. The situation envisaged is that of a liberal mainstream society which is asked to grant rights to two minority groups within that society. Both rights asked for are at least potentially internally restrictive. It goes without saying that we have already implemented Kymlicka's minimum threshold. That is, we have enriched out liberal theory sufficiently to speak about collective entities in the first place. Furthermore, to fulfil constraint 1), we assume by fiat that their acceptance is not already ruled out on the sole ground of being internally restrictive.

Example a A very small ethnic minority wants to preserve its language. Previous attempts to keep the language alive by positive incentives alone have failed (this would have been an example of external rights). The temptation to teach children only the majority language was too great: better employment prospects, no fear of bullying at school for a 'funny' accent, the general wish of some parents to assimilate ... As a result, the representatives of that community demand further action: teaching children the majority language before the age of eight, which the minority language is already firmly rooted, to be prohibited (and sanctioned by criminal law); use of the majority language in all official offices to be prohibited; mandatory language courses for everybody twice a year. And finally, the selling of newspapers written in the majority language to be prohibited in the group's territory.[11]

Example b A religious minority feels deeply offended by the 'indecent' dressing of women. To enforce the traditional dress code, the minority requires the right to send violators to one week 'enforced meditation' in a cloister.

Both regulations are, of course, deeply offensive to the liberal. They might even be wrong in an absolute sense. Nothing I am going to say now attempts to change that. However, the 'enlightened' liberal I have in mind has learnt enough from communitarian observation to accept that the preservation of these two groups might be beneficial in itself, even if this benefit is not directly distributable over the constituting group members. What conditions then must be fulfilled in addition to make an acceptable 'trade-off' and maximize the benefits? If we are going to take groups as independent entities seriously, then it seems plausible that the relation between two groups should obey the same rules which already obtain between other important collectives, especially between the classical nation states. The idea, in short, is to transfer from of the concepts of international law to the internal relations of a state towards its minorities. Two of the concepts of international law I have particularly in mind are the requirement to compensate members of other states subjected to expropriation by the host state and a modified version of the right to leave one's country. Let's begin with the latter. It has a rather obvious function in fulfilling the second constraint from above, the protection of the individual. And as I said above, it guarantees that my proposal is methodologically located in the liberal camp: not only is it up to the individual to decide whether he or she wants to be subject to the internally restrictive rights proposed above, it is also finally in the hands of the members of a group to end its existence, if necessary by mass exodus. If you doubt that possibility, remember how quickly the society of the former GDR collapsed when the borders were opened. It also means that it is not within the power of the minority group to determine to whom it extends its jurisdiction. If we think of a right as comprising two elements, the norm which is prescribed and its extension, the addressee of the norm, then internally restrictive group rights are 'incomplete rights' inasmuch as it is not up to the group but to mainstream society to determine (and restrict) their extension. Again, this shows a clear liberal element which constrains the autonomy of minority groups. The right to leave has, however, a second function. Precisely because it puts the existence of a group at risk, it also forces that group to be 'attractive' to its members, and so introduces competition. This might help to avoid the danger described above, the creation of community zoos and museum pieces. It forces a group to remain dynamic and to react to changes in the world, something which ultimately benefits the group. Again, you might think of the GDR as a concrete example. Here, severe restrictions on leaving the country allowed the ruling class to postpone necessary reforms, thus contributing to their own destruction.

In our first example, there will be no *legal* obstacles to implement that safeguard. If a community is located geographically, then simply leaving the territory is sufficient, and most states grant the right to move freely within its borders to its citizens anyway. This situation in the second example is slightly more complicated. If a group is geographically dispersed over a country, special institutions are necessary to allow members to leave that community. This could be guaranteed, e.g., but allowing members of a religious group to 'quit membership' by simple declaration of intent to an official of the state[12] (and *not* of the minority group!). (Again, this emphasises the individual element in restricting the group's ability to create obstacles to leaving it, and places the emphasis on the mainstream society.)

There is, however, a second, often overlooked, aspect of the right to leave. So far, we have discussed it as a right of the individual towards the minority group. But the right to leave one's community, together with some empirical facts about the limited space on earth, logically entails that *there must be a community which takes the person*. The claim-right of the individual against the minority group therefore entails (in Hohfeldian terms) a duty by mainstream society to accept that person. In the case of minority group versus state, this will not normally be a *legal* problem. There may, however, be *factual* obstacles to integration into mainstream society. In our first example, language would be an obvious problem. This links the discussion to the second principle, remuneration for expropriation. One thing should be clear for the liberal (and might well be a final divisive line between the schools): regardless of how beneficial we deem the existence of minority groups to be, and regardless of how minor in comparison the sacrifices for the individual in the case of internally restrictive rights are, the remain *sacrifices*. Something is taken away from the individual *to which she was entitled*. In the best of all possible worlds, groups would exist without restricting the freedom of their members. But we don't live in the best of all possible worlds, and this conflict might arise. If now it is seen as appropriate to grant such a restrictive group right, then the individual who is forced to abandon some of her rights is in the same position as someone expropriated for the common good. And if we see it as appropriate to recompense someone for his house which was expropriated to build a street, then we should surely recompense individual group members whose rights had to be restricted to guarantee the existence of the group. Normally, a considerable part of the group will make that sacrifice voluntarily and in such circumstances there is no need for interference. Typically, group members will value the existence of the group and their membership of it higher than the loss suffered from the internally restrictive right. In that situation, a true liberal must accept that individual preference, even if it is, according to his standards, slightly masochistic. It is precisely the existence of such second-order preferences which make it necessary for the liberal to contemplate even internally restrictive rights, since outright prohibition might amount to an illiberal interference with individual preferences. I do not normally want to be punished, but I might have the desire to live in such a way as to avoid that punishment, not because of simple fear of the consequences, but because of the insight that the principle is necessary to achieve something I value. And if I don't live up to that insight, I must take the consequences. Concretely, I might, in the first example, have both the desire to learn the mainstream language personally *and* the desire that the minority language survives: ideally because all the others refrain from doing as I did, practically by accepting that I might want *not* to want to learn it and motivate myself by institutional safeguards. Liberals should accept that possibility. But those who do not have these higher-order preferences might be those who choose to leave. And in that case, remuneration becomes a real possibility. That means that they are not only entitled to leave, but also that they could require from mainstream society to provide the financial means to make that possibility a reality. Back again to the example: if society grants the restrictive language rights to a minority group, it creates by doing so the moral obligation to provide, e.g., free language classes for the group leavers. We can think of other obligations of the same sort: providing the means to removing one's property from the territory of that group, providing housing, or even psychological counselling. On the one hand, this obligations supports additionally the right to leave and hence requirement 2). But it also guarantees that the granting of group rights does not come for free for those not affected by them. Therefore, it also fulfils constraint 3). As a liberal, I might with good reasons decide that a group should enjoy internally restrictive rights. Butt hen, I'm under the moral obligation to go a long way to cater for the victims of my decision.

We can re-translate that idea also to the international level. Here, the internationally recognized right to leave one's country changes the nature of asylum from a charity granted by other states to a right of the asylum seeker, a logical consequence of her right to leave her country. There is no privacy in that right between nation state and its citizens. Again, more concretely, if liberal, Western societies really refrain from interferences, say, with human right violations in Asia, for fear of an illiberal value imperialism, then they must be prepared to welcome all those who seemed to have incompletely socialized into 'Asian values'.[13]

Conclusion

As a result, we note two conditions necessary for liberals at least to discuss internally restrictive group rights. The individual must maintain the possibility of avoiding them by leaving, and the society which grants these rights must be prepared, but its own financial sacrifice, to make this choice a reality.

We have seen that there are good reasons for the liberal to take that possibility on board. Practical ethical questions about the rights of groups are not going to disappear from the agenda for the sake of theoretical ideas about methodological individualism. That was Kymlicka's starting point. Furthermore, some of these group rights are even desirable for the liberal, without being strictly distributive. This was the positive element in Kymlicka's proposal. In addition, we have seen that a restriction to these positive rights is both ethically and methodologically impossible. Methodologically, because only the possibility of internally restrictive rights means that we take groups as bearers of rights seriously. Ethically, because an a priori rejection of them might mean that the liberal does not take the preferences of the individuals involved as seriously as her ethical convictions demand. The basic paradox of liberalism, that of being illiberal towards illiberal ideas, might not be solvable. But we should at least try to evoke that argument only it if cannot be avoided. My proposal tried to move this last ditch further into 'enemy territory'. For liberal thought, as for any school of thought, the same as what I have said above about cultures holds true. They are alive only insofar as they adapt to change and take new insights seriously. To grant the possibility of less liberal forms of community, and hence the existence of alternative models of life, might thus be necessary for an animated liberal discussion itself. But human beings are not mere guinea pigs. Nor can we sacrifice other individuals to gain intellectual stimuli. Bio-diversity might be a value in itself; cultural diversity clearly isn't. Here, my own analogy from the second part breaks down for good. The constraints I have proposed intend to guarantee that we do not inflict harm on living beings of flesh and blood in the name of academic rigour. I say this to avoid a misunderstanding of what I said above: to grant the right to leave doesn't give a free ticket for inhuman internal practices of communities. Indeed, it follows from the idea of the proposal that *certain* concrete group rights are indeed ruled out; damages to the individual, for instance, which cannot be undone. This would rule out subjecting children to religiously-motivated mutilations. Nor does it mean that suddenly these internally restrictive rights become in any sense desirable or of ethical value. To grant these rights in our second example does not entail that we give up the idea that the group *should* rethink its policy towards women. Nor does it mean that any attempt by them to change the system from within is not of the highest ethical merit. It only means that we have to find *additional* arguments to argue the point, and that meta-ethical considerations about the ontological relation between group and individual alone do not decide the issue. Here, my proposals arguably face the danger which Hirschman prominently discussed in his distinction between 'voice' and 'exit' (Hirschman, 1970).[14] Some of us might remember the time when even an ever-so-cautious remark about problems in our economic system promoted the advice to emigrate to the Soviet Union as a response. The possibility of leaving might undermine the new forms of protest members of a group have. This might very well be true. The only answer I have to this is that our ethical theories should start with the victims and let the heroes look after themselves. To stay and change the system will often be the morally better solution. But we should not make it mandatory in our ethical theories. I end where I started: academic ethics should bear in mind what they require from others and what their proponents are prepared to suffer themselves. To take a risk for a better society is an honourable thing; to require it from others in the safety of our university seminars, however, is shameful.

Notes

1   The notion of 'explanatory liberalism' comes from T.E. Wilkerson's excellent book on natural kinds. This work is also the basis of most of the discussion in this chapter.

2   In the following, I refer to Kymlicka, 1995.

3   I have reformulated Aarnio's technically incomplete reformulation proposal.

4   That is, the view that groups exist independently or at least ontologically prior to their members, in an abstract Platonic heaven of ideas.

5   A good overview is provided in Simons, 1987.

6   That is, two individuals are identical if they have exactly the same properties.

7   One way to achieve this seems to be to sell these countries the more developed and hence environmentally more friendly *Western* machinery ....

8   You think I'm cynical and exaggerating? Well, I just got two glossy holiday brochures with my usual junk mail, and I'm just quoting.

9   John Gava pointed out to me that my European roots are showing here, and that for the American version of liberalism, expropriation of property is the main sin. Indeed, European legal cultures live on the whole happily with remunerated expropriation, the amount of money politically negotiated rather than presenting the real market value.

10 In analogy to the comprehension principles in set theory: they tell you which individuals are allowed to form a new 'collective' entity.

11 Not even too unrealistic, if we think of the large scale experiment currently under way in France.
12 In Germany, membership of one of the officially-recognized churches can be terminated by declaration at a registration office of the city council.
13 To take that idea, promoted by, e.g. Indonesia, seriously, if only for the sake of argument. The reader might by now have guessed that I'm not really sympathetic to restrictive group rights.
14 I owe this point to Sasja Tempelmann – it disturbed me enough to almost abandon the whole idea.

Bibliography

Aarnio, A. (1971), 'Some Thoughts on the Community of Heirs' in Aarnio, A., *From a Legal Point of View*, Helsinki University Press: Helsinki.
Hirschman, A.O. (1970), Exit Voice and Loyalty, Harvard University Press: Cambridge, Mass.
Kymlicka, W. (1995), *Multicultural Citizenship*, Clarendon Press: Oxford.
Simons, P. (1987), *Parts. A Study in Ontology*, Clarendon Press: Oxford.
Wilkerson, T.E. (1995), *Natural Kinds*, Avebury: Aldershot.

PART III

6 Citizenship Rights, Gender and Politics of Difference

ELIZABETH KINGDOM

Introduction

Feminist critiques of liberalism have focused on its preoccupation with the rights of the individual in the public sphere. On this critique, liberalism's concept of citizenship rights is predicated on a concept of the free and rational individual entering the public sphere for participation in liberal democratic politics. This concept is criticized by feminists on two main grounds. First, it undervalues the importance of the private sphere and, in particular, the interconnectedness of human beings. Secondly, the concept encourages competitiveness between individuals and masks women's social and political disadvantage.

On these two counts, communitarianism holds an attraction for feminist politics. Communitarian theory frequently mounts an attack on the concept of rights for its politics of individualism and emphasizes the values of cooperative living and mutual support in the community. Further, it identifies rights not as the private possession of insular and competing individuals but as the product of a community which promotes a vision of individuals as mutually supportive and as the product of social institutions committed to the ethics of caring and cooperation.

Yet feminists are wary of communitarianism. Put simply, they have been aghast at communitarianism's preferred institutions – variously, post-colonial America, the medieval kingdom, the Greek *polis*, the family and the church. Once the moral values promoted by communitarianism are given content in this way, it is apparent that citizenship rights are the membership badge of communities whose norms and practices have been inimical to women's interests and hostile to feminist politics.

For feminist politics, then, the problems of liberalism are not solved by communitarianism. Indeed, both positions involve a conception of citizenship rights which threaten the recognition of differences between potential subjects and potential members of the community. As Anna Yeatman has argued, liberalism's construction of group identity requires that the group assume an authoritarian character. A legitimation device is necessary for the conversion of multiplicities of people's intentions and purposes into a single voice for the representation of the group's interests (Yeatman, 1994, p. 81). On Yeatman's type of analysis, citizenship rights are accorded only to those who subordinate their individuality to the public authority of the group. Similarly, communitarianism's construction of community identity requires the subordination of differences between members of a community by the imposition of that community's norms and values. Yeatman notes that whilst few people need persuading that there is a community of interest informing the distribution of public goods, such as health and education, 'this consensus breaks down when it becomes a matter of determining which or whose community of interest we may be talking about' (1994, pp. 92–3). Again, citizenship rights will be accorded only to those who comply with community norms and practices which, however vaguely articulated, are not to be contested.

For these reasons, feminists will find little to choose between liberal and communitarian concepts of citizenship rights. It is not surprising, then, that there is, in some radical academic literature, a certain tiredness, even irritation, over the rights debate, the debate about the adequacy of appealing to and pursuing rights for the realization of progressive and radical objectives. Didi Herman (1993) advocates going 'beyond it' and Carl Stychin refers to the 'vacuity of the pro-rights/anti-rights debates often heard in the United Kingdom' (1997, p. 316). At the same time, Bryan S. Turner considers problematic 'the deafening silence about rights in sociology', on the grounds that '[I]t would be difficult to understand either the domestic or the international contestation over the nature of social membership (for unborn children, refugees, migrant labour or the chronically sick) without some elementary notion of rights' (1993, p. 163). The argument of this chapter is situated between these two positions, starting with the observation that the political use and analysis of rights displays a remarkable but unsurprising resilience to rights-scepticism. For example, the movement for the promotion of women's rights as human rights is gaining, not losing strength (cf. Kerr, 1993), and it is not possible to engage with European politics without a working knowledge of the European Convention for the Protection of Human Rights and Fundamental Freedoms (cf. Van den Berghe 1982, p. 23).

There are competing ways of characterizing these debates. For example, Renata Salecl situates 'hate speech' in the dilemma between universal human rights and the right to cultural difference (1997, p. 90); Therese Murphy positions her overview of rights strategies for feminist body politics in terms of legal feminisms' critique of essentialism and the attempt to acknowledge identity variables beyond gender (1997, p. 41); and David Berry projects his analysis of the conflicts between the rights of aboriginal women, aboriginal communities and the wider Canadian state into a proposal for a reconsideration of the meanings of 'culture' and of 'human rights' (1997, p. 12).

What these positions have in common, however, is the recognition that, like it or not, much contemporary politics is characterized by rights discourse and that, since an unreflective engagement with that discourse is problematic for radical politics, some form of reconceptualization of rights discourse has to be on the political agenda.[1] In keeping with that argument, this paper, with its focus on citizenship rights, connects the rights debate with what Barry Hindess (1993) has termed 'the realisation thesis' (henceforth RT). Briefly, the RT is the thesis that citizenship is 'a set of civil, political and social rights that have been more or less adequately realized in the democratic societies of the modern West' (Hindess, 1993, p. 19). The RT is effectively a particular characterization of a social democratic agenda nearing the completion of business: there is room for the improvement of representative mechanisms, but the principal political structures, including the political institutions for the protection of citizenship rights, do not require major alteration. On this view, the question of citizenship rights is largely a matter of tallying up progress-to-date in the extension of rights.

In what follows, four criticisms of the RT are identified: victim feminist critiques of rights, new feminist republicanism and exclusion, feminist politics of difference, and the new politics of difference. These do not exhaust the criticisms of the RT; rather they are examples which have been selected for their distinctive line on rights, and *a fortiori* on citizenship rights discourse, and for their focus on gender legal politics.

Victim feminist critiques of rights identify the prevailing political structures under which rights claims are pursued as male, or male-orientated. On this view, for example, rights as identified in formal declarations of rights, such as the American Constitution, are expressed in gender-neutral terms but conceal a male-orientated interpretation of citizenship rights.

New feminist republicanism accounts for the discrepancy between the promise of full citizenship rights held out by the RT and the reality for women in terms of the routine exclusion of women from full enjoyment of citizenship rights through the operation of certain ideologies. Examples here include the presumption of a unitary form of citizenship and the designation of certain social spheres as male and others as female.

Feminist politics of difference, whilst sympathetic to new feminist republicanism, is critical of its tendency to an essentialist separation of the interests of female contestants in the sphere of citizenship rights and its concomitant presumption that all women share the same political interests. Instead, feminist politics of difference calls for the recognition of the ways in which different groups of women, such as women of colour and poor women, have been excluded from full enjoyment of citizenship rights.

The new politics of difference is a term used here with some misgivings, in the light of the current vogue for calling almost any contemporary political phenomena new. In fact, it shares with new feminist republicanism and feminist politics of difference a concern to identify the mechanisms whereby women have been excluded from participation in democratic politics. Its newness, however, is in its refusal to be exclusively concerned with the exclusion of women. Rather it proposes that the issue of the recognition of difference and the mechanisms of exclusion relate to all possible contestants in the sphere of citizenship rights. In this way, the new politics of difference is allied with the literature of radical democratic politics.

In this chapter, I start by outlining the RT and Hindess' critique of it. I then exhibit the connections between the above four criticisms of the RT. Such is the tenacity of the RT, however, that, despite their criticisms of the RT, victim feminism, new feminist republicanism and feminist politics of difference all retain elements of the RT, though to differing degrees. The new politics of difference is not vulnerable to the criticism that it retains the RT structure, but it has been criticized on two important grounds. The first is that it necessitates the automatic disappearance of feminism from the radical democratic agenda, and the second is that it constitutes political incompetence, in the sense of removal or dispossession of the capacity to engage in political action. I attempt to defend the new politics of difference against these criticisms and to complement that argument, I propose that engagement with the topic of citizenship rights be reconceptualized as the occasion for the permanent review of inclusionary and exclusionary politics. It is my proposal that 'citizenship rights' be conceptualized as political heuristics.

The Realisation Thesis

In Hindess' analysis, T.H. Marshall's account of the development of citizenship rights as the corrective to the social divisions created by class conflict typifies the RT (Hindess, 1993, p. 20). Citizenship rights, for Marshall, comprise three basic types: the civil rights which are a condition of individual freedom, the political rights necessary to the citizens' participation in institutions of the exercise of political power, and the social rights, such as the right to a measure of economic welfare, which comprise the right to share in the social heritage. On Marshall's view, the RT can be seen as a benign, if complacent, social democratic agenda nearing the end of business.

Hindess criticizes this account of the institutionalization of citizenship rights in modern Western societies on two counts. The first is that it misrepresents the political character of these societies. For example, Hindess questions Marshall's account of Western societies as essentially democratic republics, communities of citizens, and draws attention to the fact that resident aliens now form a significant minority in Western societies, yet enjoy few or no political (as opposed to civil and social) rights in the host society (loc. cit., p. 28). The second criticism is that the RT misrepresents the role of principles, in particular the significance attached to rights. Hindess points out that, '[T]he extension of civil rights to most of the adult population does little to overcome the effects of major economic inequalities' (loc. cit., p. 25).

In making this point, Hindess might appear to be siding with those writers in the Critical Legal Studies movement who have sought to 'trash' rights, on the ground that the class nature of prevailing political structures, as the political instruments of the bourgeois state, rule out the possibility of rights being anything more than a political confidence trick. Far from it; Hindess is careful to distinguish his position from what he calls the 'mystification thesis'. According to this thesis, the fundamental role of ideas, including the idea of rights, is to misrepresent the nature of political institutions, effectively to present them as benign, thereby reproducing those institutions as crucial for the defence of democracy (loc. cit., p. 31), and effectively duping would-be citizens into a false expectation of the full achievement of citizenship rights.

Rather, Hindess' position is that the idea of citizenship rights is best viewed as one of the central organizing principles of Western political discourse, a principle which can have progressive effects but which cannot guarantee them, and a principle which can also be used for paternalistic purposes but which is not always so used. I shall return to this type of view with my proposal that to debate citizenship rights be conceptualized as the occasion, not for the tallying of rights as required by the RT, but for the review of exclusionary and inclusionary politics, so that the concept of 'citizenship rights' be treated as a political heuristic. Meanwhile, this is an appropriate point at which to start on my account of the four influential criticisms of the RT identified above.[2]

Victim Feminist Critiques of Rights

The term 'victim feminism' refers both to the distinctive feminist critique of rights associated with the work of Catherine MacKinnon (1989) and to one of the main criticisms of it. Her position is that women are systematically oppressed by men, and that the liberal state is a key instrument in that oppression, serving to promote men's interests at the expense of women's. On this view, the Constitution, the given political structure under which citizenship rights are claimed, must reproduce that oppression, with the result that women's rights campaigns are doomed to necessary and predictable failure. For example, a prima facie gender-neutral right, such as the citizen's right, protected by the Constitution, to freedom of speech is characterized as male, for it is really the male right to freedom to enjoy pornographic materials (MacKinnon, 1989, pp. 204–6). On such a view, the RT is castigated for its failure to recognize that there is a necessary and predictable gap between the official list of rights and the capacity of women to enjoy them.

The feminist critique of MacKinnon's work as essentialist in its construction of two pre-cultural populations defined as female and male is well enough known not to require rehearsal (cf. Smart, 1989, pp. 76–8). What needs emphasis here is the correlative argument that, because of men's omnipotence, MacKinnon's essentialism dooms women to occupy the status of social and political victims. So, for example, Drucilla Cornell argues that MacKinnon is 'unable to affirm feminine sexual difference as other than victimization' (Cornell, 1991, p. 2248).[3] It is for this reason that, in Cornell's view, MacKinnon is unable to develop and justify her programme for state intervention for the correction of the gender hierarchy. In a word, MacKinnon's critique of the RT converts it from being a failed political agenda for the extension of citizenship rights to being a political agenda where that extension can never succeed, an agenda on which the business of women's citizenship rights is necessarily and permanently deferred.

New Feminist Republicanism and Exclusion

In contrast to victim feminism, new feminist republicanism does not remove the possibility of the successful pursuit of citizenship rights for women. Certainly, it acknowledges that women have been excluded from the full enjoyment of citizenship rights and it deploys a powerful critique of the RT. These feminists have argued that the political structures under which citizenship rights are claimed, whether they are conceptualized loosely as rights or as rights specified in written constitutions, constitute an exclusionary political practice which has, at least so far, failed to acknowledge the routine disqualification of women from full enjoyment of citizenship rights.

So, for example, Sylvia Walby (1994) draws attention to the absence of gender from writings on citizenship and, like Hindess in his critique of the RT, Walby criticizes Marshall here, extending her criticism of Marshall to include his commentators, Michael Mann and Bryan Turner. She assembles materials on, for example, income maintenance schemes, occupational pension schemes, and the role of the (typically female) carer, to challenge the assumption made by Marshall, Mann and Turner that there is a unitary form of citizenship. For Walby, citizenship cannot be understood without a dynamic theory of gender relations and a gendered critique of access to welfare rights. In particular, she is anxious to reject the view that citizenship rights have been of no consequence for women. On the contrary, she concludes, they are crucial to the transformation of gender relations (pp. 390–1). For this reason, in her discussion of David Marquand's position on the need for full social and political citizenship rights in the interests of economic efficiency, Walby calls for a focus on women's economic participation. Such a focus, she argues, would place on the political agenda the exclusion of women from effective participation in paid work and in turn strengthen women's claim to the enjoyment of full citizenship rights (p. 390).

Similarly, Helen Irving (1994) has argued that an examination of the Australian Constitution, which came into force at the inauguration of the Commonwealth on 1 January 1901, reveals a gendered division of powers. 'National' areas of concern, such as the Federation movement and the constitutional process are located in the public, external and 'male' realm. In contrast, the common concerns of women, such as female suffrage and the social welfare of families were typically characterized as 'domestic' and accordingly relegated to the States. Irving argues that, had women gained the suffrage prior to 1901, they would have sought for the insertion into the Constitution of a range of different provisions, such as a uniform national divorce law. Indeed, Irving suggests, had women been involved directly in drafting the Constitution, a very different Constitution would have emerged (1994, p. 197). and she concludes that, 'Australian politics is not yet designed to meet the needs and interests of women, and that our very constitutional detail presents problems for women's participation' (ibid.) In terms of the RT, the Australian Constitution has failed to acknowledge women's social and economic position, it has failed to accord them the full range of citizenship rights, and Irving's political message is that contemporary women's politics requires the constant reshaping of the Constitution.

Now, this new feminist republican critique of the RT has been supplemented by the argument that the RT wrongly emphasizes rights at the expense of civic duties and responsibilities and that these political principles enhance the prospect of correcting women's exclusion from citizenship rights (cf. Sherry, 1995; Twine, 1994). But Iris Marion Young has been critical of this approach. She argues that, just as it is impossible to deny the gendered nature of citizenship rights, in the sense that their prima facie gender neutrality conceals women's exclusion from the full enjoyment of citizenship, so it is impossible to deny the gendered basis of the concepts of duty, impartiality and rationality characteristic of republican thinking (Young, 1987, pp. 60–3). Indeed, as I have argued elsewhere (Kingdom, 1996b, pp. 35–6), Young's critique can be used to show that new feminist republicanism is vulnerable to the critique that it preserves the main features of the RT. In other words, Irving's constitutional politics and the mere adding in of new political concepts or principles supports the retention of the very features of prevailing political institutions which the new feminist republicanism was concerned to challenge for their failure to accord women citizenship rights on a par with men. In fact, as will become apparent, Young's critique of new feminist republicanism also challenges its construction of citizenship rights on the grounds that it too neatly demarcates men's enjoyment of citizenship rights from that of women's. A similar critique appears in the feminist politics of difference.

Feminist Politics of Difference and Exclusion

It is Young's type of challenge to the presumption of the unity of women's experiences that provides the impetus for the feminist politics of difference. This politics rejects all forms of political discourse which suppose that the interests of women are indivisible. Instead, these feminists advance a case for the recognition of difference between women's experiences and political needs. On this view, the RT describes a set of citizenship rights from the enjoyment of which have been excluded not 'women' as a unified political category but women with a multiplicity of social statuses and experiences; the RT has failed to recognize differences between women.

One of the most powerful cases for this feminist demand for the recognition of difference is the work of those feminists who have drawn attention to the omission from feminist analysis of the ways in which black women's experiences differ from those of white women's. So, for example, Dorothy Roberts provides compelling evidence of the different effect of R v. Wade on women of colour, especially poor women, to whom the right to privacy in reproductive choice is meaningless if they have no financial resources to pay for a lawful termination (1992, p. 309), With a comparable focus on the dominance in race discrimination cases of sex- and race-privileged Blacks and on the dominance in sex discrimination cases of race- and class-privileged women, Kimberle Crenshaw argues for the centring of Black women's multidimensional experiences as a corrective to the single-axis (sex only, or race only, or class only) analyses of discrimination (1997). Similarly, Marcia Rice has argued that a black feminist perspective is necessary to understand the triple oppression of race, class and gender experienced by Black women (1990). Feminist politics of difference, then, insists that in citizenship rights debates and contests it is imperative that the multiplicity of women's experiences be recognized.

Powerful and influential as these critiques have been, however, the feminist politics of difference has itself been criticized for the political priority given to gendered difference. It is this preoccupation with gendered difference that has led Young to extend her critique of citizenship discourse, including rights discourse, to include the demand for recognition of forms of oppression other than those experienced by women. Young accordingly proposes the concept of 'group differentiated rights' to allow recognition in citizenship rights contests of groups, such as Native Americans. On Young's view, the RT is vulnerable to criticism to the extent that it fails to extend the enjoyment of citizenship rights to such groups, whether or not they present themselves in terms of gender politics.

Now, just as it is arguable that new feminist republicanism retains the structure of the RT, so a comparable case might be made against the feminist politics of difference and against even Young's critique of it. To the extent that each position retains a commitment to existing representational structures, such as the institutions and practices of constitutional politics, and a commitment to the claims of existing but under-represented political alliances, so each position could be said to retain the basic structure of the RT. For both new feminist republicanism and the feminist politics of difference, and on Young's critique, the political agenda requires only the correction of the mechanisms for exclusion from citizenship rights and the improvement of their mechanisms of inclusion. It is effectively this point that has occasioned the development of the new politics of difference.

The New Politics of Difference

The newness of this politics of difference consists not in a radical break with the prior forms of difference politics, such as feminist politics of difference, but in its commitment to extend their recognition of difference, to pursue the difference agenda, it might be said, even further. In this way, the feminist politics of difference can be seen as prefigurative for the new politics of difference.

Accordingly, the new politics of difference focuses not simply on differences between women, nor on differences between established groups, whether or not presented in terms of gender politics. Rather, the new politics of difference proposes a radical democratic politics in which no characteristic of a group, be it gender, race, or whatever, is privileged. So, for example, Mary Dietz has argued that it would be contrary to the spirit of democratic politics to launch its defence of citizenship from a position which privileges gender (1992, p. 78). Instead, what is proposed is a politics of undifferentiated difference, a politics which accords priority to no particular group of contestants in the sphere of citizenship rights.

Dietz' position here utilizes to powerful effect the anti-elitist and inclusivist discourse of democratic politics. In a similar way, Chantal Mouffe argues for the conceptualization of citizenship as a political principle which supports multiple and constantly changing identities (Mouffe, 1992, p. 372), Further, Mouffe argues, this concept of citizenship, and the correspondingly revised concept of citizenship rights, constantly subverts existing and developing forms of domination, such as the domination of ecological interests by considerations of economy. It is for this reason, Mouffe argues, that 'the political cannot be restricted to a certain type of institution, or envisaged as constituting a specific sphere or level of society' (1993, p. 3).

Now, it is this refusal to allow the political to be located in any specific institutions or practices that makes the new politics of difference resistant to any claim that it retains the structure of the RT. For the new politics of difference will not confine the sphere of the political to existing forms of representative democratic institutions, nor seek to define in advance what forms of politics are legitimate. For this reason, the new politics of difference is attractive to participants in new social movements as a conceptualization of radical democratic politics. At the same time, the new politics of difference tends to attract two serious criticisms, both from feminists and from those committed to the pursuit of citizenship rights. The first criticism is that it disqualifies feminist politics, and the second is that it leads to political incompetence.

The Disqualification of Feminist Politics

The new politics of difference is accused of making feminist politics disappear into democratic politics. On this criticism, feminist politics loses its distinctiveness, the struggle for women's full enjoyment of citizenship rights loses political legitimacy, and women are automatically disenfranchised from participation in the political. At the same time, the new politics of difference can be seen to pose a threat to what has been the great strength of feminist politics, the assertion of the politics of collective action over individualism.

This criticism, however, stems from a misreading of the new politics of difference. This politics does not disqualify feminist politics from participation in democratic politics, nor does it exclude women as contestants for citizenship rights. Further, it is not the case that the new politics of difference collapses into individualism. Rather, it insists that radical democratic politics can make no a priori judgment about which interests, whether those of an individual or a group, should be defended or supported. Indeed, as Michael Detmold has argued in connection with the democratically voted return to male suffrage in Western Australia, the democratic process itself may infringe individual and minority rights (1997: 9, n. 17). Detmold claims that 'there is little doubt that the rights of women would here prevail' (ibid.). What the new politics of difference rules out, however, is not the likelihood that women's citizenship rights will be recognized but the automatic privileging of feminist politics, the presumption that women should always have political priority over other groups in the pursuit of citizenship rights, and the presumption that gender difference has a prior political claim over other forms of difference.

In its place, the new politics of difference is a commitment to a form of politics which encourages reflection on multiple forms of difference and refuses to prejudge their competing claims. For example, Jodi Dean introduces the term 'respectful disagreement' to conceptualize the ways in which those committed to the expanded struggles of the new democracy might acknowledge their disagreements (1997, p. 11). Similarly, Anna Yeatman has argued for the introduction into decision-making processes of 'the principle of irresolvable difference', with the objective of destabilizing dominant constructions of power and supporting her emancipatory vision of radical democratic politics (1994, p. 122).

It is, of course, this type of position, with its commitment to the irresolvability-in-principle of citizenship rights contests, that has occasioned the second criticism of the new politics of difference, namely that it leads to political incompetence, to political paralysis.

Political Incompetence

The term 'political incompetence' is used here both to suggest the popular meaning of incompetence as lacking the knowledge and the skill necessary to perform a task efficiently and to suggest an analogy with legal incompetence, namely, an actor's incapacity, for whatever reason, to engage in certain activities, such as entering into a contract. The criticism of the new politics of difference that it makes activists and commentators politically incompetent is the criticism that it provides them with no point of engagement with political issues and that it affords them no justification for the pursuit of the claims of any political contestants whatever. Each political issue is sui generis and there is no political principle on which to judge the legitimacy or otherwise of the contestants' claims.[4]

The charge of political incompetence is, however, a naive interpretation of the new politics of difference. It attributes to its exponents the refusal to engage with the political history of radical democratic politics, including gender legal politics with a focus on citizenship rights. It attributes to its exponents the dismissal of the worth of political experience and the importance of evaluating, for example, the successes and failures of campaigns for the extension of citizenship rights to those groups, such as gays and lesbians, who have been excluded from their full enjoyment.

Rather, the new politics of difference restores confidence in radical democratic politics for those involved in gender legal politics. This is because, as Mouffe has argued, the radical democratic endeavour requires an engagement with the diversity and multiplicity of ways in which relations of power are constructed. For Mouffe, the theorization of multiple forms of oppression becomes not the obstacle to feminist politics but a condition of it (1992, p. 372), Similarly, Dean has argued that 'feminist work cannot focus primarily on sex and gender but must concern itself with the wider field of power relations that provide the meanings, realizations and contexts of our experiences of sex and gender' (1997, p. 3). In this way, she continues, '[T]he new democracy ... means that feminism is part of differing constellations of issues and concerns rather than a single aspect of, approach to or interpretation of these issues and concerns' (loc.cit., pp. 3–4).

Accordingly, the new politics of difference actually requires the continual review of political strategies and outcomes, including the review of the political vicissitudes of 'citizenship rights'. To facilitate that review, I now move to my outline proposal for the reconceptualization of 'citizenship rights' such that the phrase be treated as a political heuristic, a device for the constant review of exclusion and inclusion in citizenship politics and contests.

'Citizenship Rights' as Political Heuristics

Earlier in this chapter, reference is made to Hindess' characterization of citizenship as one of the central organizing principles of Western political discourse. This is not to be interpreted as the view that the employment of the idea of citizenship will automatically have the kind of political consequences envisaged by Marshall, the extension of citizenship rights to more and more members of the adult population. On the contrary, Hindess is at pains to argue that, just as human actions can have unintended consequences, so can the use of political principles.

It is consonant with Hindess' position that the use of the idea of citizenship rights is similarly prone to a variety of political outcomes. For this reason, I conclude this chapter with the proposal that 'citizenship rights' be conceptualized as political heuristics, as a mechanism for the initiation of research into the likely or possible outcomes of employing an appeal to citizenship rights in a particular context (cf. Kingdom, 1995; 1996a). Far from referring to a set of civil, political and social rights which have been or are being brought into existence and enjoyed by ever wider citizen groups, as on the RT, the term 'citizenship rights' – whether it be the title of a book, the topic of a conference, a political tract, or a provision in a state document – is conceptualized as the occasion for a review of current mechanisms and practices for the inclusion or exclusion of the groups in contestation over citizenship rights. As mechanism for initiating a review of inclusionary and exclusionary politics, 'citizenship rights' makes no automatic or a priori judgment as to who should have citizen status, who should have access to social benefits, or who has abused them. Indeed, the concept of citizenship rights as political heuristics makes no presumption in favour of a more inclusionary politics, nor a less exclusionary politics. It could be, for example, that the claim of a certain group – perhaps a neo-fascist group, or a terrorist organization – to enjoy citizen status is inconsistent with radical democratic politics.

The proposal to treat citizenship rights as political heuristics, as the trigger for a research programme into the vicissitudes of the particular right in contestation, offers no substantive political solutions. For example, to treat the right to be free from genital mutilation as a political heuristic provides no answer to whether the right should be enjoyed in all cultures and under all jurisdictions. Indeed, it can only raise a number of issues, or point to certain materials to be considered, such as whether the right is a cultural right or a right best implemented as a human right under international law.

In this respect, Berry's work is important (1997). His starting point is the conflicts that have occurred between the rights of aboriginal women, aboriginal communities and the Canadian state. This rights contest is the occasion for his consideration of the usefulness of international law for the pursuit of aboriginal self-governance. He develops what he terms 'the expanded integrationist approach' to the use of international law for the pursuit of feminist strategies. The first stage of this approach requires a scepticism towards the use of rights, a review around the globe of women's different experiences and strategies, and the contextualization of the issue in question in recognition of the fact that the effectiveness of strategies may depend on the site of their implementation. If this approach yields a positive answer to whether international law is a promising site for this instance of feminist politics, then the second stage requires the consideration of a range of strategies, such as whether to force the human rights system as a whole to accommodate women's rights or whether to formulate new rights.

To recast Berry's work in terms of my proposal here to treat citizenship rights as political heuristics, his analysis shows how the heuristic approach can introduce key legal cases, different understandings of the meaning of 'culture', greater sophistication and subtlety in the evaluation of legal, and non-legal strategies in the context of rights contests. Furthermore, his analysis can also be used to fend off any suggestion that to treat citizenship rights as political heuristics is permanently to delay political judgment, effectively to invite the sort of political incompetence which has (wrongly, in my view) been ascribed to the new politics of difference. To counter any argument that to treat citizenship rights as heuristics is permanently to delay political judgment, I would suggest that, on the contrary, the heuristic approach imposes on activists and commentators the need to organize the materials which are necessary to the development of a radical democratic politics.

Conclusion

This chapter opened with an account of Hindess' characterization of the RT; it provides a useful and insightful framework for a review of the citizenship rights debate. I have argued that three influential criticisms of the RT – victim feminism, new feminist republicanism and the feminist politics of difference – each retain certain features of it. With its emphasis on destabilizing existing forms of politics, however, the new politics of difference escapes that criticism.

Even so, it attracts other equally serious objections. My view is that the new politics of difference, as allied to the literature of radical democratic politics, survives those objections, and I have proposed that the objectives of radical democratic politics in the context of citizenship rights can be served by treating citizenship rights as political heuristics.

Notes

1   In the spoken version of this chapter, I made this point in a flippant and rhetorical way. Imagine the European Court of Justice in session, debating fundamental rights: is it a serious politics for feminists to hold up the proceedings with the complaint, 'Sorry, we don't think rights discourse is going to be any good for us – could you talk about these issues without using that word, please?'. The force of this point will be stronger, and rights discourse will be even more prominent, if the Labour government proceeds with the incorporation of the European Human Rights Convention into UK law (cf. Bynoe, 1997, p. 2).

2   In the spoken version of this chapter, again I used a frivolous 'consumerist' metaphor to represent these four criticisms of the RT. This is the supermarket model of rights, the shelves stacked with all manner of rights goods. The victim feminists stand at the turnstile, warning women that, however attractive some of the goods may appear to be, they are male goods and will invariably oppress women. The new feminist republicans complain that all the best goods are on the top shelf, typically out of reach to women and small children. Exponents of the feminist politics of difference note that the goods are mainly designed for dominant groups of women and that, since the supermarket is an out-of-town store, access to it is difficult for women who cannot drive or who find difficulty using public transport. The new politics of difference points to the constantly changing selection of goods, some of which may be usable, others not, and challenges the assumption that shopping has to be done at supermarkets anyway.

3   Cf. Dean for a summary of issues around the 'victim mentality' (1997, pp. 4–7).

4   For a brilliant attack on one form of the inertia of postmodern jurisprudence, see Veitch, 1997.

Bibliography

Benhabib, S. and Cornell, D. (1987) (eds), *Feminism and Critique*, Polity Press: Cambridge.

Berry, D. (1997), 'Contextualising International Women's Rights: Canadian feminism, race and culture' in McGlyn, q.v.

Bridgeman, J. and Millns, S. (1995) (eds), *Law and Body Politics*, Dartmouth: Aldershot.

Bynoe, I. (1997), 'Step on the rights track', *The Guardian*, 4 June, pp. 2–3.

Cornell, D. (1991), 'Sexual Difference, the Feminine, and Equivalency', *The Yale Law Journal*, 100, pp. 2247–75.

Crenshaw, K. (1997), 'Intersectionality and Identity Politics: learning from violence against women of color' in Shanley and Narayan, q. v.

Dean, J. (1997) (ed.), *Feminism and the New Democracy: resiting the political*, SAGE Publications: London.

Demaine, J. and Entwistle, H. (1996) (eds.), *Beyond Communitarianism: citizenship, politics and education*, Macmillan Press Ltd: London.

Detmold, M. (1997), 'Provocation to murder: sovereignty and multiculture', *The Sydney Law Review*, 19, 1, pp. 5–31.

Dietz, M. (1992), 'Context is all: feminism and theories of citizenship' in Mouffe, q. v.

Gelsthorpe, L. and Morris, A. (1990) (eds), *Feminist Perspectives in Criminology*, Open University Press: Buckingham.

Herman, D. (1993), 'Beyond the rights debate', *Social and Legal Studies*, 2, 25–43.

Hindess, B. (1993), 'Citizenship in the Modern West' in Turner, q. v.

Irving, H. (1994), 'A Gendered constitution?: women, federation and heads of power', *Western Australian Law Review*, 24, 2, pp. 186–98.

Kerr, J. (1993) (ed.), *Ours by Right: women's rights as human rights*, Zed Books: London.

Kingdom, E.F. (1995), 'Body politics and rights' in Bridgeman and Millns, op. cit.

Kingdom, E.F. (1996a), 'Transforming rights: feminist political heuristics', *Res Publica*, II, 1, pp. 63–75.

Kingdom, E.F. (1996b), 'Gender and citizenship rights' in Demaine and Entwistle, op. cit.

MacKinnon, C.A. (1989), *Toward a Feminist Theory of the State*, Harvard University Press: London

McGlyn, C. (1997) (ed.), *Legal Feminisms: from theory to practice*, Dartmouth Press: Aldershot.

Mouffe, C. (1992) (ed.), *Dimensions of Radical Democracy: pluralism, citizenship, community*, Verso: London.

Mouffe, C. (1993), *The Return of the Political*, Verso: London.

Murphy, T. (1997), 'Feminism on flesh', *Law and Critique*, VIII, 1, pp. 37–59.

Rice, M. (1990), 'Challenging orthodoxies in feminist theory: a black feminist critique' in Gelsthorpe and Morris, op. cit.

Roberts, D. (1992), 'The Future of Reproductive Choice for Poor Women and Women of Color', *Women's Rights Law Reporter*, 14, 2 + 3, pp. 305–14.

Salecl, R. (1997), 'Hate speech and human rights' in Dean, op. cit.

Shanley, M.L. and Narayan, U. (1997) (eds.), *Reconstructing Political Theory: feminist perspectives*, Polity Press: Cambridge.

Sherry, S. (1995), 'Responsible republicanism: educating for citizenship', *University of Chicago Law Review*, 62, 1, pp. 131–208

Smart, C. (1989), *Feminism and the Power of Law*, Routledge: London.

Stychin, C.F. (1997), Review of A. Sarat and T.T. Kearns (eds), *Identities, Politics and Rights* (University of Michigan Press: Ann Arbor), *Social and Legal Studies*, 6, 2, pp. 315–6.

Twine, F. (1994), *Citizenship and Social Rights: the interdependence of self and society*, Sage: London.

Turner, B.S. (1993), 'Outline of a theory of human rights' in Turner, q. v.

Turner, B.S. (1993) (ed.), *Citizenship in the Modern West*, SAGE: London.

Van den Berghe, G. (1982), *Political Rights for European Citizens*, Gower: Aldershot.

Veitch, S. (1997), 'Law and "other" problems', *Law and Critique*, VIII, 1, pp. 97–109.

Walby, S. (1994), 'Is citizenship gendered?', *Sociology*, 28, 2, pp. 379–94.

Yeatman, A. (1994), *Postmodern Revisionings of the Political*, Routledge: London.

Young, I.M. (1987), 'Impartiality and the civic public: some implications of feminist critiques of moral and political theory' in Benhabib and Cornell, op. cit.

7 Social Citizenship and Social Rights

CECILE FABRE

Introduction

The concept of citizenship has been the subject of increasing interest over the last few years[1] and it is not surprising that it should admit of several interpretations.[2] According to the Marshallian conception of citizenship, which I call the social citizenship conception, being a citizen means not only being able to participate in the political life of one's society, but also being able to participate in the standard lifestyle and activities of one's society. To be a citizen is to not be socially excluded from the group because one cannot consume what most members of the group consume, and it implies that one has social rights consisting in 'the whole range from the right to a modicum of economic welfare and security to the right to share to the full in the social heritage and to live the life of a civilized being according to the standards prevailing in the society' (Marshall, 1963, p. 74). Being a citizen, in short, means being a full member of society.

The aim of this paper is to assess the claim that social rights ought to be ultimately justified by appealing to the concept of social citizenship itself. The social citizenship argument for social rights has three central tenets:

1 it is a fundamental interest of mine, for various reasons, that I be a full citizen of my community, i.e. that I be able to partake in the standard lifestyle of the community. This interest is so fundamental that it justifies that I have rights to the resources necessary for me to partake in that lifestyle;

2 this standard lifestyle is defined by reference to needs. I therefore have rights to the meeting of those needs when it would help me to partake in that standard lifestyle;

3   it is against you, qua member of that community, that I have these rights.[3]

Now, I shall not dispute the claim that being a full member of the community is a fundamental interest of individuals. Nor shall I dispute the claim that citizenship should be understood as full membership in society. What I purport to do instead in this paper is to cast doubt on the claim that social citizenship can ultimately justify distribution of resources from well off citizens to badly off citizens. I shall proceed as follows. I shall first look at claim 1 and argue that the reasons most often advanced in the literature to justify turning people into full members of the community have distributive implications, but that in the social participatory argument these reasons are underpinned by a concern for autonomy, so that autonomy, and not membership in the community itself, in fact justifies the desired distribution of resources. I shall then look at claim 2, and argue that it is the strongest tenet of the citizenship argument. Finally I shall look at claim 3 and reject the claim that the fact that you and I are members of the same community justifies your having a right against me that I should help you through taxation, should you need my help. As we shall see, this claim usually rests on the idea that social cooperation between citizens is the basis upon which poor citizens have rights against rich citizens that their needs be met.

Before I start, three methodological points are in order. First, my focus is on the literature on citizenship which has mushroomed over the last 10 years or so. These writings have sought to reconstruct and to elaborate upon the writings of Marshall, Titmuss and other postwar theorists, and in doing so they have shed light on their ambiguities and problems. I shall therefore look at the later theorists rather than at their precursors. Second, I assume that it is possible to abstract the three-step argument set out above from this growing literature. This is not to deny that there are differences between contemporary theorists of social citizenship. Indeed, each of claims 1 and 3 admits of different readings (the most important, and at first sight most plausible of which I shall examine here). I believe, however, that in the form in which I have set them out they capture the fundamental tenets of the argument. Third, I am aware that other defences of the social participatory argument may have been produced, or may be will be produced, and I am not trying to reject the argument once and for all, in all its possible versions. My aim is more modest: I hope to show that the main forms of it in the existing literature are not convincing.

Self-Respect, Security and Social Citizenship

Theorists of social citizenship make the fundamental claim that it is crucial to us that we be full members of the community. Reasons differ, however, as to why it is so important. For instance, David Harris insists that preserving people's self-respect is crucial to their sense of citizenship, and that self-respect is damaged when people feel that poverty excludes them from society's standard way of life. Jeremy Waldron and Desmond King emphasize the importance of material security for people to feel that they are members of the community. Self-respect and material security are the strongest reasons advanced in the literature, and I shall look at them in turn.

Harris' claim (1987, p. 155) is that not being a full citizen of the community damages self-respect. Now, I agree that very often (although not always) feeling that one has been excluded from the standard lifestyle of society will damage one's self respect and in turn will damage one's willingness to pursue certain projects and make use of the opportunities that society offers. However, there are three problems with that argument. First, it is far from clear that all welfare benefits and services do remedy loss of self-respect. For they in fact single out their recipients to others and to the recipient themselves as being poor, as having failed. Only those services which are not means-tested can be said not to divide people into the poor and the non poor, and thus not to stigmatize the former. Furthermore, welfare services and benefits may also create a culture of dependency, which reinforces the stigma attached to poverty, thereby increasing people's lack of self-respect. Using the language of rights may not be enough to eradicate this stigma (Taylor-Gooby, 1985; Pinker, 1971; Ignatieff, 1991).

Second, assuming that giving people resources indeed fosters their self-respect and in turn makes them feel members of the community, if self-respect is so central then it does the justificatory work for social rights: citizenship does not. Indeed, self-respect is important also for people who are not citizens of the community, in the sense that they do not have the political rights of citizenship, but who live in the community. Is it not crucial then that immigrants also be able to partake in the lifestyle of the community? Of course, a proponent of citizenship could argue that they should be given citizenship. But then it is not clear to me what part is then played by this common past, common heritage that citizenship theorists often appeal to when they flesh out what common membership is.

I shall come back to such claims later. Suffice it to say now that if one argues that all people who are not citizens of the country should get citizenship, then the concept of citizenship does seem to lose much of its normative force in arguments about distributive justice. After all, by definition, talk of citizenship is not only talk about who belongs to the community but also about who does not belong, who does not share in this common identity. Someone who would wish to object to my claim that immigrants also need to partake in the standard lifestyle of the community by blurring the distinction between citizens and non citizens would have to explain what usefulness there is in invoking the concept of citizenship as the basis for distributive justice.[4]

Third, interestingly enough, Harris explains that self-respect is important because it allows people to believe that they have talents and abilities to make their life worth living, and it prompts them to pursue projects and plans (Harris, 1987, p. 155). There is an obvious connection here with autonomy, and it seems in fact that, on Harris' view, what really justifies giving resources to people is the fact that these resources are necessary for them to be autonomous.

To conclude, the reason why we should treat people as full members – it bolsters their self-respect – and not the ideal of full membership itself, seems in fact to be the justification for distributing resources.

Giving people resources and thereby turning them into full members is important also because it gives them a sense of security that they would not otherwise have. On that view, one is not a member of society if one does not have this sense of security. Thus, King and Waldron aver, in an elaboration of the claim that people should be treated as full members of the community, that there are two ways of arguing for distribution of resources on the basis of membership so conceived (King and Waldron, 1988). One looks at the expectations people currently have in a country like the UK, and argues that one ought not to deprive people of benefits they already have because doing so would threaten the view people have of what it is to belong here, to make a life here (ibid., p. 432).

This argument does not seek to prove that resources should be distributed on the basis of social citizenship in places where such distributions do not already exist; it aims to show why it is unjust to stop distributing resources. Now, I am not denying that attacking welfare provision in a country such as the UK would be to attack the way people have planned their life. However, this argument faces the same problem as the argument from self-respect. It insists on the importance for people of being able to plan and lead their life without disruption, but misses the fact that absence of disruption is also important for people who are not citizens of the country, but who live in it. In fact, insofar as immigrants cannot exercise the political rights of citizenship, and insofar as they are treated as foreigners, they can in many ways feel more insecure than citizens, so that there are strong reasons not to deprive them of the resources they have accustomed themselves to get, and thus to provide them with material security. Besides, here as well, autonomy understood as the capacity to plan one's life seems ultimately to justify not depriving people of the resources they have accustomed themselves to depend upon. The same objection I made above against the argument from self-respect applies here as well.

The second way in Waldron and King seek to justify transfers of resources on the basis of membership appeals to and draws on John Rawls' theory of justice, and it has it that a just society is a scheme of cooperation whose principles people agree to. Since no-one could be expected to agree not to 'live quiet and satisfied lives', since therefore no one could be expected to live in poverty, people should be given welfare benefits as a matter of right (ibid., pp. 440–1).

Now, I am not denying that rational people could not agree to live in deprivation and poverty.[5] However, this second argument, in seeing society as a scheme of cooperation, and in seeing people as members in such a scheme, implies that those who are not able to cooperate cannot make claims to resources. There are many reasons why people may not be able to cooperate: they might be severely disabled, or they might have been unemployed for such a long time that they are no longer employable. Since these people are often the most vulnerable in society, the most in need and the most insecure, King and Waldron's argument is flawed at its very heart: it rests on the need for material security but excludes from its scope those for whom such a need is the most pressing.[6]

To conclude this section, I hope to have shown that the two arguments under examination are not convincing. It remains to be shown that welfare benefits bolster self-respect; besides, autonomy, rather than social citizenship, seem to justify distributing resources from the well off to the badly off.

Needs and Social Citizenship

The second claim of theorists of social citizenship is that one cannot identify oneself as a full member of the community if one's needs are not met. According to Harris, one's self-respect is damaged if one is needy; according to King and Waldron, one cannot have a sense of security if one is needy. This is because needs are created socially, by reference to what others in our society have and what we do not have (Harris, 1987, p. 30).

There are problems with trying to define what the standard lifestyle is, and there is no doubt that some of our needs – that is, basic subsistence needs – are not determined by it. But there is equally no doubt that many of our needs are determined socially. For instance, nowadays, people need a television set in order to take part in the way of life of Western societies, and especially if they do not have access to other kinds of entertainment facilities. Such a claim was unthinkable 30 years ago, and is unthinkable in other types of society. It is a strength of the citizenship argument for social rights that it stresses it. So I will say no more of this here.

Duties of Citizenship

So far, I have looked at the reasons why the poor should be treated as full members of the community and given resources to partake in the lifestyle of society. In this section, I examine the reasons why, in the literature on citizenship, it is thought that the fact that you and I are members of the same community justifies that you be held under a duty to help me should I be unable to provide for my needs. As Harris (1987, p. 152) puts it:

> [O]ur right to be aided or to have certain life chances protected is derived from membership of the society per se, and not from any prior hypothetical or actual agreements, or contracts.

Now, given that membership itself is defined in terms of access to a certain lifestyle, or to certain resources, the reasoning seems to be circular. For it goes as follows: I can be a member of society only if I get these resources. Why should you give me those resources if I do not have them? Because you and I are fellow members. But since I am not a member without these resources, we are not fellow members until you give them to me. And if we are not fellow members, on what basis ought I give you these resources that you need?

The only way to rescue the argument from circularity is to modify the conception of citizenship on which it rests, by breaking it down into formal citizenship and substantive citizenship. The former would be supplemented by the latter, which would require provision of resources. If we are supposed to be citizens, and if citizenship is to mean something, then we cannot be left in poverty. Now, this move still does not rescue the claim that our common membership in the community, here understood as formal citizenship, forms the basis of our right against each other that we help each other if we need it. For the citizenship theorist still would have to show what is so important in our common formal membership that we should help one another. I examine three arguments to that effect, which all rest on the claim that contribution to society made by some members for the benefit of other members justifies transfers of resources; I show that they are not convincing.

The first argument appeals to nationality. Being a national of a certain country is to be formally a citizen of that country, and it may promise that I be given the resources necessary for me to be a national in the substantive sense that I can partake in the lifestyle of the community. On that view, the fact that you and I have the same nationality and that we both live in the country of which we are nationals justifies that I be held under a moral duty to help you should you need my help, and that this duty should be turned into a constitutional disability. Membership of the community in that thin sense justifies that we be under a duty to help others. This is the line of argument taken by David Miller in his recent *On Nationality* (1995).[7] In order to justify transfers of resources from well-off citizens to poor citizens on the grounds of nationality, he stresses the importance of historical continuity, and in particular of what our ancestors did for us. He thus justifies the special obligation that we have to help our fellow citizens,[8] arguing first that the historic national community is a community of obligations, in that we have an obligation to our ancestors, who have made sacrifices to build the nation, to continue their work (ibid., p. 23); and second, that this sense of historical continuity more specifically gives rise to an obligation to help our fellow nationals (ibid., p. 42).

I find that justification problematic. One needs a more developed argument than Miller offers us to see why the fact that our ancestors made sacrifices to build the nation puts us under the duty to help our contemporaries. Miller simply stresses the importance of the sacrifices made, but it is not altogether clear what the nature of these sacrifices is, or why, therefore, they bind descendants in the way he says they do. Does he have in mind whatever sacrifices were made to build the nation, whatever the type of nation that arose out of those sacrifices? But then it is not obvious that this should form the basis of our duties. If I find that these sacrifices were made in the name of abhorrent values, such as those of an oppressive empire, why should I feel under an obligation to acknowledge them by helping my contemporaries? Nor is it obvious, whatever the sacrifices were, even, therefore, if they were admirable, that they should be acknowledged by distributing resources to those who need help. There are other ways of acknowledging them. One could argue for instance that French governments and presidents are under the obligation to spend billions of francs to commission great architectural works, so as to continue a tradition that goes back to the Renaissance and that is integral to the French nation, even if doing that prevents them from helping the needy, as it can be argued that it actually does.

If the reason why we owe help to our fellows citizens if they need it is that our ancestors helped those of their contemporaries who were needy, then it is not very clear why we should reciprocate now what has been done in the past, and why we should reciprocate to people who have not made these sacrifices. Miller gives the example of the obligation to support a health care service in a given community, and grounds it on 'the reasons given for having the health service when it was first introduced, and reaffirmed from time to time when the health service is debated' (Miller, 1995, p. 70). Presumably then, it is enough that reasons were given in the past to hold our ancestors under the duty to make such sacrifices, and are still being given now, for us to be under the duty to support it. Now, this is very problematic. For these reasons themselves might have nothing to do with the fact that the needy are our fellow citizens, and everything to do with the fact that they are needy. And if we have to accept these reasons, then it means that we put ourselves under a duty the basis for which is radically at variance with Miller's conception.

Finally, Miller's argument cannot work generally. For if the reason why we are under a duty to help is that our first ancestors contributed to making our community what it is now, then it implies that they did not themselves have any duty to help, since they did not have any ancestors whose contribution was the basis of their duty. If it is possible, and indeed, in the case of our first ancestors, necessary to justify a duty to help on other grounds than past contributions, then it seems hard to see why we should appeal to past contributions in order to justify our duty to help our contemporaries. To sum up then, Miller's argument for distribution of resources on the basis of nationality does not hold.

If nationality cannot ground transfers of resources and thus cannot rescue the social participatory argument for social justice, what can rescue it? Unfortunately, none of the arguments to that effect that can be found in the literature adequately answers the question: what is so special about our common belonging to a community that if you are in need I should help you? I shall look at two kinds of arguments advanced in the literature on citizenship.

The first one takes the form of an analogy between relationships within the family and relationships within the community (Harris, 1987, pp. 70 ff and 152 ff). It goes as follows. Our parents give us the security and the means which are necessary to our development into full adults. We therefore owe help to them when they need it. Similarly, society and therefore all its members give us the environment, the infrastructure, the security, the language, the culture, and so on, which form our identity and enable us to have and implement plans of life. We therefore owe help to other members of our society if they need it, and this help takes the form of redistributive policies which are funded through taxation. Note that cooperation in the productive system of society is not necessary: merely being there enriches the life of the community. And even if it does not, the very fact that we belong to this community makes us eligible for help, as if the community were our family.

Citizenship-theorists do not push the analogy to the extent that help from the community is as unconditionally given as help from our family. However, this analogy plays a powerful part in the argument. But I believe that it is problematic in a very important respect. Relationships within a family are, or at any rate, ought to be, characterized by love. Claims of rights are made, or should be made, only when the love-based relationship breaks down, or fails to secure what the members of the family ought to have. By contrast, relationships within the community, as far as the provision of welfare is concerned and as citizenship theorists themselves acknowledge, are characterized by a sense of duty understood as the recognition of other people's rights (Waldron, 1993). When we vote for welfare programmes, we vote in the intention of helping strangers, not people we have any deep feeling for. The following example shows how community and family relationships ought to be understood. Consider the case of two siblings separated at birth, who do not know each other. Do they have a special duty to help each other, if they come to know of each other? Intuitively, no, precisely because they have no common past, no shared memories (Jacobs, 1993, p. 45). This is the kind of relationships that exist between citizens, who may share the same past, but in a very abstract way, in a way which may not bring them closer to one another than to foreign people.

Someone might put forward the following counter-example: if someone who has never known his father (say, because his parents split up and the father has never bothered to inquire about the child) finds him and asks for his help, it would be plausible to think that the father is under a duty to give it. If true, that would show that the absence of any close relationship does not absolve people of their duty towards others. Unfortunately, even if it were true that the father is under the duty to help his child, it would not work as a justification for help between citizens along the lines of the family model. For the reason why the father has a duty to his child is that he *is* the father, that he brought the child into existence and has to assume responsibility for it. But there is no such responsibility between citizens. To conclude then, the analogy between relationships within the family and relationships between the community cannot offer a solid arguments for distribution of resources between citizens on grounds of citizenship.

Another way of justifying redistribution of resources from some members of the community to others is to claim that cooperation between contemporary citizens in the productive system of society is the basis for distribution of resources. This argument differs from Miller's argument in that it does not take into account the contribution of our ancestors to their contemporaries' lifestyle and to ours, and it differs from the analogy between the family and the community in that it sees cooperation in the scheme of production as the sole basis for distribution. It admits of two variants. One sees distribution as compensation for the cost incurred in cooperating; the other conceives of social cooperation as a common good from which citizens ought not to be excluded and claims that distributing resources is a necessary condition for avoiding such exclusion. I shall examine them in turn.

The compensation variant goes as follows: as has been said before, members of the community all cooperate so as to build and preserve the fabric of society. In the process of doing so, some get a rawer deal than others, and they should be compensated for that. Harris, for instance, defines those who should be compensated for the situation they are in as 'members of a class or group who are making a contribution to the well-being of a class or group who are thereby under a duty to compensate' (Harris, 1987, p. 35; see also Titmuss, 1968, p. 143 and Wellman, 1982). The needy are needy because they have badly paid jobs that still benefit the better off, or because they have been trapped into a system – the market economy – which throws them on the scrap heap for the benefit of better off people. It is therefore only fair that the better off compensate them for the situation they are in now. Distributive justice, on this view, is in fact seen as an instance of compensatory justice.[9]

This claim is problematic in three respects. First, it rests on the assumption that it is possible to determine with precision what people contributed and whether their contribution meets the requirements for compensation. In increasingly complicated domestic and international economies, that sounds doubtful to me.

Second, distribution of resources by society cannot really be seen as an instance of compensation because there are social policies which are not corrective, which do not aim at restoring a status quo. Benefits for parents with dependent children and education are obvious examples.[10] This variant of the social citizenship argument fails to account for such policies.

Third, although in some cases such as unemployment it is possible to identify the situation people were in before they were harmed, in most cases it is not, precisely because pinning down the causes of people's plight is very difficult. Furthermore, talking about compensatory justice misses the fact that, in cases like unemployment, social justice does not seek to re-establish a status quo ante but to create a just situation. Most talk of compensation due by the state to individuals take place against the background of an existing system of distribution brought about by the market. When we talk of meeting the needs of the people, we do not have in mind a status quo ante that was more just and that existed before people found themselves needy. We are imagining what the most just situation would be. Compensatory justice however does not work according to just situations, but to real status quo ante. It seems therefore that in many cases, we cannot say that it is a matter of compensatory justice for the state to meet people's needs without presupposing a non-compensatory theory of distributive justice.

Furthermore, the problem with the compensation argument is that it loosens the connection between citizenship and the meeting of needs. For if the poor's contribution is defined as risk-bearing, or bearing the cost of other people's progress, then it is quite clear that in a society like ours those who bear such a cost, who are made to pay for other people's well-being, are quite often immigrants, people who are not even citizens. So presumably they should be given welfare benefits as well, whose assignment would then not depend on citizenship. Moreover, limiting claims to compensation to people living in our community seems arbitrary. For after all, in a global, world wide economy, people from poor countries bear the cost of the high lifestyle of people from Western type capitalist society. Why could it not be argued that they should be compensated before those whose standing in our society is better than theirs? Undoubtedly it would be very difficult to implement. But the conceptual issue remains: if the ground of my duty to help is that I benefit from an economic progress that would not be possible without certain people bearing its cost, then I owe help to these people, regardless of whether they are or are not citizens of my community.

The second way of justifying transfer of resources from rich citizens to poor citizens on grounds of citizenship, and via social cooperation, consists in saying that a society is a system of cooperation, that being a member of society, in other words, being a citizen, consists in being able to take part in that system of cooperation. Since the latter is a common good, in the sense that everybody has an interest in contributing to and benefiting from it, well-off people ought, for their own sake, to enable the needy, who are excluded from the system because of their neediness, to get back into the system, by relieving them of their neediness. This type of argument can be found in Bill Jordan's *The Common Good: Citizenship, Morality and Self-Interest* (1989).

The fundamental problem with this argument, for our purpose, is that it is far from clear that this conception of membership in the community has the distributive implications its holders say it has.[11] In particular it is not clear at all why well-off citizens should support a welfare system. If my motivation for partaking in that system of cooperation is that it is instrumental to the pursuit of my self-interest, why should I not rather opt for a system where the poor would have the choice between starving and accepting to perform all the menial and dangerous jobs that need to be done in a society, at a very low wages, so that they are just above starvation level? Why should I not support a society where needs would be met just at the level necessary to avoid unrest and rebellion?

Furthermore, as I have said earlier in connection with Kings and Waldron's arguments, by putting the emphasis on social cooperation, one excludes from those who should get resources those who cannot cooperate because they are severely disabled, or because they have been unemployed for such a long time that it is it is unlikely that they will ever have the capacities to go back to work and to cooperate in the social scheme. The justification for granting them benefits must lie elsewhere than in the self-interest of others, and in fact must lie elsewhere than in citizenship. For since the latter is defined in part as the ability to take part in the scheme of social cooperation, one cannot justify helping those who cannot take part in such a scheme, who cannot be citizens, on the grounds that they have to be made citizens.

Conclusion

I hope to have shown that the concept of social citizenship, as it is currently understood, cannot offer a sound justification for social rights. More specifically, I hope to have shown that in the recent literature on citizenship, distribution of resources seems to be justified not by appealing to the ideal of full membership itself but by the reasons why it is important to be treated as full members of the community; and that there are reasons to doubt that the fact of our common membership justifies that I help you should you need my help. Most importantly, I hope to have shown that some of the arguments I have examined have some disturbing implications in that, even though they stem from a deep concern for the poor, they in fact exclude from the scope of distributive justice those people who are the most in need of material assistance.

This is not to say, however, that the concept of social citizenship does not have any role to play in a theory of distributive justice. I accepted the claim that certain needs are socially created, that we have them because we live in a certain society. If it is conceptually possible to disconnect social citizenship from political citizenship altogether, so as to account for those people who live in the community without having political rights,[12] then we can see that social citizenship, understood as living in the community and sharing in (some of its) practices, can give content to social rights. The argument would go as follows: it is an important interest of mine that my self-respect and sense of security be preserved, in order for me to lead a meaningful life, to be autonomous, to fare well, etc.; and it is therefore an important interest of mine that my needs be met, including those needs which are socially determined and the meeting of which conditions my self-respect and sense of security in the specific community I live in. But it is not citizenship itself which justifies assigning social rights to resources to people: citizenship rather determines what we can do with bundles of resources, and, therefore, what resources, exactly, are needed, as well as how much of them the needy should get. This, I think, is what a theory of social citizenship should set out to address.[13]

Notes

1   For an excellent review of the growing literature on citizenship, see Kymlicka and Norman, 1994.
2   For a review of different ways of conceiving of citizenship, see Leca, 1994 and Turner, 1994.
3   Note that claim 3 does not duplicate claim 1; it asserts that the reason why you have the duty to help me is that we belong to the same community and thus explains who are the bearers of such duty and why, while claim 1 explains what it is in the rights-bearers that justifies giving them resources. One could argue that members of our community have a duty to help us if necessary because they are our fellow members, and argue, *contra* claim 1, that the reason why they should help us is not that these resources are necessary for us to be full member of the community, but, say, that they are necessary for us to be autonomous. Conversely, one could argue that we should get resources in order to partake in the standard lifestyle of our community, but that people from other communities should give us those resources, through international distribution.
4   For the claim that citizenship loses its traditional legal, political and social importance when one blurs the distinction between citizens and non citizens by assigning the latter rights of citizenship, see Bader, 1995.

5   Although one might imagine that some people might feel that their conception of the good life, for example of a life led according to certain religious principles, requires them to live in poverty.

6   This point was made by G. A. Cohen in an Oxford seminar on Rawls.

7   For the claim that one ought to divorce citizenship from national identity, see Beiner, 1995, Bader, 1995 and Habermas, 1995.

8   It is not always very clear whether in this book Miller is talking about helping citizens, or helping fellow nationals, where 'nationals' here refers to his conception of national identity, as distinct from citizenship. In the introduction, he seems to go for citizenship (see p. 11), but in chapter 3, he argues that citizenship, being simply membership in a scheme of social cooperation for the pursuit of one's self-interest, is not strong enough a basis to justify transfers of resources from the rich to the poor, and must be supplemented by the ties of national identity. This conception of citizenship, which Miller advances as if it were obvious, is certainly not the only one put forward in the literature. In fact there are conceptions of citizenship which are very similar to his conception of national identity, or to which national identity is integral. He himself develops one of those in Miller, 1989.

9   Not every claim for compensation can be honoured though: it 'must be satisfied only where not to do so undercuts one's community membership' (Harris, 1987, p. 38).

10 Obviously, the case of retraining towards getting new qualifications because the ones you have are no longer valued by the economy could, indeed, be considered as an instance of compensatory justice.

11 I owe a good deal of my argument in this paragraph to Swift, 1994.

12 That would obviously be a pretty big step to take, one which could in fact cast doubt on the propriety of using the term 'citizenship' in that context.

13 For numerous and very useful comments on earlier drafts of this paper, I am very grateful to G.A. Cohen, to Adam Swift, who also allowed me to read his typescript 'Three Conceptions of Citizenship' (which proved invaluably helpful), to the members of the Exeter University and Nuffield Political Theory Workshops, and to participants at the 1997 Annual Conference of the UK Association for Legal and Social Philosophy.

Bibliography

Bader V. (1995), 'Citizenship and Exclusion: Radical Democracy, Community, and Justice, or, What is Wrong with Communitarianism?', *Political Theory*, Vol. 23, pp. 211–46.

Beiner, R. (1995), 'Introduction' in Beiner, R. (ed.), *Theorizing Citizenship*, State University of New York Press: New York.

Habermas, J. (1995), 'Citizenship and National Identity: Some Reflections on the Future of Europe' in Beiner (ed.), op. cit.

Harris, D. (1987), *Justifying State Welfare*, Blackwell: Oxford.

Ignatieff, M. (1991), 'Citizenship and Moral Narcissism' in Andrews. G. (ed.), *Citizenship*, Lawrence and Wishart: London.

Jacobs, L. (1993), *Rights and Deprivation*, Clarendon Press: Oxford.

Jordan, B. (1989), *The Common Good: Citizenship, Morality and Self–Interest*, Blackwell: Oxford.

King, D. and Waldron, J. (1988), 'Citizenship, Social Citizenship and the Defence of Welfare Provision', *British Journal of Political Science*, Vol. 18, pp. 415–43.

Kymlicka, W. and Norman, W. (1994), 'The Return of the Citizen: A Survey of recent Work on Citizenship Theory', *Ethics*, Vol. 104, pp. 350–81.

Leca, J. (1994), 'Individualism and Citizenship', in Turner, B. and Hamilton, P. (eds), *Citizenship: Critical Concepts*, 2 vols, Routledge: London and New York.

Marshall, T.H. (1963), 'Citizenship and Social Class' in Marshall, T.H., *Sociology at the Crossroads*, Heinemann: London.

Miller, D. (1989), *Market, State and Community*, Clarendon Press: Oxford.

Miller, D. (1995), *On Nationality*, Oxford University Press: Oxford.

Pinker, R. (1971), *Social Theory and Social Policy*, Heinemann: London.

Swift, A. (1994), 'Three Conceptions of Citizenship', typescript.

Taylor-Gooby, P. (1985), *Public Opinion, Ideology and State Welfare*, Routledge and Kegan Paul: London.

Titmuss, R. (1968), *Commitment to Welfare*, Allen and Unwin Ltd.: London.

Turner, B. (1994), 'Outline of a Theory of Citizenship' in Turner, B. and Hamilton, P. (eds), *Citizenship: Critical Concepts*, 2 vols, Routledge: London and New York.

Waldron, J. (1993), 'When justice replaces affection: the need for rights' in Waldron, J., *Liberal Rights: Collected Papers, 1981–199*, Cambridge University Press: Cambridge.

Wellman, C. (1982), *Welfare Rights*, Rowman and Littlefield: Totowa, New Jersey.

8 Social Citizenship, Re-commodification and the Contract State

PAUL HAVEMANN

Introduction

The ideology of contractualism, manufactured risk, the rise of the contract(ing out) state, and the seemingly inexorable process of commodifying social relations are all dystopian features of late modernity. Yet a 'utopian realist' analysis of late modernity also yields signs of hope for global and local human welfare. Among these signs is the growing 'ethic of humanity'. This ethic is expressed in second and third generation human rights, for example, as well as in notions of social citizenship (Fraser and Gordon, 1994) – a broader concept than *social democratic* citizenship (Guild, 1996). This paper explores tensions between what I will describe as apocalyptic and utopian dimensions of late modernity.

In the contemporary New Zealand state – as the Employment Contracts Act 1991, the State Owned Enterprises Act 1986, and the State Sector Act 1988 show – contractualism rules. By contractualism I mean the intentional conflation of public and private, the blurring of the distinction between state and market, and the widespread appropriation of the latter's contract form to structure social exchange relationships in a commodified form. The model of contract between (supposedly) equal market players is used to legitimate a variety of 'contractual' transactions between decidedly unequal parties. Some of these transactions – for example in the labour market – now have gross power imbalances designed into them, contradicting their legitimating freedom-talk, while others replace relationships between citizens and state in the 'social contract' with relationships between surrogates which are neither citizen nor state in market compacts.

Citizenship status under the Keynesian welfare state (KWS) conferred benefits as of right, but this status is now seriously weakened. The individual human life is increasingly lived as an 'enterprise of the self' within a culture of contractualism (Gordon, 1991, pp. 42–5; Kelsey, 1995), and the social is reconceived in the image of the economic in the hollowed-out contract state.

Late Modernity: 'Apocalyptic' v. 'Emancipatory' Visions

Late modernity has been usefully characterized as the period exemplifying the movement from simple modernization to reflexive modernization (Giddens, 1995, 1994; Beck, Giddens and Lash, 1994). There is a considerable interpenetration and interplay among contradictory and complementary dimensions of simple and reflexive modernization on both local and global levels.

Reflexive modernization is characterized by:

* the after-Fordist economic order evidenced by an acceleration of the massive polarization of rich and poor, flexible specialization, contractualism and the enterprise culture (Heelas and Morris, 1992; Lipietz, 1992; Amin, 1994; O'Brien and Wilkes, 1993; Havemann, 1994);
* continuing local and global violence;
* continuing polarization around competing ethno-nationalisms (McGarry and O'Leary, 1993);
* mass labour migration, de-colonization and social dislocation (Richmond, 1994);
* the emergence of social reflexivity;
* the rise of the ethic of humanity and the human rights nexus;
* de-traditionalization and re-traditionalization;
* globalization and the internationalization of capitalism;
* the unprecedented manufacture of ecocidal risk (Beck, 1992);
* an epistemology acknowledging multiple truths;
* the continuing reality of democratic deficits;
* increased surveillance and control by unaccountable, public and private, entities controlling communication along the information superhighway;
* the erosion of welfare state-based citizenship rights;
* unprecedented demand for citizen-like membership of national and supranational polities, some of which were originally conceived of merely as market mechanisms, e.g. the European Union (Soysal, 1996, pp. 18–20); and
* the rise of the contracting-out state and the unprecedented re-commodification of social relations.

Social Reflexivity, De-traditionalization and Globalization

At the core of reflexive modernization are social reflexivity, de-traditionalization and globalization, and the ethic of humanity. These developments offer prospects of emancipatory 'goods' to counter the apocalyptic 'bads' – even, let us hope, the ecocidal risk being manufactured by humankind in the name of progress.

Social reflexivity (Giddens, 1994, pp. 80–97) provides the individual and the collectivity with a capacity for de-traditionalization, that is, the ability to examine – and thus to accept, reject, modify, or replace – traditional, common sense ideas which have constructed class, ethnic, nationalist, denominational and gender identities previously taken for granted and regarded as 'natural'. De-traditionalization, as used here, does not mean the radical demise of tradition conceived in terms of movement between oppositions (such as closed *v.* open, fate *v.* choice, security *v.* risk) but the construction of new traditions and coexistence of the old along with the new (Heelas, 1996a, pp. 2–3).

Globalization is the new phenomenon of 'action at a distance'. It involves the radically altered pace and direction of trajectories of change – in social contexts, cultural values, and normative justifications for institutional design – brought about by instantaneous global communication and mass transportation (Giddens, 1995).

The scenario of a global economy controlled by transnational corporations beyond the law and accountable to no organized polity is invited by the re-commodification of social relations and the contraction of citizenship. However, some suggest that it may be a mistake at this stage to conceive of the highly internationalized economy as a 'world system' (Hirst and Thompson, 1996). Even if the World Trade Organisation envisages that Multilateral Agreement on Investment is to be the constitution for a single global economy, news of the demise of the nation state is presently exaggerated.

The Ethic of Humanity

Globalization offers processes through which all kinds of alternatives get disseminated and popularized, emancipatory as well as repressive. The former include the entitlement to individual human rights. Yasemin Soysal argues that there has been an increasing intensification of the global discourse on individual human rights:

> … this emphasis on rights is expressed through codification of 'human rights'

as a world-level organizing principle in legal, scientific and popular conventions. As legitimized and celebrated by various international codes and laws, the discourse of human rights ascribes universal rights to the person, independent of membership status in a particular nation state (Soysal, 1996, p. 19).

Paul Heelas sees the 'ethic of humanity' represented by the proliferation of human rights as the essence of ideological change in the post-world war two epoch (Heelas, 1996b, pp. 207–10).

From a utopian realist perspective, the ethic of humanity is now the dominant humanistic liberal tradition of advanced modernity and can provide some of the ideological material from which to build – not unproblematically (Galtung, 1994; An-Na'Im, 1992) – both global and local social citizenship based on universal personhood rather than nationality (Soysal, 1994).

Ronald Robertson delineates phases of 'political economy' globalization culminating in the present *uncertainty phase*, which he identifies with the rise of human rights discourse. Alongside crisis tendencies in the 1990s, he also sees increasing global consciousness, inclusion of the Third World, accentuation of post-materialist values, poly-ethnicity and multiculturalism (Robertson, 1990).

Since one of the most dystopian dimensions of contemporary modernity is the 'risk society' (Beck, 1992) – the age of local and global ecocide, of manufactured threats to all life on the planet – one very evident manifestation of social reflexivity has been the counter-hegemonic, green new social movements, alongside and in tandem with the women's and peace and social justice movements. Their discourse of rights articulates a multilayered set of obligations within both national and international political and juridical structures which now inform and reinforce each other (Hunt, 1996, pp. 34–9). Underpinning this rights discourse is the universal application of the ethic of humanity to all by virtue of their personhood. Rights-based respect for personhood involves the power to participate in public affairs and to define the scope of one's autonomy and interdependency. Most of the world's population, however, experiences what David Held identifies as *nautonomy*.

Nautonomy, Social Citizenship and Utopian Realism

Held identifies seven sites of power in which *nautonomic* social relations obtain: the body, welfare system, culture, civic associations, economy, coercive relations and organized violence, and regulatory and legal institutions (Held, 1995a, pp. 54–6). Nautonomy is constituted by the asymmetrical production and distribution of life chances which erode the possibilities of political participation and options to share in socially generated economic, cultural or political goods, rewards and opportunities. Held argues that to achieve optimal *autonomy*, people require bundles of rights entrenched in democratic public law so as to be empowered to act within each of these sites of power. I suggest that such empowerment is the essence of *social citizenship*. Held's broad charter contains social, cultural, civil, economic, pacific and political rights. The body is identified as the site of power where broadly conceived rights to health and participation arm the citizen to combat the ecocidal consequences of 'manufactured uncertainty' or unprecedented high-consequence risk taking (Held, 1995b, pp. 175–6, 191–2). Universality is inherent in social citizenship thus understood, and this revised concept of citizenship must replace that based on ethnic and national identity with their concomitant denotations of exclusivity (Donald, 1996).

Autonomy through social citizenship requires a utopian realist vision informing a radical politics aimed at restructuring the major institutional dimensions of late modernity. Basic tasks which must be addressed are: the repairing of damaged solidarities – for example gender and ethnic relations; the reconciling of individuality and interdependence; the recognition of the centrality of life politics – the politics of how we live together – and of generative politics – empowering individuals and groups to make things happen; the strengthening of dialogic democracy; the entrenchment of positive welfare – that is, active mobilization rather than reactive welfarism; and respect for an overriding ethic of nonviolence in human affairs (Giddens, 1994). Social citizenship is a fundamental status and a necessary one to generate and sustain a radical new politics of autonomy in interdependence. Because the contemporary erosion of citizenship and the re-commodification of social relations perpetuates nautonomy even in societies where considerable gains had been made.

Commodification

From Status to Contract in Post-Feudal Patriarchal Capitalism

Sir Henry Maine, writing in the nineteenth century, characterized societies progressing from feudalism to capitalism as moving *from status to contract*. The feudal command chain connotes coercion and hierarchy. The liberal legal discourse of contract reflects the post-feudal ideology of individual choice, enforceable rights and obligations, and consumer sovereignty. The centre of the post-feudal universe was the new possessive (male) individual whose rationality, that of the *homo economicus*, became the template for the acquisition of identity as well as providing for post-feudal society's form of organization to accommodate his activities.

The dichotomization of public and private spheres in liberal ideology allowed those social exchange relations which are resistant to commodification, such as those in the family or altruistic caring for strangers (Titmuss, 1970), to be relegated to a peripheral realm of supposedly non-market transactions based on love and charity. The heavily gendered character of the public/private dichotomy is eloquently emblematic of the patriarchal capitalist societal paradigm (Pateman, 1991).

Nonetheless, the liberal rhetoric of contractual, i.e. consensual, choice-based transactions offers a self-enforcing exchange system in which both parties benefit and neither is exploited. The distinction between contractual transactions and feudal 'command' transactions made the post-feudal, commodified, social order ideologically 'saleable', and the market was heralded as the best guarantor of freedom from serfdom. Yet the promise of freedom of choice and equality of bargaining power, and the mutuality of being *consensus ad idem*, were always more rhetorical than real. For instance, the New Zealand Employment Contracts Act and its equivalents in Australia fundamentally weaken workers' bargaining power by atomizing the labour market. Employment contracts are made individualized transactions by all by removing the union from the negotiating table and the state from its role as the arbiter of fairness between parties (Wilson, 1997).

The Keynesian Welfare State: from Contract to Status?

The hard-edged contractualism of the first industrial revolution was mitigated by the partial de-commodification of social relations under the Fordist Keynesian Welfare State (KWS) from the 1930s until the 1970s. The KWS emerged out of '… a process of market expansion and a counter movement of protection against the market' (Therborn, 1987). Along with liberal democracy, the KWS preserved capitalism by establishing a set of institutions, rights and entitlements which transformed it (Turner, 1986).

The core idea of the KWS was the expansion of citizenship beyond eighteenth and nineteenth century civil and political rights to include *social* rights to welfare, education, health care and old age security. T.H. Marshall (1950) promoted this social democratic notion of citizenship as a means of closing class cleavages arising from both feudal and capitalist social relations to promote prosperity in postwar Britain (Hindess, 1987). *Citizenship*, the status behind the cluster of civil, political and social rights to be realized through the welfare state was to serve as the integrative and emancipatory status to counter divisive class status.

Thus *citizen status*, not contract, was revived to achieve a more egalitarian society. To sustain the legitimacy of the welfare state/market compromise, the (partial) *de-commodification* (Offe, 1984) of social relations of the Fordist KWS class compromise took the form of the proliferation of status under the umbrella of welfare state citizenship and the moderating influence of consensual contractualism in the labour market relationships (Cotterell, 1984, p. 170).

But the KWS version of de-commodification, intrinsic to the Fordist societal paradigm (or organized capitalism), was not a harbinger of a socialist future.

Crises of Legitimacy for the KWS and Citizenship

Fordism severely distorted the apparently de-commodified social status relations and notions of citizenship embedded in the welfare state (Keane, 1984, p. 264); In western Europe, North America, and countries in the advanced periphery such as New Zealand and Australia, the welfare states that emerged were ideologically compromised, fiscally crisis-prone and subservient to the *productivist mode* of capitalist development (Gorz, 1985). Among the consequences was the increased manufacture of ecological risk through unfettered economic growth. 'Full' employment in the Fordist labour market was built on a gendered and racialized hierarchy of workers that privileged white male labour's interests, and the welfare state was built on female dependency.

In the 1970s many welfare states faced two interrelated global and local crises: a fiscal crisis of the state and a crisis of legitimacy for the KWS consensus. The core contradiction of Fordism was the apparent impossibility of sustaining the compromise to allow profitable accumulation to continue yet at the same time collect sufficient tax revenue and sustain and enhance the spending power of individuals and the state in order to give legitimacy to the KWS (O'Connor, 1973).

New social movements from the Left (feminists, Marxists and anti-racists) and the Right (economic liberals and the New Right), as well as those aiming to transcend both Left and Right (Green post-materialists) roundly criticized the KWS and the Fordist compromise (Pierson, 1991). The most telling critique came from the New Right, which appropriated aspects of Left critiques. According to it, the welfare state was:[1]

- *uneconomic:* it created disincentives for capital and labour to perform rationally in the marketplace;
- *unproductive:* it encouraged spending in the public sector rather than investment in productive enterprises;
- *inefficient:* it was usurped by public service provider monopolies to perpetuate their growth rather than respond to consumer needs;
- *ineffective:* it perpetuated a 'cycle of dependence' through hugely costly and disabling social programmes in defiance of evidence that 'nothing works';
- *oppressive:* it required a progressive, i.e. confiscatory, tax regime to provide services offered by a state monopoly, thereby denying citizens choice about what to do with their money; and
- *despotic:* it intruded arbitrarily and imposed social controls, justified in paternalistic terms, which resulted in institutionalization, a culture of dependency, and alienation.

From the opposite shore, writers like Michael Ignatieff suggest that the ethical foundations of the welfare state – the Judæo-Christian (and Marxian) ethic 'from each according to ability; to each according to need' – has been eroded by the steady trivialization of rights and obligations by welfare rights talk; he calls on the Left to abandon nostalgia for the compassion of 'the old civic contract' (Ignatieff, 1989; Culpitt, 1992).

Even social democrats blamed fiscal crisis on the practice of welfare states of being needs- rather than resource-driven (Parry, 1985) and argued that the insatiable needs of diverse interest groups endemic to the welfare state culture, when translated into rights, provided no criteria to rank competing claims for priority (Culpitt, 1992, p. 52). Re-commodification and contractualism were embraced as the new societal paradigm.

Re-commodification

In the contemporary era of late twentieth-century capitalism, variously categorized as 'after-Fordist' or 'post-Fordist', disorganized, etc., advanced, high or late modernity, we are witnessing the *re-commodification* of social relations through the hegemony of the market (rather than the state) as an organizing structure and dynamic. This process is bringing about the exacerbation of 'nautonomic' social relations.

Contractualism

After Fordism, the mode of social regulation reflects and promotes the structural competitiveness of the polarized, globalized marketplace in which the state must increasingly operate. Contract is the legal form which crystallizes this competitiveness by facilitating re-commodification. All social relations and public goods can become commodities to be bought and sold. Social protections for workers are subordinated to labour market flexibility (and labour cost constraints) imposed by international competition. The KWS is hollowed out and its essential core functions sold off or contracted out (Jessop, 1994). Not only is shedding of state roles a significant technical innovation for introducing market rationality into the public sector; contractualism also signals 'a major re-drafting of some of the strongest assumptions about altruistic social exchange integral to an understanding of the welfare state' (Culpitt, 1992, p. 81).

Processes and structures which support exchange relationships are redesigned to mimic the classical contract form in a variety of settings in the 'contract state' public sector. The need for this is consistent with Claus Offe's assertion that the stability of the Fordist welfare state depended upon the reconciliation of divergent structural conditions through the incorporation of every citizen into a commodity relationship (Offe, 1984).

These only recently de-commodified status relations are now being reconstituted as vendor/consumer transactions. From the citizens' viewpoint, however, the elements of classical contracts are seldom evident in these 'contracts', which are rather inter-agency *compacts*. John Alford and Deirdre O'Neill (1995, pp. 4–6) suggest that the chief forms are:

- *intra-agency contracts within the public sector* – whereby the minister (the purchaser/funder) contracts with a dedicated public service agency (the provider) for the delivery of public services;
- *public/private service contracts* – contracting out/outsourcing the purchase by government (purchaser) of public services to be provided by a private supplier (provider);
- *privatization/corporatization* – the creation of a context in which a formerly publicly owned and provided service is provided by a private provider to the individual consumer on market contract terms.

In each instance there is an intermediary between the citizen and the state which triangulates their relationship so that it is no longer recognizable as a de-commodified, public service delivered by an accountable state official or agency to the citizen. Nor is the exchange in the form of a classical contractual relationship between citizen and provider. Vagueness abounds about specific outputs the citizen can expect, as it did under the KWS: a phenomenon which gave rise to the welfare rights movement. From the citizen's point of view, these transactions merely mimic contracts (even though the contract form does obtain between the formal parties, the funder and the provider.) Numerous questions and issues of accountability arise from the vicarious relationship which the citizen, now, increasingly has with the state arising from these 'contracts' (Martin, 1995, pp. 38–42). These questions include:

- how can the contract between the purchaser and the provider confer enforceable rights to benefits on citizens, who are not privy to the contract?
- How therefore can citizens invoke and enforce their rights against surrogates for the state?
- To what extent have citizens been given the opportunity to consent to these material changes in the characteristics of the parties involved in the delivery of services affecting them and the rights and obligations which flow between them?
- What direct benefits to citizens are guaranteed as a consequence of the changes?

The assertion of social citizenship to overcome this lack of enforceability would entail a re-politicization of rights claims, and a redesign and strengthening of rights enforcement mechanisms.

Contractualism is now integral to the public service role, manifesting itself in the 'purchase' of specified outputs desired by government from senior public servants. The idealized public servant is being portrayed as super-efficient and ultra-accountable yet driven by the positive and negative incentives of performance bonuses and rigorous output monitoring. The Schick Report raises questions about what has been lost as well as what has been achieved in this contractualist schema. Allen Schick speculates that the checklist approach to accountability may purge the ethic of public service responsibility (Schick, 1996, p. 52). Job satisfaction, promotion and recognition within the service may not be seen as sufficiently motivating to get the most out of public officials.

Contractualism encourages the discourses of competition and the freedom of contract and these become the rationale for the deregulation of activities in the market proper, as well as in other sectors such as activities with an impact on the environment, the workplace and the provision of public services where market discourses have not been preeminent. The needs of market players rather than the public good are increasingly dominant (Evatt Research Centre, 1989, pp. 81–3). The revolutionary shift represented by contractualism can be highlighted by contrasting the distinctions between private enterprise and public service (Culpitt, 1992, pp. 83–97):

- private enterprise through contract, *par excellence* between limited liability corporations, is geared to risk-taking, whereas public service is about creating social safety nets for risk regulation and limitation and about nation building, social harmony and social justice;
- private enterprise activity is geared to profit maximization utilizing borrowed capital, whereas public service is primarily non-profit and taxpayer-funded;
- commodification is the essence of private enterprise, in which the tension between supply and demand is exploited for profit, whereas de-commodification is the essence of public service, in which the goal is to maximize access, i.e. to meet needs altruistically.

In the KWS model of public service provision, the state determined the eligibility of the individual citizen for services on the basis of rights, needs, and means; the state paid for or subsidized the service provided; and the state was the provider or selected the provider. Critics of the KWS consequently emphasized the paternalistic element (or 'nanny'-ism) of de-commodified state-citizen transactions, rather than its affirmation of citizenship as a status conferring a bundle of rights associated with freedom to live as a full participant in modern society. In the private market, by contrast, where the 'consumer' or 'customer' is king, the 'customer' decides whether or not to buy the service, 'customers' pay for the service themselves, and 'customers' choose the provider of the service. Consumer choice and competition between providers supposedly ensure maximum satisfaction and maximum efficiency.

The Contract(ing {out}) State and New Public Management

The altruistic KWS ethos of (at least partial) de-commodification is replaced by the egoistic ethos of commodification in the contract state. The model of human behaviour as rationally egoistic, which was merely a heuristic device – an ideal type – for economic liberals, has become the New Right's defining paradigm for understanding human behaviour, ontologically *and* normatively.

Underpinning the re-commodification of social relations is the deliberate conflation of public service and private enterprise. The clearest articulation of this administrative-legalistic technique is the New Public Management (NPM) which has been very influential in New Zealand, the UK, the State of Victoria in Australia and the USA since the 1980s (Boston et al., 1996; Alford and O'Neill, 1995; Osborne and Gaebler, 1993; Horne, 1995; Dunleavy, 1991; Foster and Plowden, 1996).

The NPM employs the contract form to facilitate the shift from needs-driven to resource-driven public services. The assumptions about human behaviour in the market which inform classical contract theory are extrapolated into the public sphere.

At the heart of the NPM is 'rational' (public) choice theory, which depends on a particular definition of 'rationality' based on these assumptions (Dunleavy, 1991, p. 3):

- people's preferences are based on good information which they can rank and compare easily;
- people's preferences are logically consistent;
- people are maximizers seeking the greatest benefit for the least cost;
- people are egoistic and make choices based on the consequences for their personal welfare.

The needs-driven KWS is assumed to be vulnerable to 'provider capture' by self-serving bureaucracies remote from 'customer' needs, to welfare fraud, and to benefit and service exploitation by the greedy – not needy – middle class (Goodin and Le Grande, 1987); all weaknesses which lead to incessant demands for growth in public spending. To overcome these problems, 'rational choice' assumptions about individual customer and public service bureau behaviour are built into NPM agency theory and transaction cost economics.

Within this agency theory, social, political and commercial life consist of a series of contracts for labour or services. In the contractual dyad, both principal (funder) and agent (provider) are assumed to make 'rational' choices to maximize their own self-interest. This 'rationality' (including opportunism and guile) is assumed to make for efficient public service as well as profitable private enterprise.

Transaction cost economics is concerned with the optimal governance structures for organizing the delivery of goods and services. It is assumed that 'rational' actors will select structures that minimize aggregate production and delivery costs.[2]

The *form* of governance should follow the *function* to be performed by the enterprise. A key NPM paradigm is that government 'steers' (the minister decides what to purchase, from whom) while public, private, voluntary, or non-governmental organizations 'row' (provide services) (Boston et al., 1996; Osborne and Gaebler, 1993; Horne, 1995; Alford and O'Neill, 1995, pp. 4–6). Contractualism assists this split by formalizing the transaction in terms of highly specific, contracted-for *outputs* which the government pays providers to deliver. Competing providers tender for the contracts. Ministers are 'owners' of the government enterprise responsible for *outcomes;* public servants are their agents, who sell them specified *outputs* to realize these outcomes. Schick (1996, p. 62) identifies a major defect in this output-outcome nexus: it bifurcates government into (narrowly conceived) management and politics. The citizen and public service are made to disappear between them.

This approach contrasts sharply with the KWS, *outcome*-oriented, approach. From the NPM perspective, government now ceases to fund *inputs* to be processed through the 'black box' of the state apparatus and converted into nebulous *outcomes*, notwithstanding that from the KWS perspective outcomes were evaluated in terms of the provider's definition of outcome objectives, and could also be subjected to some modest cost/benefit analysis (Sunstein, 1996).

The contract state's NPM culture, in theory, promises numerous advantages over the KWS approach (Alford and O'Neill, 1995; Boston et al., 1996, pp. 19–30):

- *clear attribution of accountability* for outputs is obtained through transparent contracts, so that the opaque use of public power is reduced;
- *consumer empowerment and choice* is provided by the removal of the state monopoly on service delivery, and possibly enhanced through funding customers with vouchers instead of funding inputs to be captured by providers;
- *government bureaucracy is downsized*, since it is a steering mechanism, not a delivery system;
- *competition in government-funded activities* is achieved through the rationality of the market, leading to allocative efficiency and increased quality;
- *risk and transaction costs* are transferred to the private (perhaps privatized) sector;
- *professional and businesslike practices* rigorize public service systems, epitomized by 'customer focus' rhetoric, value-for-money evaluations and quality financial reporting systems;

- *administrative discretion* is checked, structured and reviewed more effectively.

Contract State 'Citizenship': A Customer Focus?

In empirical terms, the contract(ing {out}) state approach has yet to demonstrate its value as the cheaper and more effective way to manage the state (Culpitt, 1992, pp. 97–104; Judge and Smith, 1983; *The Economist*, 1996). The necessary links among contracts and competition, privatization, contracting out and expenditure reduction, are not proven (Culpitt, 1992, p. 29). Moreover, contractualism leads to many power-conferring 'compacts' between steerers and rowers. These compacts give enormous discretionary powers to unaccountable providers and few rights to 'consumers' or citizens.[3]

In practical terms, classical contracts frequently serve to mask asymmetrical power relationships – as the humble consumer knows from the standard form contracts governing access to necessities of life such as utilities, insurance, the mortgage, wages, and workplace health and safety (Kelsey 1995, pp. 180–206). NPM pseudo-contracts are no different. The government, not the citizen, becomes the client of the provider. Public and private are conflated to the point where everything can be commodified, even such things as prisons and optimal public service (and in some jurisdictions already, human blood and possibly human organs next). Performance as measured in outputs does not necessarily compute into accurate measures of long-term outcomes. Neither does NPM suggest ready solutions to problems endemic to societies aspiring to social and territorial justice and 'citizenship for all' – problems which can not normally be solved through market mechanisms.

How, indeed, are coherent policy and territorial justice to be achieved in a fragmented world conceived as a set of isolated quasi-markets, e.g. the health care funder-provider market, or through a series of contracts between public sector principals and private enterprise agents? 'Customer' access in such a world depends on profitability for the provider, and the quality of service is not enshrined in a universal right of citizens.

How are matters of values basic to citizenship, such as access to services, equality of treatment, the Rule of Law, social justice, and cultural sensitivity constructed as measurable and enforceable outputs? Even the KWS found achieving and measuring these outcomes elusive; how will a series of quasi-markets fare?

The trend in education to create a quasi-market by funding schools on the basis of block grants may reduce access to economies of scale such as curriculum expertise otherwise available in a national system. Budget allocation by the school within the devolved block grant/bulk funding/charter school contracts may be perverse in relation to wider citizenship goals. Schools may compete for a market share of middle class pupils at the expense of the rest.

Specified outputs in the health and welfare sectors require almost impossible specificity about what constitutes need, which services are to be regarded as 'core' services and which relegated to the penumbra, and how services are to be delivered. Need identification, monitoring and accountability – already difficult for the KWS – have proved as, or even more, difficult for the contract state as it steers a series of contracts for such services through a maze of quasi-markets. 'Contracts' have conferred new rationing powers upon providers, who have few binding obligations towards citizens. Who defines the rationing criteria (Lenaghan, 1996)?

Quasi-markets such as the health system may be colonized by insurance enterprises which have become surrogates for the 'customer/patient', as providers are surrogates for the state. Neither surrogate has an incentive to keep costs down, and the 'customer' is left out of the transaction except to pay the premium (National Advisory Committee ..., 1993; Globerman and Vining, 1996). In quasi-market health systems, unless insurance is compulsory and state subsidized, there is no universal right to quality health care. Interestingly, surveys of attitudes in the European Union found a majority of citizens willing to pay more tax for health services; citizens also rejected the notion of a mixed system based on public provision for so-called 'essential' health care and private provision through insurance for 'nonessential' services which would be available only to those people who could afford the insurance cover for them. (Abel-Smith et al., 1995)

In the steering mechanisms of the contract(ing {out}) state each ministry has now developed a contract management bureaucracy in an attempt to reduce the transaction costs of contracting out. One may ask, who ultimately bears the costs of bidding, evaluating bids and enforcing contracts, or the impact of contract failures? Who prevents provider capture by private monopolies? Who prevents 'cream-skimming'? Cream skimming appears to be endemic to quasi-markets where providers who are paid a standard fee for services will consistently look for the cheapest 'customers' to service. GPs will shun elderly patients for the healthy (and nonpregnant) young; custodial providers will cater to the most docile clients. The weakest groups of citizens may become a residual category for whom the state might, itself, provide minimalist care, e.g. health services for 'indigents' in the USA.

The fetishizing of the contract form found in the NPM culture is threatening to notions of citizenship not least because it lacks an authentic mechanism for guaranteeing accountability to citizens and the enforceability of obligations owed to them by state surrogates. Contract is a private law form, whereas citizenship is a public law status. As British analysts Ian Harden and Norman Lewis have separately pointed out, hybrid notions of public law contracts are in a very early stage of jurisprudential development (Harden, 1992, pp. 37–44; Lewis, 1996, pp. 172–7). If contractualism rules we must take contract more seriously and structure it to make citizen-state rights and obligations enforceable, not rhetorical (see also Davis, Sullivan and Yeatman, 1997).

Norman Lewis argues cogently that choice is only really possible within a framework of relative economic and psychological wellbeing in a participatory, pluralist, communitarian civic order in which second generation (social and economic) human rights, social citizenship and community are recognized as core values by the constitutional order (Lewis, 1996). This implies a fundamental commitment to the de-commodification of social relations in major sites of power even if such rights have to be conceptualized as ' new property' rights. Gøsta Esping-Andersen (1990, p. 21) writes that:

> If social rights are given the legal and practical status of property rights, if they are inviolable, and if they are granted on the basis of citizenship rather than performance, they will entail a de-commodification of the status of individuals *vis-à-vis* the market.

The bundles of social rights embodied in social citizenship are a far cry from negative rights designed to protect the atomized, possessive individual from interference from the state or another while pursuing 'his' chosen public and private activities. Yet the new contract state privileges these private rights based on classical contract assumptions, and negates social rights. At the same time, few constitutional or institutional guarantees exist in the hollowed-out contract state to enforce such 'private' contracts for public services (Harden, 1992). Even partial de-commodification continues to be vitally important for realizing opportunities to counter 'nautonomy' through an expanded definition of social rights and citizenship.

Thatcher's much vaunted 'Citizen's Charter' was set up in 1991 expressly as a quality assurance or standards-setting process, not as a rights-enforcement mechanism, despite the clever name. By 1994 there were 39 agency-specific charters, covering agencies like the London Underground, the Employment Service, and the Social Security Agency. British critics stress that despite the

Charters, the Audit Commission and other after-the-fact techniques for monitoring aggregate provider performance, a hollowed-out state is coming about with a narrow, consumer-inspired conception of citizenship with little legal underpinning – a development which must be combated with a robust Bill of (Citizens') Rights (Institute for Public Policy Research, 1990; Seidle, 1995, pp. 31–51; Bynoe, 1996).

New Zealanders have become keenly aware of this gap in the repertoire of remedies available to the citizen since the Fourth Labour Government (1984–1990) began to transform the KWS into a contract state. In the quasi-marketplace 'customers' may have considerable difficulty in invoking what rights they do have, and may even lack the right to services. Possible first steps to creating enforceable social rights have tended to be proceduralist; for example, the New Zealand Code of Health and Disability Consumers' Rights (1996) gives consumers rights in relation to *how* services are provided – but not rights as to *whether* they are provided. The Health and Disabilities Commissioner's mandate does not include scrutiny of whether or not the funder (state) ought to have purchased services from the provider on behalf of the consumer (citizen) (Health and Disability Commissioner, 1995, p. 14; Lenaghan, 1996) so no right to health care is codified and enforceable, as such.

Janet McLean, noting that relatively little is said in the New Zealand constitution about the provision of minimum services and the obligations which flow from the ownership of state assets, regards public choice theory as representing 'a very thin view of democracy'. She calculates that the New Zealand legislature is weaker than ever before (while the executive and administration are presumably stronger); provider capture and self-serving interest group politicking are thus likely to be more effective than before (McLean, 1996, pp. 213–7).

Even where the legislation enabling corporatization to take place contains expressive purposes which attempt to reconcile profit making and social responsibility, the citizen-focused obligations are subordinated to market forces. For example, the State Owned Enterprises Act 1986 section 4 (1) requires that:

> the principal objective of every state enterprise shall be to operate as a successful business and, to this end, to be–
> (a)   As profitable and efficient as comparable businesses ...
> (b)   A good employer; and
> (c)   An organization that exhibits a sense of social responsibility by having regard to the interests of the community in which it operates ... .

Yet, despite these statutory provisions, the courts have chosen to avoid the issue of obligations to citizens imposed by the 'social responsibility' requirement by saying it was too large and subjective a concept to give rise to public duties, and that any breaches of obligations were private contractual matters (Maclean, 1996, p. 220; Taggart, 1993). The citizen as a juridical person to whom public duties are owing appears to be dead in the eyes of the courts of the contract(ing{out}) state.

Mike Taggart (1992, pp. 371–2) has challenged economic rationalists on the New Zealand Court of Appeal. He identifies the need for an understanding of public law which, I would argue, sustains the proceduralist minimum guarantees for social citizenship:

> [T]he fundamental values of public law – openness, fairness, participation, impartiality and rationality – not only provide a yardstick against which to measure the activities of privatised enterprises with market power but should be embodied in the design of institutions and regulatory schemes at the outset.

Social Citizenship

Institutionalizing Altruism: Beyond Charity and Contract

Nancy Fraser and Linda Gordon identify our present predicament in the following terms (1994, pp. 60–1):

> [T]he centrepiece of the cultural mythology is an ideological opposition between two very different forms of human relationship: contractual exchanges of equivalents, on the one hand, and unreciprocated, unilateral charity on the other. These perversely appear to exhaust all social possibilities. The result is that there seems to be no conceptual space for the forms of non-contractual reciprocity and solidarity that constitute the moral basis for social citizenship.

Noncontractual reciprocity is only possible when exchange relationships are de-commodified. A truly social contract and the mutual obligations flowing from it in terms of citizen's rights must be revitalized. Richard Titmuss (1970, pp. 12–3) argued that public policy must encourage and foster the individual and communitarian expression of altruism and the regard for the rights and needs of others (intergenerationally and globally); altruism is a bastion against, and fetter on, the egoism of the marketplace.

Instruments of public policy such as social rights must enshrine values which must not and cannot be commodified. The evolving ethic of humanity must be re-institutionalized by a de-commodified set of universalized social relationships defined as a sacrosanct status for all persons, namely social citizenship. Diversity, too, can be accommodated by recognizing the right to diversity while stressing the affinities flowing from the hybridity of identity, and hence multiplicity of memberships, which are such a feature of 'the diaspora spaces' in advanced modernity (Brah, 1996; Tully, 1995). There is evidence of a growing political will to articulate justifiable second-generation social, cultural and economic citizenship rights at the national and supranational level – for example, in the Constitution of India, 1949; International Covenant on Economic, Social and Cultural Rights (ICESCR) 1966; European Community Charter of Fundamental Social Rights, 1989; Social Protocol of the Maastricht Treaty, 1989; NAPO (Canada) Draft Social Charter, 1992; Finnish Constitution (as amended 1995) and South African Constitution (1996).

Utopian Realism and Citizens' Rights Talk

The state remains, for all its many dehumanizing yet essential characteristics an important public forum for articulating the local claims of citizenship in their national and global contexts. Social reflexivity offers the intellectual capacity to conceive of alternative and emancipating identities, and globalization offers the technological medium and cultural climate of receptivity for claiming these alternative identities and potentially creating the institutional forms which make realization of them possible.

Social citizenship rights, therefore, constitute a fundamental legal form for the change of structures and for the conversion of 'nautonomy' into autonomy. Following the conceptual vocabulary of Held, Giddens, and the International Covenant on Economic, Social and Cultural Rights, a modest manifesto would include:

• economic, ecological and health rights. Recognizing the twin realities, increasing scarcities of supply and growing demands, in utopian realist *post-scarcity order*, economic growth cannot be allowed to trump other claims (Giddens, 1994, p. 101). Economic activity must be ecologically sustainable; suboptimal economic, social or cultural consequences must be avoided; and individuals and groups must be enabled to make significant life choices. 'Nautonomic' social relations have to be addressed by an alternative means of economic management reflecting democratic political participation and recognition of social rights (ICESCR, 1966, Articles 6, 11 and 12).

Equally the 'humanization' *of nature* requires that, instead of being concerned about what nature can do to us, we must worry individually and collectively about what the high risk society we have manufactured has done and is doing to nature. Ecological sustainability requires the harmonization of economic and social activities within a holistic frame of analysis in which the enforcement of the *precautionary principle in international environment law* and the *principle of inter-generational rights* to a clean, bio-diverse ecoystem are crucial;

- political and social rights. *Dialogic democracy* requires public dialogue between citizens and mutual tolerance coming from a continuingly developed social reflexivity (ICCPR, 1966; ICESCR, 1966, Articles 8, 13, 14 and 15).

Meaningful participation in political processes is a key to citizenship. Generative politics, to achieve dialogic democracy, requires that individual autonomy must be nurtured in spaces where hierarchies are flattened, active trust is earned, and power is decentralized and de-traditionalized. Authoritarianism manifested in the control of knowledge and information must be rejected. Meaningful economic participation is also crucial for social citizenship to serve as an integrative force. It is not liberation from work, or even from joblessness, that is required, so much as a radical redefinition of work and de-commodification of social worth (Pixely, 1993, pp. 268–9);

- cultural rights. *Negotiated power* must replace global, local and interpersonal violence in its psychological and physical manifestations. Damaged solidarities dividing people along ethnic, gender, sexual-orientation and class lines must be obliterated and new compromises achieved which are far more inclusive than the KWS could be (ICESCR, 1966, Articles 9 and 10).

Universal social citizenship is a necessary, though not sufficient, condition for bringing about the radical, albeit disjointed and incremental, change from the present commodified contract state order towards a peaceful, socially just and ecologically sustainable world order.

Notes

1   Adapted from Pierson, 1991.
2   By separating the parts of a vertically or horizontally integrated enterprise, for instance.
3   Although there are some proceduralist (Bynoe, 1994) and substantive (Coote, 1992) strategies available for citizens to combat this situation.

Bibliography

Abel-Smith, B. *et al.* (1995), *Choices in Health Policy: An Agenda for the European Union*, Dartmouth: Aldershot.
Alford, J. and O'Neill, D. (eds) (1995), *The Contract State: Public Management and the Kennett Government*, Centre for Applied Social Research, Deakin University: Geelong, Australia.
Amin, A. (ed.) (1994), *Post-Fordism: A Reader*, Blackwell: Oxford and Cambridge, Mass.
An-Na'Im, A.A. (ed.) (1992), *Human Rights in Cross-Cultural Perspectives: a Quest for Consensus*, University of Pennsylvania Press: Philadelphia.
Beck, U. (1992), *Risk Society: towards a new modernity*, Sage Publications: London; Thousand Oaks, New Delhi.
Beck, U., Giddens, A. and Lash, S. (1994), *Reflexive Modernisation: politics, tradition and aesthetics in the modern social order*, Polity Press: Cambridge.
Boston, J., Martin, J., Pallot, J. and Walsh, P. (eds) (1996), *Public Management: the New Zealand Model*, Oxford University Press: Auckland.
Brah, A. (1996), 'Difference, Diversity and Differentiation' in *Cartographies of Diaspora: contesting identities*, Routledge: London.
Bynoe, I. (1996), *Beyond the Citizens Charter: New Directions for Social Rights*, IPPR: London.
Camilleri, J. and Falk, J. (1992), *The End of Sovereignty: The Politics of a Shrinking and Fragmenting World*, Elgar: Aldershot, UK.
Cesarani, D. and Fulbrook, M. (eds) (1996), *Citizenship, Nationality and Migration in Europe*, Routledge: London and New York.
Constitution of India, (1949 as amended), Part IV.
Coote, A. (ed.) (1992), *The Welfare of Citizens; Developing New Social Rights*, IPPR and Oram Rivers Press: London.
Cotterrell, R. (1984), *The Sociology of Law: an Introduction*, Butterworths: London.
Culpitt, I. (1992), *Welfare and Citizenship: beyond the crisis of the welfare state?*, Sage: New York.
Donald, J. (1996), 'The Citizen and the Man About Town' in Hall, S. and Du Gay, P. (eds), *Questions of Cultural Identity*, Sage: London.
Dunleavy, P. (1991), *Democracy, Bureaucracy and Public Choice: Economic Explanations in Political Science*, Harvester: New York.
European Community Charter of Fundamental Social Rights (1989).
Esping-Andersen, G. (1990), *Three Worlds of Welfare Capitalism*, Polity Press: Cambridge.
Evatt Research Centre (1989), *State of Siege: renewal or privatisation for Australian state public services*, Pluto Press: Leichhardt, NSW.
Foster, C.D. and Plowden, F. (1996), *The State under Stress: Can the Hollow State be Good Government?*, Open University Press: Buckingham.

Fraser, N. and Gordon, L. (1994), 'Reclaiming Social Citizenship: Beyond the Ideology of Contract versus Charity' in James, P. (ed.), *Critical Politics*, Arena Publications: Fitzroy, Melbourne.

Galtung, J. (1994), *Human Rights In Another Key*, Polity Press: Oxford and Cambridge, Mass.

Giddens, A. (1995), 'Brave New World: The Context of Politics' in Miliband, D. (ed.), *Reinventing the Left*, Polity Press: Cambridge.

Giddens, A. (1994), *Beyond Left and Right: the future of radical politics*, Polity Press: Cambridge, UK.

Globerman, S. and Vining, A. (1996), *Cure or Disease? Private Health Insurance in Canada*, CPA monograph, University of Toronto: Toronto.

Goodin, R.E. and Le Grande, J. (1987), *Not Only the Poor: The Middle Classes and the Welfare State*, Allen & Unwin: London.

Gordon, C. (1991), 'Governmental rationality: an introduction' in Burchell, G., Gordon, C. and Miller, P. (eds.) *The Foucault Effect: studies in governmentality*, The University of Chicago Press: Chicago.

Gorz, A. (1985), *Paths to Paradise/On the Liberation from Work*, Pluto Press: London.

Guild, E. (1996), 'The Legal Framework of Citizenship of the European Union' in Cesarani, D. and Fulbrook, M. (eds), *Citizenship, Nationality and Migration in Europe*, Routledge: London and New York.

Harden, I. (1992), *The Contracting State*, Open University Press: Buckingham.

Havemann, P. (1994), 'Regulating the Crisis: from Fordism to Post-Fordism in Aotearoa/New Zealand 1984–1993', *Humanity and Society*, Vol. 18 (1), pp. 74–96.

Health and Disability Commissioner (1995), *A Proposed Draft Code of Rights for Consumers of Health and Disability Services*, Department of Health: Wellington.

Heelas, P. (1996a), 'Introduction: Detraditionalisation and its Rivals' in Heelas, Lash and Morris, q. v.

Heelas, P. (1996b), 'On Things not being Worse, and the Ethic of Humanity' in Heelas, Lash and Morris, q. v.

Heelas, P., Lash, S. and Morris, P. (eds) (1996), *Detraditionalisation: critical reflections on authority and identity*, Blackwell Publishers: Oxford and Cambridge, Mass.

Heelas, P. and Morris, P. (eds) (1992), *The Values of the Enterprise Culture: the moral debate*, Routledge: London and New York.

Held, D. (1995a), 'Inequalities of Power, Problems of Democracy' in Miliband, D. (ed.), *Reinventing the Left*, Polity Press: Cambridge, Mass.

Held, D. (1995b), 'Sites of Power, Problems of Democracy' in *Democracy and the Global order, From the Modern State to Cosmopolitan Governance*, Polity Press: Cambridge.

Hindess, B. (1987), 'Citizenship and the Market' in *Freedom, Equality and the Market: Arguments on Social Policy*, Tavistock Publications: London.

Hirst, P. and Thompson, G. (1996), *Globalisation in Question: The International Economy and the Possibilities of Governance*, Polity: Cambridge.

Horne, M. (1995), *The Political Economy of Public Administration*, Cambridge University Press: Cambridge.

Hunt, P. (1996), *Reclaiming Social Rights: International and Comparative Perspectives*, Dartmouth: Aldershot and Brookfield, USA.

Ignatieff, M. (1989), 'Citizenship and Moral Narcissism', *The Political Quarterly*, Vol. 60 (1), p. 72.

Institute for Public Policy Research (IPPR) (1990), *A British Bill of Rights*, IPPR: London.

International Covenant on Civil and Political Rights (ICCPR) (1966).
International Covenant on Economic, Social and Cultural Rights (ICESCR), (1966):
  Article 6: the Right to Work;
  Article 8: Trade Union Right;
  Article 9: Right to Social Security;
  Article 10: Protection of the Family, Mothers and Children;
  Article 11: The Right to an Adequate Standard of Living;
  Article 12: The Right to Physical and Mental Health;
  Article 13: Right to Education;
  Article 14: The Principle of Compulsory Education Free of Charge to All;
  Article 15: Right to Take Part in Cultural Life and to Enjoy the Benefits of Scientific
    Progress and the Protection of the Interests of Authors.
Jessop, R. (1994), 'Post-Fordism and the State' in Amin (ed.), op. cit.
Judge, K. and Smith, J. (1983), 'Purchase of Services in England', *Social Service Review*, Vol.
  57 (1), pp. 209–33.
Keane, J. (1984), 'Reflections on the Welfare State and the Future of Socialism: an interview'
  in Offe (1984), q. v., pp. 252–99.
Kelsey, J. (1995), *The New Zealand Experiment: A World Model for Structural Adjustment?*,
  Auckland University Press with Bridget Williams Books: Auckland.
Kymlicka, W. (1995), *Multicultural Citizenship*, Oxford University Press: New York.
Lash, S. and Urry, J. (1987), *The End of Organised Capitalism*, Polity Press: Cambridge.
Lawler, P. (1994), 'Constituting the Good State' in James, P. (ed.) *Critical Politics*, Arena
  Publications: Fitzroy, Melbourne.
Lenaghan, J. (1996), *Rationing and Rights in Health Care*, IPPR: London.
Lewis, N. (1996), *Choice and the Legal Order: Rising Above Politics*, Butterworths: London.
Lipietz, A. (translated 1992), *Towards a New Economic Order: Postfordism, Ecology and
  Democracy*, Polity Press: Cambridge.
Marshall, T.H. (1950), *Citizenship and Social Class and other essays*, Cambridge University
  Press: Cambridge.
Martin, J (1995), 'Contracting and Accountability' in Boston, J. (ed.), *The State under Contract*,
  Bridget William Books: Wellington.
McGarry, J. and O'Leary, B. (eds) (1993), *The Politics of Ethnic Conflict Regulation*, Routledge:
  London.
McLean, J. (1996), 'The Contracting State' in Peters, M. et al. (eds), *Critical Theory,
  Poststructuralism and the Social Context*, Dunmore Press: Palmerston North.
Mercury Energy v. Electricity Corporation of New Zealand Ltd [1994] 2 NZLR 385.
NAPO (Canada) (1992), Draft Social Charter.
National Advisory Committee on Core Health and Disability Support Services (1993), *Core
  Services for 1994–5*, Department of Health: Wellington.
O'Brien, M. and Wilkes, C. (1993), *The Tragedy of the Market*, Dunmore Press: Palmerston
  North, New Zealand.
O'Connor, J. (1973), *The Fiscal Crisis of the State*, St. Martin's Press: New York.
Offe, C. (1984), *Contradictions of the Welfare State* (ed. J. Keane), Hutchinson: London.
Offe, C. (1996), 'The Utopia of the Zero Option: modernity and modernisation as normative
  political criteria' in *Modernity and the State: East, West*, Polity Press: Cambridge.
Osborne, D. and Gaebler, T. (1993), *Reinventing Government: How the Entrepreneurial Spirit
  is Transforming the Public Sector*, Addison-Wesley: Reading, Mass.

Pateman, C. (1991), *The Sexual Contract*, Stanford University Press: Stanford, CA.

Phillips, A. (1993), *Democracy and Difference*, Polity Press: Cambridge.

Pierson, C. (1991), *Beyond the Welfare State: the new political economy of welfare*, Polity Press: Cambridge.

Pixely, J. (1993), *Citizenship and Employment: Investigating Post Industrial Options*, Cambridge University Press: Cambridge.

Richmond, A.H. (1994), *Global Apartheid: Refugees, Racism, and the New World Order*, Oxford University Press: Toronto.

Robertson, R. (1990), 'Mapping the Global Condition: Globalisation as the Central Concept' in Featherstone, M. (ed.), *Global Culture: nationalism, globalisation and modernity*, Sage Publications: London, Newbury Park and New Delhi.

Schick, A. (1996), *The Spirit of Reform: Managing the New Zealand State Sector in a Time of Change*, The Public Service Commission: Wellington.

Seidle, L.F. (1995), 'Transforming the Public Sector in the United Kingdom: executive agencies and the Citizen's Charter' in *Rethinking the Delivery of Public Services to Citizens*, Institute of Research on Public Policy: Montreal.

Social Protocol of the Maastricht Treaty (1989).

Soysal, Y.N. (1996), 'Changing Citizenship in Europe: Remarks on postnational membership and the national state' in Cesarani and Fulbrook, op. cit.

Soysal, Y.N. (1994), *Limits of Citizenship: migrants and postnational membership in Europe*, The University of Chicago: Chicago and London.

Sunstein, C.R. (1996), 'The Cost Benefit State', John M. Olin Program in Law and Economics, University of Chicago, Working Paper 39.

Taggart, M. (1993), 'State Owned Enterprises and Social Responsibility: A Contradiction in Terms?', *New Zealand University Recent Law Review*, pp. 343–64.

Taggart, M. (1992), 'The Impact of Corporatisation and Privatisation on Administrative Law', *Australian Journal of Public Administration*, Vol. 51 (3), pp. 368–73.

The Economist (1996), 'Cradle to Grave', 21 September, pp. 15–7.

Therborn, G. (1987), 'Welfare State and Capitalist Markets', *Acta Sociologica*, Vol. 30 (3/4), pp. 237–54.

Titmuss, R. (1970), *The Gift Relationship, from human blood to social policy*, Allen & Unwin: London.

Tully, J. (1995), *Strange Multiplicity: Constitutionalism in an Age of Diversity*, Cambridge University Press: Cambridge.

Turner, B.S. (1986), *Citizenship and Capitalism: The Debate over Reformism*, Allen & Unwin: London.

Wilson, M.A. (1997) 'New Contractualism and the Employment Relationship in New Zealand' in Davis, G., Sullivan, B. and Yeatman, A. (eds) *The New Contractualism?*, Centre for Australian Public Sector Management: Brisbane.

9 The Corporate Republic: Complex Organizations and Citizenship

MARK BOVENS

[T]he good citizen must have the knowledge and ability both to rule and be ruled. That is what we mean by the goodness of a citizen – understanding the governing of free men by free men (Aristotle, *The Politics,* III, 4).

The Corporate Republic

The twentieth century has been the century of the complex organization. The number of such organizations has risen at an explosive rate. Nowadays, more than half of the hundred largest economies in the world are not countries, but corporations.[1] Complex organizations have come to dominate the front pages of most serious newspapers and outnumber natural persons as participants in court cases (Coleman 1982, pp. 10–3; Bovens, 1998, pp. 14–5). They are strongly professionalized and bureaucratized; their size, complexity, and social importance is enormous (Coleman, 1990).

However, most contemporary political currents act as if we were still living in the nineteenth century. Many modern liberals, social democrats and communitarians still take the contrast between public and private, between government and market – with civil society as bogeyman or buffer in between – to be the central issue in political theory.[2] Many citizens, however, could not care less whether they lose their way in the bureaucratic corridors of the national health or of a private health-insurance company, of a state university or a private university, a social service or a private insurance board, a ministry or a multinational enterprise. From the point of view of social and political power, the antithesis between natural persons and corporate bodies, or between citizens and organizations, is nowadays at least as important as the antithesis between government and market.

Modern society is thus as much a republic of corporate bodies as it is a republic of citizens. What is more important, modern society is an asymmetrical

158

society, as there is a large imbalance of power between corporate actors and individual citizens (Coleman 1982, 1990; Bovens 1998). Complex organizations have laboratories and teams of researchers, they can afford to wage advertising campaigns, run extensive lobbies, and can resort to legal specialists and attorneys. Individual citizens usually have to fight for themselves. Complex organizations are, in the words of Marc Galanter (1974), 'repeatplayers'– they are frequently involved in the same sort of legal procedures and become adept in the field. Citizens usually are 'one-shooters'. Complex organizations have an unlimited life-span. Citizens are mortal.

One of the important issues for contemporary political thinkers ought therefore to be the rise and social dominance of complex organizations. What does citizenship mean in a world ruled by complex organizations? In this paper some possible answers to this question will be explored. In exploring them, I shall take as my point of departure an emphatically (neo-)republican, humanistic notion of citizenship. By that, I understand a notion of citizenship in which the political community of independent and free citizens is central. That implies a strong emphasis on the individual rights and claims of the citizen in relation to the government and on the citizen's independent power of judgment in personal and public affairs. Coupled to this is a strong emphasis on the public interest and on the participation of the citizen in public affairs and in the political debate. The republican view rests on the basic premise that citizens administer themselves. Modern authors such as Arendt (1958, 1965 and 1972), Sullivan (1982, 1995), Barber (1984), Ignatieff (1984), Van Gunsteren (1992), and Sandel (1996) plead for an actualization of the classical ideal of the *polis* and of the *vivere civile*. They plead for the conservation and restoration of the public domain, for room for what Arendt has called 'action': speaking and acting together on the basis of shared values and with an eye to public affairs. Politics is in that sense more than the promotion of personal or group interests, it is also '[a] way of living – as, namely, the way that human beings with variable but malleable natures and with competing but overlapping interests can contrive to live together communally not only to their mutual advantage but also to the advantage of their mutuality' (Barber 1984, p. 118).

How can we reconcile these classic ideals of citizenship with the reality of organizational dominance? What we need in fact is a revival of the political economy of citizenship (Sandel, 1996, p. 329). In this paper two possible reactions to the social dominance of complex organizations are explored: citizenship *of* complex organizations and citizenship *in* complex organizations. In the first case, the complex organization itself acquires a civic status; in the second, the civic status of natural persons within organizations is emphasized.

Citizenship of Complex Organizations

This strategy is inspired by corporate law and takes as its starting point the idea that 'if you can't beat them, let them join you'. Monasteries, parishes, churches, and guilds, and later also trading companies, foundations, associations, and corporations, have been treated over the centuries in a number of areas of law as if they were natural persons. Gradually these corporate bodies, first with regard to property and later also with regard to contracts and crimes, have acquired the same rights and duties as natural persons. One can decide to extend this personification to public law and to the sphere of politics. If in a number of areas of law we can, with relative ease, treat organizations as fully-fledged legal subjects, why should we not also be able to treat the same organizations as citizens in the political sphere? In various European legal systems steps in this direction have been taken. The explanatory statement attached to the revised version of the Dutch Constitution says, for example, of basic human rights that '[t]he proposed stipulations are aimed at bestowing rights and claims also on corporate bodies and on groups and organizations without corporate status in so far as to do so can be meaningful with regard to the nature of the relevant basic right' (TK, 1975–1976, 13872, no. 3, p. 11). The German Constitution is even clearer on this point: '[T]he basic rights are also valid for corporate bodies, as far as they, given their nature, are applicable to them' (Art. 19, paragraph 3). In the case law established by the European courts one also sees that, step by step, corporate bodies and (other) organizations are independently acquiring the protection of a number of basic rights. That is true, for example, of the right to a fair trial, the right to privacy, the freedom of worship, the freedom of association, and – above all – the freedom of expression (Finaly, 1991). In business too, and in particular on the fast growing terrain of 'public affairs management', one regularly and repeatedly comes across the idea of the company as citizen, for example in the form of a 'corporate citizenship model' (Peterse, 1990, pp. 34, 218–22).[3]

From a republican perspective a case can be made for this extension of the circle of citizens. After all, at the end of the day organizations keep the economy going and determine a large part of socioeconomic and political developments. Why should the old adage of the pioneers of the American independence struggle – 'no taxation without representation' – not also hold for them? In the nineteenth century, one could still insist that most big private organizations were represented in the political sphere by their owners, who were often at the same time their directors. Nowadays, however, there is little or no connection between property, management and political representation.

Most companies are managed by professional executives who are in paid employment. They have little in common with the Lockean 'freemen' who, cleansed by their experiences on their estate and without having to pay lip-service to others, could devote themselves in all freedom to the pursuit of politics. To begin with, the modern managers simply have no time for it. Would it therefore not be better to conceive of the corporate body itself as a 'freeman' and thus to open up the possibility for organizations to participate directly in the political debate?

The application of modern civic rights to organizations is, moreover, quite feasible. Marshall (1950) distinguished three categories of civic rights: civil, political and social. Most civil rights are not difficult to apply to organizations. Think of due process, the right of petition, the freedoms of speech, association, and assembly, the inviolability of the home and the right to privacy. Only a few civil rights are difficult to transpose to non-natural persons; they include, for example, the right to freedom of travel and to a passport and the right to equal eligibility for public service. National citizenship, an important condition for the exercise of nearly all civil rights, can also be a problem in the light of the increasing internationalization of companies. These objections need not, however, be insurmountable. In criminal and private law the equation of natural and corporate bodies has also been far from complete.

Awarding political rights to organizations is also quite easily conceivable. Passive suffrage could be realized by means of constructions of representation. One could, for example, give each corporation a certain number of votes, in proportion to the number of its personnel, to be exercised by the management, the executive council or the workers' council. In the case of active suffrage, one could institute comparable measures. Within a sort of semi-corporatistic structure one could, for example, reserve seats on representative bodies for representatives of organizations. An example of such constructions is the way in which voting is carried out in the contemporary Dutch Water Boards. Companies that are enrolled in a Chamber of Commerce in the region and that have company premises in the area of water conservancy have the right to vote in the elections for members of the general council. There is even the possibility to weigh the votes according to the scale of the organization.

The most difficult to realize are the social rights – but this is in fact also true for natural persons. Basic social rights, such as a right to social assistance, education and work, and the general right to self-fulfilment, are, by their very nature, not easy to apply to non-natural persons.

Corporate citizenship implies, moreover, not just rights but also duties. A number of important civic duties – obedience to the law and the duty to pay taxes – already apply to corporate bodies. Citizenship can also mean, however, that private organizations can be addressed regarding their responsibilities to their fellow citizens. Companies can then no longer hide behind the division between the public and the private sector and in that way push off their responsibility for public affairs onto the government. Citizenship of organizations could offer an extra framework for environmental and social policy making. Such a framework would be more compelling than the noncommittal plea for 'corporate social responsibility', by means of which companies over the past few decades have been persuaded to cooperate. Citizenship for organizations would not only be a logical next step in the development of corporate law and an acknowledgement of the important social role of organizations, but would also represent a means by which a number of public goods could be produced or preserved.

The introduction of citizenship for organizations is thus quite feasible and is already taking place in some areas. Should we continue along such a path? Three important considerations speak against so doing. In the first place, one could above all object to the granting of the classic rights to freedom (Marshall's civil rights) on the grounds that the reason for the granting of these rights to ordinary citizens in many respects does not hold for organizations. Generally speaking, one could say that they are directed toward the protection and the advancement of the autonomy of individuals in respect of government. That autonomy is due them above all on the grounds of their humanity. For that reason, we often speak of 'human rights'. On the basis of such a legitimation of fundamental rights, often inspired by notions of natural law, it is easy to see why these rights should not be granted to corporate bodies and other organizations. After all, they are not people and they therefore cannot, any more than (for example) plants and animals, claim as such any right to individual autonomy.[4] Which fundamental human values are at stake in the case of an independent freedom of speech for companies or an independent right to privacy for companies?[5]

Nor are complex organizations self-evidently eligible for the more procedural rights that have their roots above all in the tradition of the rule of law, such as for example, due process, the right to a fair and timely trial, no punishment without law, the right to legal aid and so on. These more procedural rights aim predominantly at setting limits to the inequality of power between government and individual citizens. Although they can easily be applied to corporate bodies, the reasons for doing so are less compelling than in the case of natural persons. Most companies, for example, are far more powerful than individual citizens and some are more powerful even than local or national authorities. The turnover of General Motors is larger than the GNP of Denmark, Ford's is larger than South Africa's GNP and Toyota's returns are larger than Norway's GNP. The classic image of the lonely citizen who needs protection against the powerful judicial apparatus, the image that underlies many safeguards in criminal procedure, does not apply in many big environmental and fraud cases. In such cases, it is the relatively lonely public prosecutor who has to take on wealthy companies which, with the help of teams of specialists, can make optimal use of the guarantees that the criminal procedures and the rules of evidence offer (Stone, 1975; Vaughan, 1983; Fisse and French, 1985; Fisse and Braithwaite, 1993).

These observations bring us to a second objection. Would the recognition of civil rights for organizations be a solution for our problem of the asymmetrical republic? In a society in which the inequality of power is above all between organizations on the one hand and individual citizens on the other, the equal recognition of a number of fundamental rights to the strongest party, the organizations, could disturb the social balance of power even further. It would make intervention by the government on behalf of natural persons in economic affairs even more difficult than it already is (cf. Lindblom, 1977); and it might even, within the framework of the horizontal effect of basic rights, further weaken the formal position of natural persons in relation to corporate bodies.

This objection is even more applicable with regard to political rights. According a number of such rights to corporate bodies would, given the current inequality of power, further weaken the position and participation of the 'old' citizens, the natural persons. The individual citizen would be completely outflanked if complex organizations, with their wealth of information and resources and their repeatplaying skills and stamina, were to participate on a formally equal footing in the political arena. Here we are therefore confronted with the danger of the complex organization as a modern Leviathan.

Alongside these general philosophical objections, there are, in the third place, also a number of important practical objections. Which organizations are admitted to citizenship? Obviously, public organizations must under all circumstances be excluded from citizenship. After all, such organizations were called into being exclusively in order to assist citizens. If the servants themselves become citizens, who will then serve the citizens? Public organizations are the slaves of the modern polity. In the case of private organizations, the question arises as to what the minimum conditions are. A charter of incorporation cannot in itself suffice, for then every corner-shop owner who, for fiscal or other reasons, turned their company into a one-person limited company would in so doing have doubled their citizenship. It would not be easy, however, to set a basic limit for admission to citizenship (number of personnel, turnover, social importance?). Even more difficult is the question of what to do with the growing number of multinational and transnational organizations. In which country should a multinational enterprise exercise its citizenship and what is the relationship, for example, between the citizenship of subsidiaries to that of the holding company? And what about the orientation toward the public interest in the case of actors whose principal concern is profit and who operate in a competitive situation? Even if their actual intention is to serve the public interest, many companies will because of the 'logic of collective action' feel themselves forced to give priority to the preservation of their own competitive position. Moreover, the internationalization of the business community also makes the recognition of citizenship at the national level not only impractical but in many respects even undesirable. After all, where do the loyalties of those transnational concerns lie and in how far does it make sense to address them regarding their national or even local civic duties?

From the point of view of liberal or (neo-)republican visions of citizenship, there is thus little reason to accord direct, primary citizenship to companies and other private organizations. The most they can be is secondary citizens (Schmitter, 1994). Corporate actors can emerge in the *polis* only in a disguised fashion, as wolves in sheep's clothing. In the words of the title of an article by Van Gunsteren (1987), 'companies are political monsters'. They do not fit within the classification schemes of liberal or republican thinking. Their place is in the private sphere, the sphere of contracts, torts and property. Political rights and political freedoms are reserved for natural persons, the authentic political beings.

Citizenship in Complex Organizations

A second reaction to the emergence of an asymmetrical republic could consist in making possible or facilitating the exercise of citizenship by natural persons within complex organizations. If organizations interfere in the lives of citizens, citizens must also have the opportunity to interfere in the life of organizations. This citizenship within organizations can take a number of very different forms, depending on what you define as community, as polity, and to whom you assign citizenship.

The first quadrant, ordinary citizenship in a *liberal democracy*, is not

Table 9.1   Citizenship in complex organizations

	Polity	
	State	**Organization**
Residents	liberal democracy	civic management
	1	2
Citizenship	4	3
Employees	employee citizenship	corporate democracy

important for us here. The second quadrant implies the most radical form of citizenship within organizations: alongside the state the organization is also understood as a polity. In the various forms of *civic management* of companies, it is the ordinary citizens and not (or not only) the managers of the organization who, in one form or another, have a say in important decisions of the organization. In the third quadrant, the organization is likewise understood as polity, but citizenship is on the other hand reserved for the employees of the company. Marshall (1950, p. 80) speaks anachronistically of industrial citizenship, but a better term is economic or *corporate democracy*. This quadrant accounts for many of the proposals and structures that give the members of a company more say in the policy of the company. In the fourth and final quadrant, the national citizenship of employees is the central issue. This will be referred to as *employee citizenship*. This notion emphasizes that functionaries even within the framework of their own organization remain members of the larger community of citizens – which is why it is legitimate that in working hours too they should pay attention to issues such as the preservation of the political community and the protection of their fellow citizens.[6]

Civic Management: Citizens as Managers

In Western countries, the activities of companies have enormous effects on the life of society. New products and technologies, shifting capital streams, plant closures and mass sackings often have a greater influence on the structure of society than the efforts of governments (cf. Lindblom, 1977). Following Bozeman (1987), one could hold that all organizations, to greater or lesser extent, are public. Given this fact and given the republican viewpoint that citizens are deemed to administer themselves, why should one restrict the domain of citizenship to public organizations?[7] Since companies have such a big influence on public life, citizens should for their part have a big influence on companies. Citizens should, directly or by way of representatives, have a say in important company decisions. The company is thus seen as a partial polity of which all citizens are residents.

Yet this is a problematic form of citizenship within companies. The objections to it are above all of a practical nature. After all, how will this civic management of companies take shape? The experiences in the former Eastern European states with *Volksbetriebe* (nationalized firms) were disastrous. But in the West, too, experiences with nationalization and state enterprise have been far from happy. Direct political interference in the management of companies often puts the wrong people in the right places because of the emergence of patronage and spoils systems. The involvement of public managers in the company is often small and the chance of irresponsible business decisions large because the public purse will cover for the private losses.

Perhaps public representatives can provide a workable compromise on this point. One could appoint one or several public commissioners or representatives in companies of a certain size. These have in the first place the task of promoting the general interest in the decision-making process. Stone (1975, pp. 152–73) has come up with a rather elaborate proposal for appointing General Public Directors, a sort of government commissioner, in the case of companies whose capital turnover exceeds a given indexed limit. Candidates for such posts are nominated by the government, but can be vetoed by a majority of votes cast by the other directors. Once appointed, they can, under certain conditions and with qualified majorities, again be removed by the board of directors. These public directors should not be civil servants but should have the same (business) background as the directors who serve in the big companies. They should function as the 'public conscience' of the organization and see that it keeps to the law, but they should also play an advisory role in the emergence or modification of legislation in their own sector. Alongside their ordinary role as member of the board, they should particularly look to the functioning of the internal information system and act as confidants for internal whistle-blowers. In order to be able to fulfil these roles properly, the public directors should have at their disposal their own staff and a number of special powers; these would include free access to all committees and to all company data and documents, the right to overturn sackings or other disciplinary penalties that might result from people contacting them or their staff and the right to recommend bonuses for employees who have acted in the public interest. Finally, there should be a right of appeal to a judge or arbiter.

However, the experiences with public directors in the Netherlands suggest that functionaries of this sort are in a structurally difficult position. In practice, public directors are confronted with different rationalities and with vague, or mutually conflicting, responsibilities. Too much involvement with the organization can lead to an identification with the interests of the company; too much attention to the public cause can lead to an alienation from the organization and to a position of relative isolation. If they are appointed for long periods of time to the same company, which is necessary if they are to acquire reliable information and a proper insight into the enterprise, they will presumably regularly encounter conflicts of loyalty. Only strong characters will be able to withstand such schizophrenia-inducing conditions for any length of time (Glasz, 1991).

Hirst (1994, p. 151) has suggested appointing public representatives not to the executive board but to a special Supervisory Board. This Supervisory Board (consisting of one-third shareholders representatives, one-third employee representatives and one-third community representatives) would then appoint the Management Board charged with the operational running of the company. This would diminish the pull from operational responsibilities and might thereby alleviate the conflict of loyalties for the community representatives. Hirst also suggests that both boards should have a legal duty to 'consider and to give due regard to the interests of shareholders, employees, consumers, the community and the environment when making decisions' (1994, p. 151).

Corporate Democracy: The Organization as a Separate Polity

In the case of corporate democracy, the organization is understood not as a part of public life but as a separate polity; only its own employees acquire the rights and duties of citizenship. In such cases, we are therefore dealing exclusively with citizenship that is internal to the company. A serious case can be made for the introduction of this form of citizenship. An ordinary employee in a big enterprise in many respects resembles an inhabitant of a nineteenth-century authoritarian state. The enterprise lays claim during working hours and sometimes even outside working hours to a large part of his activities and restricts many of his freedoms. S/he is 'subject to authority, he [sic] is part of a legal community in which many rules apply that can be unilaterally imposed on the part of the authority and in the emergence of which he as an individual had no part whatsoever' (van der Heijden, 1988, p. 21). Most complex organizations are hierarchies or oligarchies that are administered in an absolutely autocratic manner, while changes in the leadership usually take place on the basis of co-optation. The question then arises as to why the arguments that eventually led to the democratization of most Western states in the nineteenth and twentieth centuries are not equally valid in the case of large-scale modern enterprises. Why should employees, who are presently treated in the realm of public affairs as citizens capable of independent judgment, get no say in matters that concern their daily work?

The champions of this form of citizenship take this factual parallel between state and enterprise seriously and argue for a democratization of companies. One of the modern exponents of this current of thought is Robert Dahl (1985). He discusses two arguments for economic democracy that one constantly encounters in the discussions.[8] In the first place, the argument of the favourable external effects: citizenship within companies would help maintain and improve the quality of citizenship in the public realm. It would increase the political skills and sense of community of citizens, raise the level of participation in the national administration, lessen social polarization and promote equality of income. Dahl himself admits (1985, pp. 94–110) that there are few indications that these positive external effects actually happen. Other studies are also negative on this point (Mellor et al., 1988, p. 146). Experiences in a number of companies with a large measure of workers' self-management provide little evidence of an increase in civic competence and participation.

Alongside this somewhat weak instrumental justification, Dahl also comes up with an intrinsic argument: '[I]f democracy is justified in governing the state, then it must also be justified in governing economic enterprises; and to say that it is not justified in governing economic enterprises is to imply that it is not justified in governing the state'. There is, according to Dahl, no difference in principle between big companies and (lower-level) government. The decisions of companies are *de facto* often just as binding on employees as are the decisions of government on citizens, while for most employees the exit-options are not significantly greater than for the residents of any municipality or state. 'Like a state, then, a firm can also be viewed as a political system in which relations of power exist between governments and the governed' (1985,

p. 115).

But, one could object, have the experiences with all sorts of productive associations not shown that democratization leads to the downfall of the company? After all, employees do not have the education and skills to lead a company; such tasks must be left to professional managers, directors, and shareholders. Moreover, joint management impairs the company's readiness for the fray, since painful decisions often get no majority or are delayed in various ways. In the business world, meritocracy and not democracy is the best form of government. According to Dahl, such an objection does not, however, detract from the principled parallel between government and enterprise. It is after all the same argument which, from Plato through to Pareto, has again and again been brought against the democratization of public administration. If one no longer accepts this elitist argument in the public sphere, why should one then accept it in principle for private organizations? Moreover, according to Dahl, research suggests that, unlike in the difficult circumstances of the nineteenth century, 'participation by workers in decision-making rarely leads to a decline of productivity; far more often it either has no effect or results in an increase in productivity' (1985, p. 133). After all, joint management does not automatically need to imply that each employee should have a full say in the daily administration of the enterprise. Oligarchization and a certain measure of meritocracy are inevitable in every modern democracy and in every big organization. Corporate democracy in bigger companies, just as in bigger public organizations, is often feasible only by means of representation, delegation and other devices. The role of the ordinary employee-citizen will therefore in practice be more comparable with that of a shareholder than of a manager. There is no reason to assume that the average employee, who if his company goes bankrupt loses not only his investment but his very means of livelihood, would not fulfil that role at least as carefully as the average shareholder (Dahl, 1985, pp. 116–33).

It is not possible on the basis of the available research into forms of economic democracy to say definitively whether Dahl is right on the point of practical feasibility, but the odds are against him. Most of the empirical literature in this field is by researchers who are at the very least sympathetic to producers' cooperatives, workers' self-management, and other forms of corporate democracy (Poole, 1986; Mellor et al., 1988; Lammers and Széll, 1989; Oakeshott, 1990). Nevertheless, they must all concede that the number of successful cooperatives has over the years been relatively small.[9] Typical of this literature is the wishful conclusion, also reached by Dahl, that there is no reason to assume that cooperatives cannot work, that there is a great need for non-capitalist forms of production and that, in coming years, things will certainly get better. However, they do not positively answer the question of whether cooperatives generally can cope with the competition from traditional companies.[10]

Here, however, it is important not only whether far-reaching forms of economic democracy *can* work, but also whether they *should* work. From the point of view of republican citizenship, there is at least one important objection that can be raised to the large-scale introduction of far-reaching forms of Dahl's economic democracy.[11] If one treats discrete organizations as small polities, one legitimates the emergence of states within the state. Employees acquire a double citizenship and, therewith, double loyalties. There is a chance that this will lead to a further atomization of society. If everybody, as a result of his or her work, is a member of a separate political community, who will have time left over for the collective, public affairs? Corporate democracy legitimates reasoning on the basis of sectoral interests and may as a result lead in the long run not to a strengthening but to a splintering of the political community.[12] Also, there is the real danger that the already substantial gap in economic, social and political resources between the employed and non-employed part of the citizenry will further widen. What arises is an image of society as 'a series of tight little islands, each evolving towards political self-sufficiency, each striving to absorb the individual members, each without any natural affiliations with a more comprehensive unity' (Wolin, 1960, p. 431).

Employee Citizenship: The Employee as Citizen of the State

Employee citizenship, on the other hand, might give less occasion to a splintering of the community of citizens. After all, it refers to ordinary, *company-external* citizenship whose sphere of operation is extended to the organization. The external effects of civic rights and duties are to the fore here. The idea is to promote the participation of employees in the public debate and to protect the interests of one's (fellow) citizens or of the political community as a whole. In a society dominated by complex organizations, the sphere of bureaucracy and the sphere of politics cannot remain entirely separate. The activities of corporations, laboratories and public agencies are, in the end, politically relevant activities. However, because of the politics of expertise (Fischer, 1990) ordinary citizens and politicians are often not able to fully comprehend and assess the nature and extent of the risks that flow from the organizational activities. Enabling all sorts of self-criticism and discussions from within organizations is vital to protect society from these risks (Beck, 1992, p. 234). Employees and civil servants are therefore also treated as citizens, i.e. as members of the political community, with the rights and duties associated with that membership. This employee citizenship can take various forms.

In the first place, it can consist quite simply of an extension of the scope of a number of basic rights. Whereas most civil rights were originally intended to offer protection in the sphere of the vertical power relations between government and citizens, they must now also work horizontally in the relationship between private corporate bodies and employees. Alongside the freedom to strike, which they have long had, employees would also have to be able to claim from their employers the protection of other civil rights, such as the freedom of religion, the freedom of speech, the freedom of association and meeting, protection of the privacy of letters, telephone communication and e-mail. Companies permit themselves a number of infringements of the freedoms of individual employees that in most cases would be deemed inadmissible if the government were to practice them against citizens. Think of the obligation, on penalty of dismissal, to work on religious holidays, the imposition of bans on public speaking, the prohibition on membership of professional associations or of other legitimate organizations, the imposition of penalties without due process, or the uninvited opening of mail, listening to telephone conversations or spying on employees by means of video cameras (Ewing 1977, 1983; van der Heijden, 1988). Such an extension of the scope of a number of civil liberties is a legitimate and logical supplement to the catalogue of civil liberties recognized by the modern democratic state. The inequality of power between individual employees and complex organizations and the weak position of most employees on the labour market in practice minimizes their contractual freedom (van der Heijden, 1988, p. 22; Gersuny 1994). Most employees cannot afford to give up their jobs in order to regain complete command over their civil rights. *De facto* their position does not differ all that much from that of a citizen in an authoritarian state. Given the reason behind the classic civil liberties, a horizontal effect on complex organizations is therefore quite easy to defend.

However, employee citizenship consists of more than just the extension of a number of rights. It provides at the same time a basis for external responsibilities.[13] Acknowledgement of the citizenship of employees and civil servants also implies that individual functionaries may and sometimes even must play a role in the preservation of the community of free and independent citizens (Burke 1986). That means on the one hand that functionaries, as citizens, can be held to account by their fellow citizens for their contribution to the activities of their organization. The acknowledgement of the citizenship of employees implies that they, just like civil servants, police officers, and soldiers in the public sphere, can no longer so easily hide behind the orders of their superiors.

On the other hand, it also implies, as a complement to that external accountability, a legitimation of certain forms of 'civil disobedience' within working hours. If one wants functionaries to behave as responsible citizens, one must also provide them with the space in which to do so. Citizenship of functionaries implies that the democratic control of organizations need not always happen indirectly, by way of the top political levels or of the company management, but that in some circumstances a direct role is also set aside for lower functionaries. Some forms of employee disobedience, such as refusal to work or whistle-blowing, can be legitimate when important public interests are at stake. Possible grounds for employee disobedience are for example (the threat of) an evident violation of rules and regulations, a substantial and specific danger to public health, safety or the environment, a large-scale waste of public funds or, in the case of civil servants, a deliberate obstruction of democratic control.

These interests not only offer grounds for disobedience but also set emphatic limits to those grounds. Indiscretion and disloyalty are justifiable only when the rule of law or democratic control is thereby served. That means that a large number of forms of disloyal behaviour are not legitimate at all, such as, for example, thwarting your minister or parliament as a civil servant for party-political, personal or institutional reasons, or employees refusing to submit to examination by a judge. It also means that a functionary acts responsibly only when the control, and where necessary the correction, by public bodies of his or her own behaviour does not become impossible. This will, in most circumstances, mean that it can be demanded of the functionary that: a) his or her conduct takes place in the open; and b) s/he is prepared and in a position to answer for his or her behaviour on the basis of public considerations. Secretly leaking or selling confidential documents so as to make a policy change desired by a minister impossible in advance, or doing the same thing for reasons of personal gain, will hardly satisfy this demand. But refusing certain assignments on the basis of strictly personal, conscientious objections will also be difficult to reconcile with these demands.[14]

Citizenship and Complex Organizations

Of the different venues discussed here, employee citizenship, including limited forms of employee civil disobedience, offers the most promising and feasible way of overcoming the antithesis between the ancient ideal of individual citizenship and the modern reality of organizational dominance in society. It opens up the most powerful actors in society for public scrutiny and political debate, without a further extension of the formal and informal powers of corporate actors, as would be the case with corporate citizenship. Neither does it give rise to a general and substantial reduction of the efficiency and effectiveness of complex organizations, as would civic management or corporate democracy. Last but not least, it directs the exercise of civic rights and duties towards the public domain and thus contributes to the central tenet of citizenship: 'the governing of free men by free men'.[15]

Notes

1 According to a study by S. Anderson and J. Kavanah of the American Institute for Policy Studies (quoted in *The Sun* in Baltimore).

2 With the exception of Wolin (1960, ch. 10), Dahl (1985), Schmitter (1994) and Sandel (1996).

3 Even Rawls makes room for 'associations (states, churches, or other corporate bodies)' in the negotiations in the 'original position' (1971, p. 146).

4 From a natural-law or creationist perspective on rights, plants and animals would have an even greater right to protection than organizations.

5 The individual employees, managers, owners and shareholders, given that they are people, do of course have these rights. In many cases, one might derive some rights for corporations from these individual rights. From the point of view of legal theory, however, that is a very different justification of organizational rights.

6 This employee citizenship must not be confused with 'organizational citizenship behaviour' (Organ, 1988). In the latter case, citizenship behaviour is viewed not in the political but in the social-psychological sense. It exclusively concerns the question of why some employees are more assiduous and altruistic than others. This is also called 'the good soldier syndrome': some employees are prepared to do more than their duty for the organization. It is therefore a question not of citizenship but of a sense of responsibility.

7 See for forms of civic administration within government bodies Fredrickson and Chandler (1984), Barber (1984, pp. 290–3); Wamsley et al. (1987); and Stivers (1990, pp. 99–103).

8 See for example the pleas of Louis Brandeis and Woodrow Wilson for industrial democracy in the early decades of the twentieth century (discussed by Sandel, 1996, pp. 211–6).

9 The only still successful large-scale cooperative is the Mondragon Group in the Basque Country – and this example crops up again and again in all the literature on the subject. However, the Mondragon companies have over the years developed such indirect forms of democracy and such orthodox management structures that it is very doubtful whether they can still be reckoned as genuine cooperatives (cf. Mellor et al., 1988, p. 174).

10 Recently introduced collaborative forms of corporate governance, in which employees own (part of the) stock seem to be more efficient than traditional, hierarchical forms of

corporate governance (Alcaly, 1997). However, these are basically management tools and not political forms of corporate democracy.

11 One can find the following objection in rudimentary form in Bonger (1936, p. 127) and very explicitly in the work of Wolin (1960, pp. 429–34).

12 A second objection of a more principled character is less convincing because of its essentialist character. Wolin (1960) and Stivers (1989) object to the idea of corporate democracy also on the grounds that such a politicization of daily life leads to a loss in meaning of the idea of politics. If everything is political, politics is nothing. This is in general a potent argument against tendencies to politicize everything. It is not clear, however, why the limits have already been reached. After all, in the case of corporate democracy personal life remains untouched. Moreover, this objection disregards the important political power of complex organizations in contemporary society.

13 See for similar reflections, mostly in the public sphere, Fleishman, Liebman and Moore (1981), Nielsen (1984), Burke (1986), Wamsley et al. (1987) and Cooper (1991).

14 See for an extensive legal and organizational analysis of several forms of employee civil disobedience, such as refusal to work and whistle-blowing, Bovens (1998, chs 9–11).

15 This article is based on a paper presented at the 24th Annual Meeting of the UK Association for Legal and Social Philosophy, Edinburgh, 3–5 April 1997. Minor parts of it are based on chapter 9 of my *The Quest for Responsibility: Accountability and Citizenship in Complex Organisations* (1998). An early version of the paper was published in H.R. van Gunsteren and P. den Hoed (1992), *Burgerschap in praktijken, WRR voorstudies en praktijken*, SDU: Den Haag.

Bibliography

Arendt, H. (1958), *The Human Condition*, University of Chicago Press: Chicago.

Arendt, H. (1965), *On Revolution*, revised 2nd edn, Viking: New York.

Arendt, H. (1972), *Crises of the Republic*, Harvest/HBJ: New York.

Barber, B.R. (1984), *Strong Democracy: Participatory Politics for a New Age*, University of California Press: Berkeley.

Beck, U. (1992), *Risk Society: Towards a New Modernity*, Sage: London.

Bonger, W.A. (1936), *Problemen der democratie: Een sociologische en psychologische studie*, 2nd popular edn, Arbeiderspers: Amsterdam.

Bovens, M.A.P. (1998), *The Quest for Responsibility: Accountability and Citizenship in Complex Organisations*, Cambridge University Press: Cambridge.

Bozeman, B. (1987), *All Organizations Are Public: Bridging Public and Private Organizational Theories*, Jossey-Bass: San Francisco.

Burke, J.P. (1986), *Bureaucratic Responsibility*, John Hopkins: Baltimore.

Chandler, R.C. (ed.) (1987), *A Centennial History of the American Administrative State*, Free Press: New York.

Coleman, J.S. (1982), *The Asymmetric Society*, Syracuse University Press: Syracuse.

Coleman, J.S. (1990), *Foundation of Social Theory*, Harvard University Press: Cambridge Mass.

Cooper, T.L. (1991), *An Ethic of Citizenship for Public Administration*, Prentice Hall: Englewood Cliffs.

Dahl, R.A. (1985), *A Preface to Economic Democracy*, University of California Press: Berkeley.

Ewing, D.W. (1977), Freedom inside the Organization: Bringing Civil Liberties to the Workplace, Dutton: New York.

Ewing, D.W. (1983), *'Do it My Way or You're Fired!': Employee Rights and the Changing Role of Management Prerogatives*, Dutton: New York.

Finaly, R.A.R.S. (1991), 'Grondrechtsbescherming van rechtspersonen', *NJCM-Bulletin*, Vol. 16, pp. 105–20.

Fischer, F. (1990), *Technocracy and the Politics of Expertise*, Sage: Newbury Park, Ca.

Fisse, B. and French, P.A. (eds) (1985), *Corrigible Corporations and Unruly Law*, Trinity University Press: San Antonio.

Fisse, B. and Braithwaite, J. (1993), *Corporations, Crime and Accountability*, Cambridge University Press: Cambridge.

Fleishman, J.L., Liebman, L. and Moore, M.H. (eds) (1981), *Public Duties: The Moral Obligations of Government Officials*, Harvard University Press: Cambridge Mass.

Frederickson, H.G. and Chandler, R.C. (eds) (1984), 'Citizenship and Public Administration, Proceedings of the National Conference on Citizenship and Public Administration, April 14–16, 1983', *Public Administration Review*, Vol. 44: special issue.

Galanter, M. (1974), 'Why the "Haves" Come Out Ahead: Speculations on the Limits of Legal Change', *Law and Society Review*, Vol. 9, pp. 95–160.

Gersuny, C. (1994), 'Industrial Rights: A Neglected Facet of Citizenship Theory', *Economic and Industrial Democracy*, Vol. 15, pp. 211-26.

Glasz, J.R. (1991), 'De overheidscommissaris heeft het moeilijk', *Nederlands Juristenblad*, Vol. 66, pp. 1541–5.

Gunsteren, H.R. van (1987), 'Bedrijven als politieke monsters' in Twijnstra, A. and van Dijk, J.W.A (eds), *Management and Politiek: Samenspel en tegenspel*, Stenfert Kroese: Leiden.

Gunsteren, H.R. van (1992), *Eigentijds burgerschap*, WRR publication: The Hague.

Heijden, P.F. van der (1988), *Grondrechten in de onderneming*, Kluwer: Deventer.

Hirst, P. (1994), *Associative Democracy: New Forms of Economic and Social Governance*, Polity Press: Cambridge.

Ignatieff, M. (1984), *The Needs of Strangers*, Chatto: London.

Lammers, C.J. and Széll, G. (eds) (1989), *International Handbook of Participation in Organizations. Volume I: Organizational Democracy: Taking Stock*, Oxford University Press: Oxford.

Lindblom, Ch. E. (1977), *Politics and Markets: The Worlds Political-Economic Systems*, Basic Books: New York.

Marshall, T.H. (1950), *Citizenship and Social Class: and other Essays*, Cambridge University Press: Cambridge.

Mellor, M., Hannah, J. and Sterling, J. (1988), *Worker Cooperatives in Theory and Practice*, Open University Press: Milton Keynes.

Nielsen, R.P. (1984), 'Arendt's Action Philosophy and the Manager as Eichmann, Richard III, Faust, or Institution Citizen', *California Management Review*, Vol. XXVI, pp. 191–201.

Oakeshott, R. (1990), *The Case for Workers' Co-ops*, 2nd edn, Macmillan: Basingstoke.

Organ, D.W. (1988), *Organizational citizenship behavior*, Lexington.

Peterse, A.H. (1990), *Onderneming en politiek in liberale democratieën*, Wolters-Noordhoff: Groningen.

Poole, M. (1986), *Towards a New Industrial Democracy: Workers' Participation in Industry*, Routledge: London.

Rawls, J. (1971), *A Theory of Justice*, Harvard University Press: Cambridge, Mass.

Sandel, M. J. (1996), *Democracy's Discontent: America in Search of a Public Philosophy*, Belknap: Cambridge, Mass.

Schmitter, P.C. (1994), 'Interests, Associations and Intermediation in a Reformed Post-Liberal Democracy' in Streeck, W. (ed.), *Staat und Verbaende*, Westdeutscher Verlag: Opladen.

Stivers, C. (1989), 'Organizational Citizenship: A Problematic Metaphor', *Administration and Society*, Vol. 21, pp. 228–33.

Stivers, C. (1990), 'The Public Agency as Polis: Active Citizenship in the Administrative State', *Administration and Society*, Vol. 22, pp. 86–105.

Stone, Ch. D. (1975), *Where the Law Ends: The Social Control of Corporate Behavior*, Harper & Row: New York.

Sullivan, W. (1982), *Reconstructing Public Philosophy*, University of California Press: Berkeley.

Sullivan, W. (1995), *Work and Integrity: The crisis and promise of professionalism in America*, Harper: New York.

Vaughan, D. (1983), *Controlling Unlawful Organizational Behavior: Social Structure and Corporate Misconduct*, University of Chicago Press: Chicago.

Wamsley, G.L. et al. (1987), 'The public administration and the governance process: Refocussing the American dialogue' in Chandler (ed.), op. cit.

Wolin, S. (1960), *Politics and Vision: Continuity and Innovation in Western Political Thought*, Little Brown: Boston.

PART IV

10 Civil Society as the Community of Citizens: Adam Ferguson's Alternative to Liberalism

JOHN VARTY

Civil Society and Despotism

The rebirth of the concept of civil society dates from the 1980s, when dissidents in Eastern Europe began to use the term. The concept has also been taken up in the West, especially by those on the Left who have seen certain parallels between the situation in Eastern Europe and in the West during the neo-liberal revolution. Civil society theorists share with neo-liberalism the opposition to statist visions of socialism. But if neo-liberalism can be seen as a mixture of the free market and the strong state, civil society theorists see both as possible threats to a 'strong' civil society. Neo-liberalism has led an assault on a number of the associations within civil society that civil society theorists wish to defend and strengthen. The concern has been to reassert the distinction between state and civil society and to argue for the ethical priority of the latter, for the purposes of limiting state power and defending citizens' freedoms. There is a long tradition in political thought of delineating a terrain of human association, a notion of 'society' distinct from, and with moral claims independent of, and sometimes opposed to, the state (Wood, 1990, p. 61). Most commentators point to Locke's concept of the state of nature as the historical starting point. It is the value of this liberal and potentially 'anti-political' conception of civil society that the paper questions, proposing instead a republican or more strongly 'political' conception of civil society. Paradoxically it may be that we can best defend civil society from the state by pointing to the necessary mediations between civil society and the state.

In order to advance my argument I first turn, as many contemporary civil society theorists do, to the eighteenth century roots of this debate. Historically, the concept civil society has been directed more against despotism and in favour of limited government than against the state per se (Keane, 1988a). Adam Ferguson's *An Essay on the History of Civil Society*, the text around which my own reflections are based, is very much an argument as to how citizens can, and must, 'contain' despotism. Yet Ferguson did not draw the conventional distinction between state and civil society. This suggests that it is possible to put forward an argument against despotism that does not rely on counterposing society against state.

In what follows I shall first briefly outline Ferguson's discussion of why despotism arises and how it is to be prevented or opposed. Then I consider what Adam Ferguson's concept of civil society can bring to contemporary debates; more specifically, the communitarian and republican responses to liberal political theory. I will consider the sceptical intervention of Krishan Kumar who has questioned the usefulness of the concept of civil society. Then I shall turn to the different perspectives of John Keane and Ernest Gellner as to the relationship between civil society and liberty. What I wish to draw out of this is the continued relevance of Ferguson's republican argument that: i) insists upon the importance of citizens' participation in maintaining liberty and preventing despotism; ii) focuses on the limits of institutional – whether legal or political – defences of freedom; and, iii) realistically appraises the conflictual nature of community and the motivations behind people's political action.

Ferguson followed Montesquieu in treating different forms of government as arising out of different forms of society – systems of manners, property and subordination. Both thinkers were concerned with, and opposed to, the possibilities of the rise of despotism. Ferguson differed from Montesquieu in providing more of a dynamic and 'sociological' model than a simple political typology of government forms: he gave greater emphasis to property, social stratification and social conflict in the development of government. State despotism arises out of a corrupt society – 'the rules of despotism are made for the government of corrupted men' (Ferguson, 1996, p. 228). So, for Ferguson, one can only understand when and how despotic governments might develop by considering the relationship between state and society and remaining sensitive to the possible sources of corruption which would tend towards despotism.

How then is despotism to be prevented? Despotism exists when government is no longer subordinate to the rule of law. Ferguson quotes Montesquieu's definition of despotism as that form of government 'in which one man, without law, or rule of administration, by the mere impulse of will or caprice, decides, and carries every thing before him' (ibid., p. 66) Civil society is counterposed to despotism in that, by definition, it includes the rule of law. As Philip Selznick notes, to define it thus is already to see it in relation, not just in opposition, to the state. Civil society is sustained by, even in some respects constituted by, law. The counterposition of state and society is thus not absolute (Selznick, 1992, p. 509).[1]

Ferguson observes that Rome and England are 'the great legislators among nations'. The former has provided Europe with 'the foundation, and great part of the superstructure of its civil code'. The latter has brought 'the authority and government of law to a point of perfection' which they had not attained before. In England 'known customs, the practices and decisions of courts, as well as positive statutes, acquire the authority of laws; and every proceeding is conducted by some fixed and determinate rule'. Precautions are taken to ensure that rules are impartially applied to particular cases. However, despite their differences, the two systems of law share something in common: in both cases the people reserved 'the office of judgement to themselves, and brought the decision of civil rights, or of criminal questions, to the tribunals of peers, who, in judging of their fellow-citizens, prescribed a condition of life for themselves' (Ferguson, 1996, pp. 159–60).

Crucially for Ferguson though, one cannot rely on political and legal establishments such as the rule of law for the prevention of despotism and the preservation of freedom. Ultimately, despite appearances, they are not independent of the will and arbitration of men. For Ferguson 'liberty is a right which every individual must be ready to vindicate for himself' (ibid., p. 251).[2] He observes that liberty, we say, is a consequence of the government of laws. People tend to consider statutes as not only the 'resolutions and maxims of a people determined to be free' and the written record of their rights but also a 'power erected to guard them' and a 'barrier against which the caprice of men cannot transgress' (ibid., p. 249) The rule of law can help to restrict political abuses and secure citizens' civil liberties and rights. This alone, though, cannot guarantee the civil freedoms of citizens. Those who exercise power directly can always abuse it (Keane, 1988b, p. 43). If laws are no longer 'enforced by the very spirit from which they arose[,] they serve only to cover, not to restrain, the iniquities of power'. A corrupt magistrate respects the laws only when they 'favour his purpose' not 'when they stand in his way'. Ferguson insisted that the effect that laws have in preserving liberty is not some 'magic power descending from the shelves that are loaded with books'. Instead it is the 'influence of men resolved to be free'. Once they have set in writing the terms which will regulate their relations to the state and between themselves, it is up to them to ensure 'by their vigilance and spirit' that these terms are observed (Ferguson, 1996, p. 249).

Thus, despite institutional defences, the prevention of despotism ultimately comes down to the virtuous action of the citizenry. All legal systems both arise from and are dependent upon the citizen who makes the laws and is free in as much as s/he abides by them. It is important, however, not to overstate Ferguson's position. He is not saying that the rule of law is of no purpose. Nor is he arguing against it. It is simply that, without the continued existence of the spirit of liberty, the resolution to be free, the laws that codify this spirit can be, not a barrier to, but a cloak that hides despotic power. Ferguson doubts whether rights are necessarily well protected by an 'intricate system' which it then becomes the task of a separate profession to interpret (ibid.). Once this is the case it then becomes difficult to see how the rule of law differs from the discretionary powers of a despot. Ferguson's position is an argument against reifying law, of projecting onto it 'magical' power and thus denying the essential role both of lawyers and citizens in creating, upholding and preserving law. Once in existence the power that any statute may have comes from those who act to maintain and enforce it. Ferguson's argument is that objectivizing political will in the form of law can become a means for abdicating individual, intellectual responsibility and capacity in opposition to despotism and the maintenance of liberty (Mason, 1988, p. 200).

It helps to understand Ferguson's perspective in contrast to that of his contemporaries David Hume and Adam Smith, who shared a political vision that was much more strongly 'institutional', 'a matter of legal and constitutional machinery' (Winch, 1978, p. 177). Both saw politics in terms of machinery not men. Hume stressed 'the institutional character of politics'. He thought that the lesson one should draw from the ancient world is that basing social life on people's personal qualities is disastrous. 'Virtue unassisted by institutional structures was no match for vice' (Haakonssen, 1994, p. xxiv). It is too fragile a base on which to erect a system of government. Thus he was primarily concerned with political machinery, checks and controls. Ferguson was not willing to agree with this perspective and put his sole trust in legal and political machinery as to do so would be to risk giving up liberty. He was an opponent of theories of legal-constitutional mechanisms that deny the necessity of the active participation of citizens; which is not to say that institutional defences do not play an important political role.

For Ferguson, a system of law 'by which the person and property are ... perfectly secured to individuals' honours the 'genius of a nation' and can only have been established by those of a 'resolute and vigorous spirit'. Yet, if individuals think they are secure through no attention or effort of their own, this 'boasted advantage' may only provide them with an 'opportunity of enjoying, at leisure, the conveniencies and necessaries of life'. Ferguson goes onto argue that such people may secretly grow tired of a free constitution which they may constantly boast of in conversation but which, in their actions, they always neglect. Liberty can never be in greater danger than from the 'remissness of a people, to whose personal vigour every constitution, as it owed its establishment, so must continue to owe its preservation'. Liberty is never less secure when men 'think that they enjoy it in safety, and who therefore consider the public only as it presents to their avarice a number of lucrative employments' for which they are ready to forsake their rights (Ferguson, 1996, p. 212).

Within the liberal tradition rights are conventionally seen as the barrier to despotism. Though he makes use of the language of rights in his discussion, Ferguson was not a proponent of natural rights and his argument against despotism is not rights-based. Nevertheless, he admitted that people have a sense of their rights and, in as much as they act to defend them, this acts as a barrier to despotism. These though are rights and duties that one has as a member of a particular social group of a certain standing. They cannot be said to exist regardless of and prior to our social and political existence. Nor can these rights be used as trumps over and above duties.

If, then, in the end it is only citizens themselves who can prevent despotism from arising, what kind of citizens are needed? The answer is those who have received the kind of political education one only gains by participating in politics. Those who are sensitive to, aware of and actively promote and defend the public good. If citizens lacked this awareness they would be blind to the rise of corruption and despotism. A lack of public spirit generates a loss of citizens' suspicion of power and thus paves the way for despotic government (Keane, 1988b, p. 42). The problem that commerce and private pursuits raises is that citizens may not then respond to the 'calls of the public'. Wealth in itself is not a problem, what matters is that citizens retain their political personae (Oz-Salzberger, 1996, p. xvi). J.G.A. Pocock has defined the 'Machiavellian Moment' as 'the moment in conceptualized time in which the republic was seen as confronting its own temporal finitude' (Pocock, 1975: viii). Ferguson's worry was that his contemporaries would no longer be aware of such a moment. His purpose when writing his *Essay* was both to warn his readers of the continuing possibilities of corruption and to suggest how to stave them off. He was worried that people no longer recognized such a danger. Naturally, if they did not do so this only increased the likelihood of corruption.

Unfortunately it is not just that people are no longer aware of the dangers of despotism. In as much as they value stability and efficiency over liberty, they can come to think that despotism is favourable to other forms of government. There are reasons why they may think so. Commerce creates a desire for efficiency, peace and stability – which is required for the continued acquisition of private wealth – and this may outweigh the love of liberty. A dominant view of government arises that gives absolute priority to the cessation of strife and the achievement of security and the rule of law. Not only are people able to devote their whole attention to the pursuit of material betterment, but it becomes their exclusive concern. As Ferguson notes: '[T]he best constitutions of government are attended with inconvenience'. The 'exercise of liberty' often creates complaints. Despotism 'has certain advantages': 'in time of civility and moderation' it may 'continue with so little offence, as to give no public alarm' (Ferguson, 1996, p. 255). He goes on to suggest that, under the influence of such ideas and of philosophical justifications of a selfish private life as represented by Mandeville and Hume, people may go on to make 'dangerous innovations' that, though they may not of themselves usher in a despotic regime, certainly lead in that direction. Despotism can emerge from the unintended consequences of actions whose goals are unrelated to this end (Hamowy, 1987, p. 40).

It is not only that despotism arises out of corrupt society: it is itself corrupting. Hence, as it is only citizens themselves who can transform such a system, should despotism take root fully it is that much harder to get rid of. It is difficult to imagine how a corrupted citizenry can shake off its corruption (Keane, 1988b, 43). On this point Ferguson rather optimistically assumes that despotism, in the long run, sows the seeds of its own destruction.

Civil Society as a Community of Citizens

In his argument Ferguson insists upon the importance of citizen's participation in public, political life to prevent the rise of despotism. No government arrangement is free of the dangers of the abuse of power. The effectiveness of the rule of law ultimately rests upon the resolve of the citizenry. If citizens are solely concerned with their private lives there is a greater likelihood both that government will become more despotic and that citizens will either be unaware of such trends or even tend to favour them.

Ferguson defends participation on instrumental grounds – we need to participate, to be active, in order to prevent the rise of despotism. Liberty only exists in proportion to citizens' willingness to sustain the 'burden of government' (Ferguson, 1996, p. 252). There is a price to pay for freedom: taking on the burden – and it is a burden – of government. A free, participatory regime calls on citizens to provide themselves things that a despotism may provide for them. Citizens are required to do things that mere subjects can avoid. Free regimes are more onerous because they require service in public life, both military and political, that the unfree do not (Taylor, 1995, p. 193). Having said this Ferguson also sees participation as intrinsically good: political activity is part, indeed the best part, of human nature. As Charles Taylor (ibid., p. 141) notes, civic humanists consider the life of the citizen, a person who is not simply subjected to power but participates in his/her own rule, to be an essential component of human dignity. For Ferguson, a life concentrated solely on private pleasures and pursuits is a life without value.

From such a perspective the issue then arises, can we expect people to take on this extra burden? Why do, or should, people participate in public affairs? What is it that motivates them? According to Ferguson, it may not always be for the highest of reasons. Political action is not meant to necessitate the suppression of personal or sectional interests. Whilst certain constitutions cannot survive in the absence of 'disinterested' public spiritedness, in modern commercial societies it is the citizen's desire for profit and promotion that motivates his entrance into public affairs and that guides his political conduct. Ferguson comments that it is only in philosophy that virtue is a 'task of severity and self-denial' (Ferguson, 1996, p. 59). The cause of virtue has not been promoted by people's zeal to prove that it is disinterested (ibid., p. 55). It is only thanks to these theoretical errors that calls for increased participation in politics appear to rest upon unrealistic expectations about people's motivations or equally unlikely hopes that human nature will be transformed so that people will become more benevolent than they currently are. It can be ambition that draws people into politics. Whilst Ferguson argues that politics has to be 'above' interest in some sense, he is not such a utopian as to argue that it is unconnected to interest and that our reasons for participating in politics must be only the purest ones. As we have seen, part of the reason is instrumental: that is, if citizens do not participate, they will lose their liberty. This does not mean, on the other hand, that political action is purely instrumental. By its very nature involvement in politics requires qualities that are admirable. Ambition and the desire for personal standing and fame involves people in pursuits that call forth some of the best human qualities (ibid., pp. 244–5).

Krishan Kumar has recently downplayed the significance of the concept of civil society, arguing that its multiple meanings lead to confusion. For radicals wishing to deal with contemporary issues and problems, Kumar argues that there is more mileage in the concepts of citizenship and the public sphere. As Kumar himself notes, the concepts of civil society and citizenship are linked, yet it does seem, contrary to Kumar's position, that the concept of civil society adds something extra: a focus on the preconditions and the terrain of citizenship. Civil society is the medium through which individuals become active citizens. It make more sense to suggest that discussion of citizenship supplements rather then replaces the civil society debate. Citizenship is inherently about membership of and participation within a political community. The advantage of such a concept is, as Kumar suggests, that it forces one to start thinking in terms of the mediations between civil society and the state and not just in terms of civil society against the state. Unfortunately for Kumar, though, the same problem of multiple meanings arises with, for example the concept of citizenship (Kumar, 1993; Bryant, 1993).

A number of authors have made a distinction between liberal and republican theories of citizenship, the latter drawing on a stronger theory of participation, public goods and civic virtue. For liberals citizenship is merely life's outer frame. It is a status that entitles us to a set of rights passively enjoyed. For republicans citizenship is, or should be, the core of our life. It is a burden proudly assumed (Walzer, 1989, p. 216). Communitarians share this concern with citizenship and political participation and have seen parallels between their ideas and that of the historical tradition of civic republicanism.

Michael Sandel (1984, p. 7) insists that 'our most pressing moral and political project is to revitalize those civic republican possibilities implicit in our tradition but fading in our time'. So what does Ferguson have to offer a communitarian perspective on civil society? There are a number of similarities of approach and concern. In both cases there is a focus upon developing a model of citizenship which posits an alternative to market relations as the basis of moral community and a politics that is not simply reducible to individual or sectional interests. Ferguson criticized utilitarian theories of motivation and of happiness and insisted upon the importance of the public sphere. He was vehemently opposed to a purely 'private' way of life. Ferguson argued that man's happiness is to make his social dispositions the ruling spring of his actions. Man should:

> state himself as the member of a community, for whose general good his heart may glow with an ardent zeal, to the suppression of those personal cares which are the formation of painful anxieties, fear, jealousy and envy ... (Ferguson, 1996, p. 56).

Moving to where Ferguson departs from current communitarian assumptions, it is noteworthy that Ferguson saw a link between solidarity and conflict. His perspective is coldly realist compared to some of the romantic notions of community held by communitarians. Ferguson focused on the role conflict plays in the growth of individual personality and social institutions. He saw humanity as having a 'mixed disposition to friendship or enmity', 'union' and 'dissension', 'war' and 'amity', 'affection' and 'fear'. Members of one society 'derive, from their union, and joint opposition to foreign enemies, a zeal for their own community, and courage to maintain its rights' (ibid., p. 37).

> Our attachment to one division, or to one sect, seems often to derive much of its force from an animosity conceived to an opposite one: and this animosity in its turn, as often arises from a zeal on behalf of the side we espouse, and from a desire to vindicate the rights of our party (ibid., p. 22).

From these conditions of war and struggle are derived an intense passion of solidarity. Affection, fellow-feeling and solidarity are derived from opposition to others. The sources of dissension are not just the conditions people find themselves in but are part of their essential make-up, part of human nature. Ferguson does not see conflict as a necessary evil or an ingenious dialectic device leading to a higher, harmonic level of existence, but as a good thing in its own right. He 'described (and prescribed) it on all levels of human interaction – between individuals through play or hunting, between political parties as an unintended means of securing liberty, and between rival nations' (Oz-Salzberger, 1995, p. 114).

Ernest Gellner has focused on civil society as a precondition of liberty in Western societies and has drawn upon Ferguson's understanding of civil society. He differs from Ferguson though as to his interpretation of the 'conditions of liberty'. Gellner (1994, p. 80) argues that whilst eternal vigilance was once the price of liberty, now

> even the absent-minded, or those preoccupied with their private concerns or for any other reason ill-suited to the exercise of eternal and intimidating vigilance, can look forward to enjoying their liberty.

Gellner's confidence – which, due to the precarious nature of certain civil liberties under neo-liberalism, seems misplaced – flies in the face of Ferguson's insistence that 'liberty is a right which every individual must be ready to vindicate for himself, and which he who pretends to bestow as a favour, has by that very act in reality denied' (Ferguson, 1996, p. 251). John Keane is sympathetic to this republican stress upon the necessity of political activity to preserve liberty. On the other hand, he does not want to deny the importance of the freedom not to participate and would thus temper any republican desire to 'force people to be free'. For Keane, we need more complex and differentiated concept of liberty. He argues in favour of dividing decision-making powers into a variety of institutions within and between civil society and the state. Maximizing citizens' liberty requires enlarging their choices which, in turn, necessitates increasing the various social and political spheres in which they can participate, if and when they wish (Keane, 1988b, pp. 12–3).

Kumar (1993, p. 390) advises those who wish to retain the concept civil society 'to avoid the use of civil society as a general category abstracted from particular social philosophies'. He argues that such a complex concept is best situated in some 'definite tradition of use that gives it a place and a meaning'. This is what I have done in this paper, yet Ferguson's discussion of civil society did have an influence on others, most notably Hegel and Marx. Marx commented favourably on Ferguson's ideas on the division of labour in *The Poverty of Philosophy* and *Capital*. Hegel never directly mentioned Ferguson but his reflections on human needs, the economy and the division of labour are marked by his reading of the Scots (see Dickey, 1989; Waszek, 1988).

Ultimately for Kumar (1993, p. 392) rediscovering and retrieving the concept civil society may be an 'interesting exercise in intellectual history but it evades the real political challenges at the end of the twentieth century'. Here Kumar is being unnecessarily harsh. No theoretical concept is going to come out too well if it must address all the political challenges we currently face. The debate has not been seen by its participants as a panacea and Ferguson's account should weigh against any such tendency. The debate is aimed at one of the challenges: the issue of the threat of state power for political liberty. I take it that Kumar accepts that this is and will remain one of the challenges of the late twentieth century. Furthermore, whilst it is correct that we cannot simply rely on past texts to provide solutions for what are contemporary problems, I would suggest that recovering some of the themes in the *Essay* enables us to evaluate what some of these challenges are and from where we might expect responses to come, even if the specific solutions Ferguson put forward are no longer timely. For example, few will wish to take up his proposals for a citizen's militia: Keane argues that the alternative to the continued existence of standing armies is the militarization of civil society, which is incompatible with its democratization, and thus he favours the former as the lesser of two evils (Keane, 1988b, p. 23). Despite the distance that separates us from Ferguson, a number of themes raised in the *Essay* are pertinent and are ones that have re-emerged in recent years: namely the importance of political responsibility and civic alertness, and the dangers of blind reliance on laws and institutions, manufactured or natural (Oz-Salzberger, 1996, p. xxv).

The most common criticism of republicanism is that, ever since the demise of the old city-states, it is backward-looking and out of date. Ferguson provides an example of a thinker who overturns this expectation. He was writing during, and trying to make sense of, the transition to commercial society. He attempted both to assess this transition through the vocabulary of the civic republican tradition and update the tradition in light of the transition. Rousseau had already written of the advent of commercial society in terms of a revived republicanism, yet he did not attempt to update any of the civic notions – such as luxury – so that he could articulate a politics that was more than just negative and 'preventive' (Shklar, 1976). It would seem that Rousseau's advice to societies about to become commercial boiled down to 'don't'. If it is possible to avoid making the transition one should do so. In this sense Rousseau seems to have been in agreement with Hume and Smith that commercial society and the politics of virtue are incompatible; it is just that Rousseau rejected the former, Hume and Smith the latter. Ferguson rejected both options and tried to update the republican tradition so that it was relevant to the new circumstances, but was insistent, *contra* Smith and Hume, that it was both relevant and necessary. In the same sense, the task for current communitarians and republicans, if they are to match up to Kumar's strictures, is to show that their calls for greater political participation and involvement in community life are relevant to today's circumstances and that the conditions exist for such a politics.

Conclusion

Contemporary definitions of civil society are based on a contrast with and opposition to the state. In Eastern Europe the concept of civil society was, for good reason, tied to a notion of 'anti-politics'. Dissidents wished to bypass the official realm of politics which they understood to be unalterably driven by the impersonal demands of power, bureaucracy and technology, and defend an ethical 'anti-political' politics wholly independent of the state system (Havel, 1988). It seems that certain advocates of civil society in the West share a similar 'anti-political' conception: wishing to not only be independent of but to ignore the conventional political system. Those civil society associations that are currently most active normally are so only in a negative and resolutely single-issue sense: for example, anti-roads campaigns that oppose certain government policies but do not themselves take part in the formation of policy and public opinion. The rejection of the official political system makes sense in terms of its distance from and perceived irrelevance to many people's lives, yet it this a solution to such a problem? A more politically-minded conception would consider only as a part of civil society those organizations that take on responsibility for, and control over, the process of legislation and policy formation. Ferguson's alternative to liberalism is to argue that civil society only exists where there is community of citizens; citizens who take part in public, political life, 'command as well as obey' (Ferguson, 1996, p. 144) and take on 'the burden of government' (ibid., p. 252). Such citizens are best equipped to preserve their liberty and most aware of the dangers that threaten it. Such a definition leads us to stress the continuities between civil society and the state as much as the distinction between the two. My argument is not that people should give up on the distinction between civil society and the state; rather it is to warn against the neglect of the important mediations that should take place between the two. We should not always insist on the separateness of civil society from the state. We can understand Ferguson's argument as part of a republican desire to lessen, rather than abolish, the separation between state and civil society, as it is only through the active involvement of the citizenry *in politics* that state power can be controlled and liberty preserved.

Notes

1   Selznick adds that this continuity between state and civil society does not negate the moral primacy of society.
2   For Ferguson, as with others in the civic republican tradition, freedom is understood not in the sense of negative liberty but in a wider sense as the antonym of despotism.

Bibliography

Bryant, C.G.A. (1993), 'Social Self-Organization, Civility and Sociology: A Comment on Kumar's "Civil Society"', *The British Journal of Sociology*, Vol. 44, pp. 397–401.
Dickey, L. (1989), *Hegel: Religion, Economics and the Politics of Spirit 1770–1807*, Cambridge University Press: Cambridge.

Ferguson, A. (1996), *An Essay on the History of Civil Society*, Cambridge University Press: Cambridge.

Gellner, E. (1994), *Conditions of Liberty: Civil Society and Its Rivals*, Hamish Hamilton: London.

Haakonssen, K. (1994), 'Introduction' to Hume, D., *Political Essays*, Cambridge University Press: Cambridge.

Hamowy, R. (1987), *The Scottish Enlightenment and the Theory of Spontaneous Order*, Southern Illinois University Press: Carbondale and Edwardsville.

Havel, V. (1988), 'Anti-Po*litical Politics' in Keane, J. (ed.),* Civil Society and the State: New European Perspectives, Verso: London.

Keane, J. (1988a), *Democracy and Civil Society: On the Predicaments of European Socialism, the Prospects for Democracy, and the Problem of Controlling Social and Political Power*, Verso: London.

Keane, J. (1988b), 'Democracy and Despotism: The Origins and Development of the Distinction Between Civil Society and the State 1750–1850' in Keane, J. (ed.), *Civil Society and the State: New European Perspectives*, Verso: London.

Kumar, K. (1993), 'Civil Society: An Inquiry into the Usefulness of an Historical Term', *The British Journal of Sociology*, Vol. 44, pp. 375–95.

Mason, S. (1988), 'Ferguson and Montesquieu: Tacit Reproaches?', *British Journal for Eighteenth-Century Studies*, Vol. 11, No. 2, pp. 193–203.

Oz-Salzberger, F. (1995), *Translating the Enlightenment: Scottish Civic Discourse in Eighteenth-Century Germany*, Clarendon Press: Oxford.

Oz-Salzberger, F. (1996), 'Introduction' to Ferguson, op. cit.

Pocock, J. G. A. (1975), *The Machiavellian Moment: Florentine Political Thought and the Atlantic Republican Tradition*, Princeton University Press: Princeton.

Sandel, M. (1984), 'Introduction' to Sandel, M. (ed.), *Liberalism and its Critics*, Blackwell: Oxford.

Selznick, P. (1992), *The Moral Commonwealth: Social Theory and the Promise of Community*, University of California Press: Berkeley and Los Angeles, California.

Shklar, J. (1976), *Men and Citizens: A Study of Rousseau's Social Theory*, Cambridge University Press: Cambridge.

Taylor, C. (1995), *Philosophical Arguments*, Harvard University Press: Cambridge, Mass.

Walzer, M. (1989), 'Citizenship' in Ball, T., Farr, J. and Hanson, R.L. (eds), *Political Innovation and Conceptual Change*, Cambridge University Press: Cambridge.

Waszek, N. (1988), *The Scottish Enlightenment and Hegel's Account of Civil Society*, Kluwer: Dordrecht.

Winch, D. (1978), *Adam Smith's Politics: An Essay in Historigraphic Revision*, Cambridge University Press: Cambridge.

Wood, E.M. (1990), 'The Uses and Abuses of "Civil Society"' in Miliband, R. and Panitch, L. (eds), *Socialist Register 1990: The Retreat of the Intellectuals*, Merlin Press: London.

11 'Baffling' Criticism of an 'Ill-equipped' Theory: An Intervention in the Exchange Between MacIntyre and Taylor

ARTO LAITINEN

In the recent literature connected with the liberal–communitarian debate, Alasdair MacIntyre and Charles Taylor (along with Michael Walzer and Michael Sandel) have come to be regarded as 'philosophical communitarians', although both have refused this label (see, e.g., Bell 1993, p. 17).[1] Whatever the label, it is clear that Taylor and MacIntyre have a lot in common. They both hold that conceptions of justice and right always presuppose some particular conceptions of good. They also hold that a cultural or communal context plays a central role in the justification and interpretation of goods. They both view their teleological, hermeneutic or neo-Aristotelian position as lying somewhere between 'universalist' (Kantians, utilitarians) and 'relativist' (neo-Nietzscheans) moral theories.[2] In this chapter I will not deal with the arguments between these different 'camps'. Instead, I will concentrate on the differences within the communitarian camp.

MacIntyre is a more pessimistic 'knocker of modernity', while Taylor is a moderate critic of our times (Taylor, 1991a, chs 1 and 2). It is intuitively harder to agree with MacIntyre's pessimistic conclusions, but it is not clear how Taylor can avoid these conclusions from the teleological position: does not the 'fact of pluralism' (Rawls) or plurality of goods make it impossible to have a modern teleological ethics? And if one does not follow the Kantian deontological path, could it be that the only remaining options are postmodern Nietzschean subjectivism and premodern MacIntyrean Aristotelianism?

Taylor's moral theory is an attempt to show that one can take the teleological starting point while retaining a grasp of modern phenomena.

MacIntyre does not acknowledge such an option. Thus we have every reason to think that MacIntyre's criticism of Taylor's theory would be relevant in evaluating this possibility.

A short-cut into the centre of these differences is an exchange between the two, published in *Philosophy and Phenomenological Research, March – 94*, which on the face of it appears highly paradoxical. I will summarize the main points in what follows.

In his 'Critical Remarks on *The Sources of the Self* by Charles Taylor' MacIntyre claims that Taylor's moral theorizing provides first of all no criteria for telling which judgments about goods are mistaken; and, secondly, that Taylor's theory provides no criteria for the choice between rival goods. Moreover, MacIntyre claims that Taylor's theorizing 'seems peculiarly ill-equipped to do so' (MacIntyre, 1994, pp. 188–9). MacIntyre thereby states that Taylor's moral theory cannot deal with the plurality of rival and incommensurable conceptions of good and right.

MacIntyre is worried about a kind of erosion of our moral frameworks from within, because of 'the multiplication of goods and alternative possibilities of realizing different sets of goods in different types of life'. Here he sees a danger of a slide to emotivism or subjectivism (ibid., p. 189; MacIntyre, 1985, chs 2 and 3; Taylor, 1991a, ch. 6). According to him, this multiplication of goods

> gradually frees the self from commitment to any one such set or type of life and leaves it bereft of criteria, confronting a choice of type of life from an initial standpoint in which the self seems to be very much what Sartre took it to be (MacIntyre, 1994, p. 189).

There are simply too many ways of making sense of our lives; too many goods.

In his reply Taylor states that he has given his account of practical reason in a paper published later, not in *Sources of the Self* (Taylor, 1994c, p. 205).[3] Taylor goes on to say that 'the contemporary philosopher from whom I have learned most in this account is none other than Alasdair MacIntyre' (ibid.). Taylor in fact states that he has translated MacIntyre's views of tradition- or context-dependent practical rationality into his own moral theory. And the best part is yet to come. On the basis of this MacIntyrean view of rationality, Taylor states the following: 'I find baffling MacIntyre's call for "criteria." Because it seems to me that, in one common sense of this term, these have no place here' (ibid., p. 206).

There is thus an air of paradox here: MacIntyre claims that Taylor's moral theory is ill-equipped to provide an adequate account of practical rationality in order to deal with a plurality of rival goods, and Taylor seems to argue that not only is his account borrowed from MacIntyre, but that his views are more MacIntyrean than MacIntyre's own talk about 'criteria'.

In this chapter I shall first try to make sense of this 'baffling' criticism of an 'ill-equipped' theory by examining Charles Taylor's moral theory in more detail. Then I shall evaluate this criticism and see how it affects our views on the possibility of modern teleological ethics in general.

One way to summarize Charles Taylor's moral theory is as follows: 1) people have 'conceptions of good' that are not a matter of choice but rather of upbringing and being-in-the-world. 2) These goods are not always fully linguistically articulated but can be partly implicit in moral reactions and practices. 3) The goods are plural and potentially in conflict and 4) to some extent are or can be ordered by their relative worth. 5) The framework of 'goods' is based on some ontological vision the articulation of which makes sense of the goods or which forms a background to the goods. 6) The conceptions of good can be criticized and compared rationally.

In what follows I shall analyse these six claims in more detail, trying to evaluate how adequate they are as answers to MacIntyre's criticism. I will also point out their connection with Taylor's reply.

I will analyse these six claims one by one, and use them to clarify and evaluate the actual exchange between Taylor and MacIntyre. I hope to show that MacIntyre's criticism is not that 'baffling' after all. I will also argue that Taylor's theory is not that 'ill-equipped'. When taken together, these six claims are adequate as answers to most parts of MacIntyre's criticism. The crucial point that they do *not* answer adequately is the MacIntyrean view that *quantity* of different goods affects the *quality* of our commitment to them: if there are too many goods we simply can't take all of them seriously. This, I will argue, is a question that Taylor does not deal with sufficiently and this is also what makes sense of MacIntyre's criticism. But although this criticism makes sense, it must be qualified.

Analysing these six claims in more detail will also show that Taylor *does* have an account of how to choose between rival goods and how to tell which judgments of goods are erroneous.

Taylor's starting point is the Heideggerian thesis that understanding is a mode of being-in-the-world (see Taylor, 1995, pp. 100–26; 1995, pp. 61–8; 1993, pp. 317–36). Our self-understandings to some extent constitute our selves, we are 'self-interpreting animals' (Taylor, 1985a, pp. 45–76). For

Taylor, the world is always a moral world, or a moral space, and in this moral space we cannot but orientate towards some good (Taylor, 1989, ch. 2, passim). To use another catch phrase, we are 'strong evaluators' (Taylor, 1989; 1985a, pp. 15–44; see also Flanagan, 1996, pp. 142–70). In Taylor's theory 'selfhood and the good, or in another way selfhood and morality, turn out to be inextricably intertwined themes'(Taylor, 1989, p. 3).

This is in sharp contrast to Sartre's position (or at least to Sartre as conceived by Taylor and MacIntyre): Taylor discusses Sartre's example of a young man who is torn between staying with his ailing mother and going off to join the Resistance. According to Taylor, this example cannot be made sense of within Sartre's doctrine's claim that ethical commitments are based on a choice, because clearly the existence of the conflicting demands is not a matter of decision.

> We see a grievous moral dilemma because the young man is faced here with two powerful moral *claims* ... *But* it is a dilemma only because the claims themselves are not created by radical choice. If they were the grievous nature of the predicament would dissolve, for that would mean that the young man could do away with the dilemma at any moment by simply declaring one of the rival claims as dead and inoperative (Taylor, 1985a, pp. 29–30).

The fundamental level of Charles Taylor's moral theory is not our choices or decisions but our moral reactions, experiences, instincts or intuitions, i.e. the way we respond to the challenge of orientation in the moral space. For Taylor, these intuitions are historically and culturally formed; they are a result of upbringing and participation in social practices. Some intuitions may have instinctual roots, but even they receive variable shapes in culture. To make sense of moral reactions and intuitions is to articulate the 'evaluative framework' or the 'horizon of significance' embodied in them (Taylor, 1989, ch. 1; 1991a, pp. 31–41; 1985a, pp. 15–44).

Thus, Taylor claims that we cannot choose our values or conceptions of the good; there is nothing voluntary about them. We live in a moral space which is dependent on our culture or civilization. Taylor, therefore, strongly opposes the kind of subjectivism or emotivism that MacIntyre sees Taylor as coming close to represent.

The 'self' in Taylor's moral theory is actually quite far from the 'emotivist' picture that MacIntyre tries to superimpose on it. True, Taylor acknowledges that emotions play a part in morality. Moral emotions, however, embody a moral framework in a way that MacIntyre does not take into account.

MacIntyre seems to view emotions as arbitrary, but according to Taylor emotions, intuitions and moral reactions are embodiments of moral wisdom and virtues. They are not open to any arbitrary re-descriptions, but guide the possible re-descriptions in a hermeneutical manner (Taylor, 1989, chs 1–4 and passim; 1985b, pp. 15–57).

Thus conceived, the inner life of individuals lessens the need for collective or shared truths.[4] In MacIntyre's view, collective truths can survive only if tightly-knit communities survive: because there is no universal epistemic point of view from which to tell the difference between rival goods, we have to have social limits or otherwise all we are left with is an emotivist picture. But for Taylor, inner convictions do have a role. Of course, they are dependent on 'horizons of meaning', recognition and dialogical relationships with 'significant others', i.e. one can be a self or a strong evaluator only amongst others, but that can happen also in looser relationships than what MacIntyre describes in his account of 'traditions' (see, e.g., Taylor, 1989, chs 4–5). In any case, what is relevant here is that Taylor is quite far from Sartre, and we have to study further aspects of Taylor's theory in order to make sense of MacIntyre's criticism.

The second relevant feature is the already-mentioned distinction between implicit and explicit embodiment of the moral framework (see, e.g., Taylor 1985a, pp. 15–44). The framework is first of all tacitly or implicitly expressed in our moral conduct, moral reactions and our inarticulate moral know-how. These are the implicit embodiments of the framework. Perhaps one can say that Taylor's moral theory is a hermeneutical, linguistically and historically interpreted variant of Hutcheson's theory of moral sense.[5] For Taylor, what is called 'moral sense' is different for different people in different times and places, but it is still the ultimate foundation of our morality.[6]

The framework is also linguistically articulated and thus has an explicit, more-or-less-accurate, expression in language. There is a two-way causality between the implicit and the explicit; they are connected by a hermeneutical circle. In articulating our intuitions we make sense of them and clarify their meanings, and this process of articulation at the same time modifies these intuitions. Taylor calls this process 'engaged reasoning'. It is engaged to our intuitions and does not try to justify them externally (see, e.g., Taylor, 1989, pp. 162–4).

This distinction is relevant in making sense of Taylor's claim that morality and practical rationality do not necessarily have 'explicit criteria'. It is more a matter of implicit grasp or insight. Lack of criteria in that sense does not threaten Taylor's moral theory. If this were what MacIntyre meant in his critique, then his 'call for criteria' would be baffling indeed. And if this were the critical point, Taylor would have no difficulty answering it.

But in fact there is more to the critique. In another sense, this tacit knowledge or implicit grasp has to work as criteria or standards. It is important to realize that implicit criteria are also criteria. Thus the distinction between implicit and explicit in the end merely begs the question. If we take MacIntyre's challenge seriously, we have to ask: do we really have the sufficient implicit grasp of the rival conceptions of good?

The third claim is that genuine goods can be, and very often are, in conflict. The nature of goods is such that sometimes we cannot avoid conflict, but still the goods in conflict can be genuine goods. Thus the existence of conflicts as such does nothing to refute Taylor's theory. Again, a crude form of criticism can be answered easily.[7]

But, again, nothing suggests that MacIntyre had this kind of criticism in mind when he claimed that Taylor's theory cannot deal with a plurality of incommensurable goods. MacIntyre, too, opts for what he calls the 'Sophoclean insight': that genuine goods can conflict with each other. MacIntyre (1985, pp. 163–4, 222) even defines a tradition as an embodied conflict.

However, MacIntyre draws out a difference between a conflict concerning goods we are committed to and one between two goods, only one of which we are committed to. For us, the members of our tradition, the latter is no conflict.[8] There are limits to what counts as good within a MacIntyrean tradition. The fact that something is good for someone else does not make it good for us. MacIntyre seems to claim that Taylor's theory gives no account of this kind, no account of where the limits of a moral framework ought to be.

This is strong criticism against Taylor's theory: perhaps there are simply too many conflicts? Perhaps Taylor's theory would allow more conflicts than is humanly bearable, more than moral frameworks can take?

According to Taylor, we can understand and evaluate foreign cultures in a non-ethnocentrical way, thanks to a 'fusion of horizons' which we can attain after careful comparison and a construction of a common 'language of perspicuous contrast' (see Taylor, 1985b, pp. 134–51). Thus, we can learn from foreign cultures. Within one framework genuine goods can conflict, and this applies to conflicts between different frameworks, different cultures as well. What is good for one culture can be good for all others as well. Underlying Taylor's pluralism of contexts there is a possibility of one universal context which would come true if all cultures and frameworks were carefully to study and evaluate each other, on a 'one-to-one' basis, and then fuse into one single culture. But, of course, there is an even bigger danger that such a culture would be full of conflicting ideas of good (see Taylor, 1995, pp. 146–64; 1995, pp. 225–56).

This is central to MacIntyre's worry that there are simply too many conceptions of good and not enough coherence, and no criteria for choosing between the goods. According to Taylor, modern culture is indeed a fusion of the Enlightenment ideals and the ideals of Romanticism, and to a lesser extent some premodern goods rooted in Christianity and ancient Greece (Taylor, 1989, ch. 25, passim; 1975, chs 1, 2 and 10; 1979). MacIntyre agrees, but rather than regarding this as a well-ordered fusion, he sees it as a collection of fragments without any internal coherence (MacIntyre, 1985, chs 1–2). Thus, linked with Taylor's and MacIntyre's basic disagreement about moral theory there is a disagreement about the modern moral situation: is it genuine pluralism or an ill-assorted melange of fragmented, incommensurable viewpoints?

Now we are in a position to understand MacIntyre's argument that Taylor's theory comes close to Sartre's. The point is that there are limits as to how many goods can effectively command our respect. MacIntyre's worry was 'the multiplication of goods and alternative possibilities of realising different sets of goods in different types of life'. According to him, this

> gradually frees the self from commitment to any one such set or type of life and leaves it bereft of criteria, confronting a choice of type of life from an initial standpoint in which the self seems to be very much what Sartre took it to be (MacIntyre, 1994, p. 189).

Thus the whole of Taylor's theory is at stake here. Taylor must show how a self committed to goods can deal with the vast variety of goods and either make a commitment to all of them or judge some of them inferior. In MacIntyre's theory this is not a problem, because of the clear boundaries of different traditions.

To anticipate the conclusion, one must say that Taylor has not said much on this precise issue of 'the limits of a framework', and this counts as a weakness of his theory. But there are other points which are relevant here and which strengthen Taylor's case: the issue of the priority of goods, the issue of 'ontological background pictures' and the issue of practical rationality. We must go through these points before we can evaluate whether they actually suffice to compensate for the missing account of the limits of a framework. After all, as we have seen, in Taylor's theory 'the self' and 'inner life' have some of the functions that 'tradition' has in MacIntyre's. Taylor might thus make recourse to 'experience' and claim that we can experience only some goods as genuine. He might claim that the criteria implicit in our experiences and moral reactions in fact do the job. Before the final evaluation of this claim, we must proceed further.

Fourth, Taylor does think that some goods are more important than others. These goods that are of central importance to us and our identity he calls *hypergoods* (Taylor, 1989, pp. 63 ff).

Taylor does not subscribe to the dogma of many modern moral theories that justice is a hypergood or that questions of justice always override those of the good life. He says that the goods within a moral framework lie on three different axes because they answer three different questions: i) our sense of respect for and obligations to others, i.e. morality in the narrow sense, and in the sense in which Habermas uses the term 'morality'; ii) our understanding of a full, meaningful, good or virtuous life, i.e. the 'ethical issues' in Habermas's terminology; and iii) our sense of our own dignity or status, i.e. our sense of ourselves as commanding the 'attitudinal respect' of those around us. Taylor calls these the 'three axes' of our moral framework (ibid., p. 15). The hypergoods can be found from any of these three axes and thus the question of the order of goods is a separate issue from that of the existence of the three different axes.

As we have seen, according to Taylor the diversity of goods gives rise to moral conflicts, but these conflicts do not invalidate the goods in question. The hypergoods provide us with a standpoint from which the goods in conflict can be ordered. This ordering is a continuous task:

> [t]he domain of ultimately important goods has a sort of prescriptive unity. Each of us has to answer all these demands in the course of a single life, and this means we have to find some way of assessing their relative validity, or putting them in order of priority. A single coherent order of goods is … something we always try to define without ever managing to achieve it definitely (Taylor, 1985b, p. 244).

The notion of hypergoods answers directly one of MacIntyre's critical claims: here we have a standpoint from which we can deal with conflicting goods. The claim that Taylor has no account of how to order goods is unfair, and although Taylor didn't use the notion 'hypergoods' in his reply to MacIntyre, he made this point by reference to Aristotelian 'architectonic' goods (Taylor, 1994c, pp. 204–5).

Of course, MacIntyre could go on and claim that there is a plurality of rival hypergoods as well. If there are too many rival ways of ordering, there is no way of ordering. Thus Taylor's theory has not yet answered MacIntyre's worry in a way that would satisfy MacIntyre. This only adds to the relevance of the issue of the 'limits of traditions'. But again, Taylor might claim that we in fact experience only some goods as more important than others, i.e. that everyone has a limited number of hypergoods.

The next point about the structure of our moral frameworks is that they include an ontological background picture (Taylor, 1989, ch. 1–4).

Taylor draws a distinction between 'life goods' and the ontological pictures, which he calls 'constitutive goods'. Life-goods are ordinary goods and part of a good, moral or admirable life. They include goods like authenticity, autonomy, justice, and virtues. Hypergoods are the most important life-goods.

Constitutive goods, by contrast, are ontological accounts with which we try to make sense of the phenomenon of moral goodness in general. Taylor insists that the abstract question 'what constitutes the goodness of the goods' must be answered by giving an ontological account: in Plato's theory it is the 'Idea of Good'; in Christian tradition it is God the creator; in modern times it has often been Nature. The notion of constitutive goods is a complex one, and we need not go into details here. What is relevant here is that the notion of constitutive goods helps to qualify MacIntyre's worry, because constitutive goods lend 'circular' or hermeneutical (albeit not decisive) support to the accounts of life-goods (Taylor, 1989, chs 4 and 18).

Constitutive goods contribute to the content of our life-goods by giving them a background. This means that we can, for example, try and define which property or set of properties of humans, or animals, demands moral responses from us (see Taylor, 1985b, pp. 187–210). In answering this question we are articulating the ontological picture we have. These pictures form a background to our intuitions and thus, in a circular or hermeneutic way, also in some sense justify them, offer reasons for them.

Taylor distinguishes this from 'giving a basic reason'. The basic reasons are the endpoints in the chains of reasoning when we say that something is good or right, because they are special cases or applications of some more basic goods, rights or duties. The basic reasons are the endpoints in our search for more basic standards or criteria of rightness or goodness (Taylor, 1989, pp. 75–90).

Background pictures are not simply one step further in this chain. For example, we offer a basic reason for not manipulating someone by stating that this manipulation would violate human rights. And here respect for human rights is a criterion, a basic reason. But it is another thing to ask just what makes human beings worthy of 'rights'. And the answer can be, for example, that humans are rational agents, or they have a capacity to choose a conception of a good life or that they are God's creation. What sort of justification is this? Human rights do not logically follow from our acknowledging this human capacity or predicament. In a different way, however, acknowledging this throws light on our moral intuitions concerning human rights. Thereby human rights give hermeneutical support to our moral intuitions.

But MacIntyre could claim that his worry still remains unanswered. He would say that Taylor and Taylor's moral agents simply belong to one tradition among many: he would stress that different traditions give different accounts not only of life-goods, but also different accounts of constitutive goods. MacIntyre states in his remarks on Taylor that we can make sense of our lives in many different ways. And thus in order to avoid fragmentation and incoherence we must belong to only one of them, i.e. commit ourselves to one tradition only. Taylor himself comes close to noting this in *Sources of the Self*. Taylor claims that there is more consensus about life-goods than constitutive goods, and that we are not very likely to come into agreement about constitutive goods (Taylor, 1989, pp. 513–21). Taking this into account decreases the relevance of constitutive goods as an answer to MacIntyre's worry of fragmentation.

The final point – the one that Taylor emphasizes in his reply to MacIntyre – is Taylor's account of practical rationality (see Taylor, 1995, pp. 34–60; 1989, pp. 71–3). We have seen that the five points mentioned so far give some kind of an answer to MacIntyre but still leave some version of MacIntyre's worry alive. We still have to address the question of justifying our account of goods, hypergoods and constitutive goods against competing accounts.

Taylor opposes any attempts to create a procedural account of practical rationality. He tries to give an account of a substantive rationality, where rationality means in the first place simply 'getting things right'. Thus moral judgment is rational when it gets things right. And what is right is determined by one's evaluative framework.

Justifying one's evaluative framework can proceed in three directions. First, as we have seen, one can try to clarify one's moral intuitions concerning what is good or right, give them better articulations and make better sense of them. These articulations always also modify the intuitions, and we can always try to articulate our intuitions better. Taylor calls this kind of clarification 'engaged reasoning'. This is not justification in any external sense.

Second, one can try to articulate the constitutive goods. As already mentioned, articulating constitutive goods in a sense can support one's account of the life-goods. This is still engaged reasoning, i.e. reasoning engaged to existing intuitions. If this were the whole story, Taylor's account of practical rationality would be really conservative and also unable to answer to MacIntyre's worry.

But this is not the whole story: one can use moral arguments concerning the errors in our moral intuitions, and this is the third dimension. But for this argument we cannot have universal or formal criteria, we can only compare our intuitions or evaluative frameworks with others. Here we get to what Taylor has borrowed from MacIntyre:

> [p]ractical reason can't 'establish' goods by arguing from the ground up. Arguing from the ground up would mean offering an argument meant to convince anybody and everybody, no matter where they start from in their moral views and sensibilities (Taylor, 1994c, p. 205).

Instead,

> the arguments must be directed at particular positions or sensibilities. The arguments are ad hominem, and in an important sense comparative. Our attempt will be to show that the interlocutor's moral outlook could be improved by some error-reducing move. The goal of my argument is to show that the interlocutor's position flips over into mine, once you carry out the error-reducing move on it (ibid.).

This is the sense in which Taylor's picture has room for critical argumentation, in this *ad hominem* or comparative sense. Thus one can argue for one's own framework and against one's competitors.

It is important to note that for Taylor this comparison and *ad hominem* argumentation works cross-culturally as well. Taylor leaves it open a priori whether different moral outlooks are incommensurable or whether these error-reducing moves point in one and the same direction (Taylor, 1995, pp. 34–60).

Now we can sum up all the three aspects of moral judgments in Taylor's moral theory:

i   we have a more or less implicit sense of the goods in the three axes, including hypergoods;

ii   we have a more or less implicit sense of constitutive goods or background pictures; and

iii there can be arguments about the possible errors in our moral intuition.

Of the relation of these different aspects Taylor says that 'none of these has primacy. It is a matter of achieving reflective equilibrium, to use the Rawlsian term' (Taylor, 1994c, p. 213).

Thus, moral arguments and moral theories have relevance only in the context of intuitions. The balance between arguments and intuitions can only be found in a reflexive equilibrium, in a 'best account so far', the best interpretation that makes most sense. We never get out of the circle of interpretations: arguments are merely new 'input' into it. This is a holistic account: what is decisive is the whole, and this whole cannot ever be fully articulated into explicit criteria (see, e.g., Taylor, 1985b, pp. 15–57).

Now, in what sense is Taylor's account of practical rationality relevant particularly as a reply to MacIntyre? At the level of particular goods, hypergoods and constitutive goods, practical rationality can also make comparative *ad hominem* claims about the genuineness and relative order of the goods. Thus it seems that this finally answers MacIntyre's worry. We can argue against rival and mistaken accounts.

Conclusion

In this chapter I have tried to make sense of the exchange between MacIntyre and Taylor. I think the seemingly paradoxical elements of the exchange have become clearer: there is a point in MacIntyre's worry about subjectivism and the overload of conflicting goods, although it has to be qualified. It is unfair to say that Taylor gives no account of how to choose between rival goods. The notions of hypergoods and practical rationality do provide such an account.

It is also unfair to say that Taylor gives no account of how to tell which judgments about goods are erroneous: according to Taylor's account of practical rationality, this is done by our intuitions and arguments in a reflective equilibrium.

However, the claim that Taylor's theory is ill-equipped to deal with the multiplicity of goods is more acceptable. Although Taylor agrees that there are genuine conflicts, and although he discusses hypergoods, constitutive goods and practical rationality, he has no account especially of the limits of a moral framework. Taylor simply assumes that a moral framework, limited to some goods, exists to begin with, and this moral framework is embodied in the moral reactions of a person. All the notions mentioned above (hypergoods, constitutive goods and practical rationality) presuppose this. MacIntyre's criticism reveals that this is a supposition that needs further justification.

The implicit/explicit distinction makes it possible for Taylor to claim that in fact everyone has a moral framework, and I think this is a valid point against neutral theories of the self which in a way claim that the moral framework contains nothing. But it is not a valid point against MacIntyre, who claims that the framework contains too much. It seems that this is a possibility that Taylor has not considered.

And Taylor's account of learning from other cultures makes things even more complex: if we can learn more goods from other cultures, then the framework contains even more conflicting goods. Also, as we saw, there is a point in the claim that a multiplication of goods would lead to a situation where the Sartrean account of the self would come true

Thus MacIntyre's criticism is not that baffling after all. One reason why Taylor found it baffling was that he thought MacIntyre was talking about explicit criteria, which I think was not the case. Taylor didn't think that the existence of implicit criteria might be in question, while this is precisely what *is* in question: can Taylor's theory show that we can count on the existence of criteria implicit in the inner life (moral reactions, insights, experiences, intuitions) of the moral self, despite the multiplication of goods? Or is this assumption all-too-optimistic?

These questions are closely connected with the fate of modern teleological ethics: if we do not opt for Kantian or Nietzschean moral theory, do we need tightly-knit communities with shared traditional criteria of what counts as good? Or can the teleological theory count on the existence of individual moral persons whose moral capacities are sufficient even in the conditions of modern plurality?

I think that MacIntyre's position, though useful as a critical device, is further from truth than Taylor's. MacIntyre reduces an individual to a member of a community and is very sceptical towards accounts of 'the self' or 'inwardness'. But it seems that modern individuals are capable of being members of many communities at once, and able to use their moral capacities even in the conditions of modernity. Thus, when the problem of the 'limits of tradition' is translated into Taylor's theory, it splits into two: first, the problem of how individuals can develop their moral capacities in modern times. Taylor has expressed sensitivity to this problem in his critical writings about the modern tendencies of instrumental rationalization, loss of freedom, loss of meaning, loss of belonging, and individualization (see, e.g., Taylor, 1989, ch. 25; 1991a). And second, the problem whether any individual can have the capacity to deal with the overload of conflicting goods. To repeat, I think this is something that Taylor has not sufficiently taken into account, although the notions of hypergoods, constitutive goods and practical rationality help to qualify the accusation of being 'ill-equipped'. Thanks to these notions, Taylor can state that conflicts can sometimes be resolved (1994c, p. 205).

> Conflicts can be resolved, but does this mean that all conflicts can be resolved? This doesn't seem to me to follow either. An *a priori* answer either way seems misplaced ... We have to recognize the full stretch of goods which have a claim to our allegiance, and not artificially shorten the list through bogus "refutations". Then we have to face the conflicts that arise, without the *a priori* certainty either of resolvability or irresolvability.

The question remains open whether too many irresolvable conflicts will force one to 'shorten the list' of goods to less than a 'full stretch'. Taylor leaves it open whether modern moral agents or 'strong evaluators' might have reasonable criteria for such occasions, for drawing limits to moral frameworks, or whether 'bogus "refutations"' will remain the only option. And this question which has yet to be answered seems to be a central one for any modern version of teleological ethics.[9]

Notes

1   Bell quotes MacIntyre's letter to the periodical *Responsive Community*, Summer 1991, p. 91: '[i]n spite of rumours to the contrary, I am not and never have been a communitarian. For my judgment is that the political, economic, and moral structures of advanced modernity in this country, as elsewhere, exclude the possibility of realizing any of the worthwhile types of political community which at various times in the past have been achieved, even if always in imperfect forms. And I also believe that attempts to remake modern societies in systematically communitarian ways will always be either ineffective or disastrous'. See also MacIntyre 1995.
     Taylor (1994b, p. 250) criticizes the moral thinking of Kant and Bentham (and their political equivalents) for looking for a single principle of morality. Taylor continues: '[t]hat's (one of the many reasons) why I'm unhappy with the term "communitarianism". It sounds as though the critics of this liberalism wanted to substitute some other all-embracing principle, which would in some equal and opposite way exalt the life of the community over everything. Really the aim (as far as I'm concerned) is more modest: I just want to say that single-principle neutral liberalism can't suffice.'
2   In Richard Bernstein's (1983) vocabulary both Taylor and MacIntyre went 'beyond objectivism and relativism'. They themselves use different terms for this classification, but usually there are two extremes they want to avoid. In *After Virtue* MacIntyre calls the positions he opposes 'Emotivism' and the 'Enlightenment Project'. In MacIntyre's

description of emotivism, Sartrean empty selves are free to choose their conceptions of the good, to choose their morality. MacIntyre argues that the Enlightenment project of providing a universalist justification to morality had to fail because it denied all conceptions of human telos. MacIntyre also argues that a logical conclusion of emotivism would be a Nietzschean destruction of morality. In this situation he calls for Aristotelian virtue-ethics. In *Whose Justice?* MacIntyre prefers a Thomist version of Aristotelianism to the moral philosophies of Scottish Enlightenment or liberalism. In *Three Rival Versions* he defends 'Tradition' as a method of moral enquiry against 'Encyclopedia' and 'Genealogy'.

    In *Sources of the Self* Taylor criticizes, amongst others, the modern moral philosophies ('Kantian' and 'Benthamite', p. 87) and 'Neo-Nietzscheans' (e.g., pp. 71–103).

3   I would claim that the main insights in fact are present in *Sources of the Self*; see pp. 71–3. But even if *Sources* did not contain this section, we would have to evaluate MacIntyre's claim that Taylor's theory 'seems peculiarly ill-equipped' to provide criteria of practical rationality.

4   On 'inwardness', see Taylor, 1989, chs 5–11.

5   On Taylor's views on Hutcheson, see Taylor, 1989, ch. 15.

6   On MacIntyre's critical views on Hutcheson, see MacIntyre, 1988, ch. 14,

7   In his 'Reply to MacIntyre', Taylor (1994c, p. 204) mentioned this point that genuine goods can be in conflict.

8   On the difference between internal and external challenges to a tradition, see MacIntyre, 1988, ch. 18.

9   This article is based on papers read at the ALSP conference 'Communitarianism and Citizenship', Edinburgh, 3–5 April 1997, and at the 'History of Practical Reason' conference, Oslo, 21–23 February 1997.

Bibliography

Bell, D. (1993), *Communitarianism and its Critics*, Clarendon Press: Oxford.

Bernstein, R.J. (1983), *Beyond Objectivism and Relativism*, University of Pennsylvania Press: Philadelphia.

Flanagan, O. (1996), *Self-Expressions*, Oxford University Press: Oxford.

Horton, J. and Mendus, S. (eds) (1994), *After MacIntyre: Critical Perspectives on the work of Alasdair MacIntyre*, Polity Press: Cambridge.

MacIntyre, A. (1985), *After Virtue*, 2nd edn, Duckworth: London.

MacIntyre, A. (1988), *Whose Justice? Which Rationality?*, Duckworth: London.

MacIntyre, A. (1990), *Three Rival Versions of Moral Enquiry*, University of Notre Dame Press: Notre Dame, Indiana.

MacIntyre, A. (1994), 'Critical Remarks on the Sources of the Self by Charles Taylor', *Philosophy and Phenomenological Research*, Vol. LIV, pp. 187–90.

MacIntyre, A. (1995), "The Spectre of Communitarianism", *Radical Philosophy*, 70, pp. 34–5.

Taylor, C. (1975), *Hegel*, Cambridge University Press: Cambridge.

Taylor, C. (1979), *Hegel and Modern Society*, Cambridge University Press: Cambridge.

Taylor, C. (1985a), *Human Agency and Language: Philosophical Papers vol. 1*, Cambridge University Press: Cambridge.

Taylor, C. (1985b), *Philosophy and Human Sciences: Philosophical Papers vol. 2*, Cambridge University Press: Cambridge.

Taylor, C. (1989), *Sources of the Self: the Making of a Modern Identity*, Cambridge University Press: Cambridge.

Taylor, C. (1991a), *The Ethics of Authenticity*, Harvard University Press: Cambridge, Mass.

Taylor, C. (1991b), 'Comments and Replies', *Inquiry*, 34, pp. 237–54.

Taylor, C. (1993), 'Engaged Agency and Background in Heidegger' in Guignon, C. (ed.), *The Cambridge Companion to Heidegger*, Cambridge University Press: Cambridge.

Taylor, C. (1994a), 'Justice After Virtue' in Horton and Mendus, op. cit.

Taylor, C. (1994b), 'Reply and Re-articulation' in Tully, J. (ed.), *Philosophy in the Age of Pluralism: the Philosophy of Charles Taylor in Question*, Cambridge University Press: Cambridge.

Taylor, C. (1994c), 'Reply to Commentators', *Philosophy and Phenomenological Research*, Vol. LIV, pp. 203–13.

Taylor, C. (1995), *Philosophical Arguments*, Harvard University Press: Cambridge, Mass.

12 The Community of Friends

SANDRA E. MARSHALL

> For without friends no one would choose to live, though he had all other goods
> … when men are friends they have no need of justice, while when they are just
> they need friendship as well, and the truest form of justice is thought to be a
> friendly quality (Aristotle, viii 1).

> The self is both made and explored with words; and the best for both are the
> words spoken in the dialogue of friendship. In default of that, the debate with
> the solitary self comes limping far behind (Taylor, 1989a, p. 183).

Liberalism, as a political ideology, might be thought to have reached a kind
of apotheosis in the remark (possibly apocryphal) attributed to Margaret
Thatcher, that there is 'no such thing as society, only individuals and their
families'.[1] What makes such a remark by an active politician so striking and
seemingly significant is the way it appears to distil complex liberal thought
down to its purest essence and to capture the fundamental metaphysical
assumption at its heart: the detached individual, the autonomous locus of
interests, to be understood independently of any particular context as that to
which any complex of social relations is ultimately reducible.[2] For a
philosopher there is, no doubt, something intensely gratifying in such a
convergence of the metaphysical and the apparently practical concerns of the
ordinary politician on the streets, as it were. Doubly so if that philosopher is
of communitarian persuasion, since it is precisely this conception of the self
which has been the focus of the philosophical struggle with liberal theory.

The fundamental criticism of liberal theory which has emerged from this
philosophical battleground, and been dubbed 'communitarian', has to do with
the conception of the self which lies behind the substantive liberal claims
made at the level of political theory. The structure of rights, for instance,
derived from such fundamental liberal values as liberty and equality, depends,
so it is claimed, upon a construction of the 'self': the metaphysical self suitable
for hiding behind the veil of ignorance. Such a self is a metaphysical
construction, of course, because no such detached individuals are to be found
strolling the streets of even the largest and most anonymous city, let alone the

narrow lanes of a small village. Such a metaphysical conception is the very stuff of philosophy, however, and informs more than just the debate between liberals and communitarians. The epistemological self which is required to take up the position of the 'view from nowhere' or the moral self seeking 'the absolute conception' are versions of the same idea and subject to the same kind of criticism: that ultimately it is an incoherent notion. In the case of Rawlsian political theory,[3] this incoherence becomes apparent the more closely we peer at what is supposed to be going on behind the veil of ignorance.

One kind of communitarian argument is concerned with ontology, and it is as well to keep clearly in mind the distinction between such ontological concerns and normative concerns.[4] The core ontological claim, that the liberal conception of the self fails to recognize the way in which our selves are socially embedded and constructed within a community, does not by itself say anything about the nature of that community. To be sure it is the embeddedness that gives the self its identity, understood as a structure of values, but nothing yet follows about what those values are. As far as this strand of the communitarian argument goes, such values could still be standardly liberal ones. However, it should not be supposed that this leaves liberalism unscathed. Any acceptance of the ontological version of communitarianism will require the abandonment of the anti-perfectionist claims of liberalism; the liberal could no longer claim to be neutral as between competing conceptions of the good. The ontology of the self that functions behind the veil of ignorance had liberal values built into it: once that ontology is abandoned, and the liberal self is embedded in a liberal community from which it draws its identity and commitments, then it embodies just one conception of the good which may compete with others. Any attempt to give it priority risks being driven back towards the rejected ontology. Rawls' own attempts to avoid the metaphysical charge by characterizing his view as political rather than metaphysical remains plausible just so long as the question of its priority over other conceptions of the good is left unasked. Granted that the political is an aspect of the embedded self, we still need some account of why it might take priority over other values which might well conflict with political values. Embedded values are likely to be 'thicker' than the supposed unembedded political values of neutral liberalism.

Rawls, and others like him, make it clear that the theories have to be seen against a background of assumptions about how things are in the world and purports to elaborate on what a human society would be like given these assumptions. Rawls thus offers a theory of justice for a society in which, as a matter of fact, there is no shared conception of the good. Justice is the standard through which competing conceptions of the good are balanced. Rawls does not rule out the possibility that there might be a society in which there is a shared conception of the good; so justice is not part of the definition of 'society'. Thus it may seem that such a theory is neutral as to whether a plurality of conceptions of the good is a good or a bad thing, as against a single and universally accepted conception. That, however, is too simple; plurality is not merely the background assumption of liberalism but an important liberal value. A commitment to the individual as *fundamentally* , not merely accidentally, the autonomous rational chooser is central even to Rawlsian theory; it is central to the idea of liberty. It belongs with the idea that what we aspire to is the fulfilment of our desires and the development of our individual selves through our own conceptions of our interests. The individual is required to choose, not to discover, her conception of the good. The ideal society is one which maximizes the opportunities for the rational chooser. This is an ideal in the sense of something to which we ought to aspire, not just in the sense that it pictures something that does not in fact exist. It provides us with a measure against which our existing societies are to be judged. It is a normative ideal and not in the least bit neutral.

All this shows the way in which the ontological and the normative interweave, for the communitarian as well as the liberal, and it is the relationship between the communitarian's ontological and normative arguments that are most in need of attention in the debate about communitarianism. The communitarian claim is that the conception of the self as rational chooser, and thus the rights based conception of moral life which flows from it, leave no room for and cannot account for those affective relations which form a substantial part of human lives. These affective relations provide us with our identity, with our self. The self cannot be given independently of these relations; the bare self lurking behind the veil of ignorance is too skimpily clad to be a self at all. Reciprocity of rights cannot capture the bonds of love and affection, the concern for the 'weal and woe' of others, as Blum puts it, without which we cannot flourish (Blum, 1980). The values which form such relationships do not admit of a re-description in terms of justice and fairness.[5] So, here we can already see a difference in what each side will count as 'human flourishing'. These accounts will necessarily depend upon the values embedded in the theories. Liberal theory characteristically relegates affective relations to the sphere of the private lives of individuals: this is not to say that they need be seen as unimportant, but they do not belong to the individual self which inhabits the public sphere; that public, political space is entirely taken up by justice and rights.

At this point a problem for the communitarian begins to emerge: the ontological claims which form the basis of the communitarian account may seem to eliminate the private sphere altogether. If everything we are is given in our social relations with others, can there be any room left for a private self which is not anyone else's business? The communitarian ideal begins to look somewhat oppressive.

One communitarian response to this criticism might well be that it presupposes liberal values and conceptions: that a view is inimical to liberal values is not *by itself* a complete objection since the question of why liberal values should be taken as fundamental needs an answer. A more congenial response, however, would be one which tried to give an account of community and the relations between individuals which has room for privacy (and other values) but which rests upon the communitarian account of the self. A community in which each one's identity is totally subsumed in the collective is hard to imagine and does not sound much like a community of human beings (more like a community of bees). There needs to be some boundary between the self and others to make sense of the self at all and to make sense of the relationship between selves. Privacy is given in relation to that boundary between self and others. The communitarian argument is only that the self cannot be understood as being independent of social relations, and it may even be argued that it is not the communitarian story that erodes the idea of separate selves but rather the liberal, since if we take the idea of the 'original position' seriously there is nothing which individuates the selves behind the 'veil of ignorance'. The rational choosers there choose as one; the only identity available to them is numerical identity, and even that may look problematic since it is not clear that they have bodies which would enable such numerical identification.[6]

So, the problem for philosophical communitarian constructivism comes when the self as embedded is read back into political theory. The liberal fails, according to the argument, to offer a suitable model, or picture, because it fails to depict a community. But what exactly is a community? Plato, who is one kind of communitarian, offered a detailed account of an ideal community but one which no contemporary philosopher is likely to take very seriously in its details. Rather, they have seemed all too often to take Lady Bracknell's[7] view that identity depends on family, and thus to try and flesh out the concept of community by appealing to the family as a model for social relations.[8] It is not always clear, however, just what an appeal to the family amounts to. For one thing, and this applies as much to the critics of communitarianism, it is not clear just what anyone means by 'the family'. The family that Lady

Bracknell requires before she can recognize Mr Worthing as a member of society is not one constructed by affective relations but by legal ones. The foundational relations of society for her are defined by marriage and the family relations which spring from that. Marriage is a contract, thus identity is arrived at through a properly sanctioned contract. The ideal family of communitarian thought cannot be of that form. Indeed, marriage as a contract may seem closer to a liberal conception than a communitarian one.

The family as community must consist not just in parents but grandparents, cousins, aunts, uncles, sisters, brothers and so on. Marriage is not the foundation of this community but blood relationships are. This conception of the family provides a rich network of relations of kinship within which people care for one another and which extends outwards to include relationships of kin which are based not on blood but upon association. There are, for example, honorary 'aunts' and 'uncles'. As one belongs to a family so, in much the same way, does one belong to a community. The crucial insight of communitarianism is that individuals do not choose to belong to communities any more than they choose to belong to families; these are what one is born into. The idea of choice, which necessitates the cumbersome apparatus of social contract, tacit consent, and all the rest of it, simply makes no sense here. The demands which each makes upon the other are not seen as demands at all but as occasions for giving. Once the members of a family see their relationships in terms of rights then the relationship of family has already broken down. In divorce, where it is appropriate to speak of the rights of the parties, this is an indication that one kind of relationship has failed and has to be replaced by a quite different one.

Now it cannot have escaped the notice of the communitarian philosopher, as it certainly has not her many vociferous critics, that this picture of the extended family, consisting of the complex network of affective relations, does not necessarily describe families as we experience them. Much can be made of the ways in which parents in particular may treat children badly, but the point of the picture is that it portrays a kind of relationship informed by values which provide the grounds for the judgments we make of actual families. When parents abuse children, when children neglect elderly parents – treat them cruelly as they sometimes do – these are grounds for criticism of a particular kind. The criticism is not that they have failed to recognize the rights which parents or children have but that they did not care enough, or care in the right way. If those who neglect their parents say that nothing is owed to parents, or that the duties have been discharged long ago, the response must be not 'That's all right then' but that they do not understand the criticism.

This conception of the family is an ideal one – just as the society of free, rational choosers is an ideal one. No one is ever that rational; no one ever has that clear a grasp of what constitutes their interests. Ideals may be striven for, not necessarily ever achieved. The question is: 'to which ideals shall we aspire'?

The problem for the communitarian ideal then, as for the liberal one, is not whether we can achieve it but whether it is coherent, whether it makes sense and how far it embodies those values which we think are important. Thus if the criticism from feminist writers is that communitarianism bolsters a defective institution, one which is patriarchally oppressive of women, it has to be shown that this is built into the very concept of the family, not merely that the family as it happens to function is so. The conception of the family given above does not seem to be susceptible to this criticism, i.e. it is no more obviously patriarchal than matriarchal, which is not to say that it is not susceptible to any criticism at all. The version of communitarianism which concerns me here does not say that community consists in nothing but families, or that the family is the foundation of community. Rather the idea is that we can read the values of family into the wider community. We may thus think of it as being like the family in respect of the values which underpin it, and in terms of which we should see ourselves as connected to one another as citizens. This vision, I shall suggest, is no more plausible now than when Socrates appeared to argue something of the kind in the *Crito*.

One response to the family ideal is that the network of relationships which provide a background of security and comfort, and which feel like a warm embrace to some, will suggest to others tentacles which choke and repress leaving no room for development and change in the individual. Whilst the family model recognizes the interdependence of individuals and the necessity of nurturing bonds for the development of the self, it leaves little room for the idea that we must grow up and leave home. All that a person is is given over to the family, it is where one's self begins and ends. In this community there are no strangers: everyone belongs, and there can be none of the excitement of discovery which we experience when we meet strangers.

These reservations involve a misunderstanding of the conception of family which is in play here. Whilst it is true that there are no strangers, it is not true that every relationship of a familial kind is a close one. The whole point about the picture sketched, no doubt rather roughly, here is that it includes the distant cousin along with the parents and siblings with whom I grow up. My relationship with those siblings may become less close and the one with the distant cousin may become closer. Change comes about by the fact that new members enter the family through marriage and other kinds of association. Relationships change as people grow older; family life is not static. Furthermore, a respect for another's privacy, a sense of when to leave well alone, is one of the ways in which members of a family show their concern and regard for one another. The idea that love and affection attempt to devour their objects was an idea much paraded by Sartre: but it is no coincidence, I suggest, that these ideas were worked out though characters so self-absorbed and etiolated that is it difficult to see how even their own mothers could have loved them.

The problem for the family model lies elsewhere, in its projection onto the larger society. Any model of community will require projection: we need to know how the pattern of relationship exhibited in the model is to map onto society as a whole; and thought the fit might not be perfect, sufficient points of contact are necessary.

In two respects, however, the projection of the family model is problematic. First, even if (which is anyway hardly plausible) the wider community consists solely of families, we could need some explanation of how the families are related to, and deal with, one another – an explanation which the family model itself does not seem to provide. Second, some people, like the unfortunate Mr Worthing, do not have families in any ordinary sense; and families cannot, pace Lady Bracknell simply be acquired.

Perhaps, however, the idea is that the wider community itself is in some sense to be seen as a family. The European family, for instance, living in the European home? Encouraging though the idea of a 'common European home' is, as a piece of rhetoric now replacing the old political rhetoric of the 'Cold War' period in European history, it still does not help much in filling out the communitarian ideal. How am I to understand my relation to the elderly women whom I occasionally meet or who are my neighbours?[9] Am I to see these women as like my mother? Do I stand to them as I stand to aunts or to grandmothers? What is noticeable here is that it does not seem very plausible to suggest that my relation to them is one of *sisterhood* . The trouble with the family is that it is a community with a hierarchical structure; one that is most obviously exhibited in the relationship between parents and children. This hierarchy continues, in a modified way, into adulthood. The family is not a community within which ideas of equality have a natural home. Read this back onto the political community and we may have exactly the opposite of the 'worst excesses of the French Revolution' (Wilde, 1948): the suffocating paternalism of the monarchy. It is not for nothing that the Czars were called 'Little Father'.

Alternatively, members of a community which has a shared religious background may see themselves as a family, as all God's children, and in that sense all equal. This may make internal sense, but communitarian theories are more usually concerned with secular society.

A communitarian might respond to this by rejecting equality as a value and with it ideals of a roughly democratic kind, as Plato did, though presumably without the metaphysics which allowed for the Philosopher King. My concern here, however, is with a communitarian response which *does* accept the democratic ideal and with it some notion of equality and some concern with liberty. The point of the exercise is to provide a reinterpretation of such values, not simply to deny them.

The return to Aristotelianism which is noticeable in some of the communitarian arguments (MacIntyre, 1981) might indicate that we should look to Aristotle for a suitable human relationship on which to construct the ideal picture. Aristotle, unusually amongst philosophers, gave particular emphasis to friendship as a necessary component of human flourishing; friendship is placed above justice and, according to the quotation with which I started, friendship should inform justice itself. Will friendship do the trick for the communitarian?

Most commentators on Aristotle's account of friendship note that *philia* seems to cover a wider range of cases than we include under 'friendship'.

> Its field covers not just the (more or less) intimate relationships between persons not bound together by near family ties, to which the words used in modern languages to translate it are ordinarily restricted, but all sorts of family relationships (especially those of parents to children, children to parents, siblings to one another, and the marriage relationship itself); the word also has a natural and ordinary use to characterize what goes in English under the somewhat quaint-sounding name of 'civic friendship' (Cooper, 1980, p. 302).

The very broadness of this concept may be just what the communitarian needs; it will enable her to spell out a conception of a relationship which avoids the restrictiveness that was seen to be a fault in the family model. It is worth noting, moreover, that although we may not take the familial relationship to be straightforwardly reducible to friendship, it is by no means unusual for people to speak of coming to see their parents as friends, and to count themselves as lucky in having been able to develop their relationship in that way.[10] Our 'ordinary' notion of friendship is, then, broader than the supposed contrast with the Aristotelian notion suggests; and the communitarian need then have no fears about foisting an alien concept upon us. Moreover, friendship is not simply an individualistic relation of a one-to-one kind since friendship may take a group form. It is important too for the communitarian, that, as Cooper points out, whilst Aristotle does not argue that there could not be completely self-sufficient individuals for whom friendship is not a necessity, such individuals would not be *human* individuals. For us friendship forms a part of our nature and is related to the development of the self.

However, there is a problem for friendship as the communitarian model for a community. Are we to imagine that a community is made up of groups of friends? This is the problem of projection which I raised earlier in connection with the family model. However one looks at it, friendships are relationships which include some and exclude others. How are we to understand the connections between the groups, and what about those who do not fall into any group? It is all very well to speak of group friendship where one is speaking of small communities united by shared interests and geography, where the values are shared by all the members by virtue of their membership of the group: but how is it possible to read this back onto large industrialized societies? Is communitarianism only possible if one envisages a small scale community? One of the important claims of justice and rights is that they apply to everyone; is it *really* possible for me to be a friend to everyone? Such an idea may seem to make no sense. At first sight it is difficult to see how my relationship with the shopkeeper could be described as one of friendship. If one thinks of something like a village shop where the shopkeeper sees herself as providing a service for the benefit of the community as much as being in the business of making a profit, the idea of friendship might begin to gain some purchase. But, again, this depends upon the idea of small scale communities. How am I to understand my relationship to the person at the check-out in Tesco as one of friendship? Does it make *any* sense to claim that this person is my friend? Surely my contact with the check-out person is far too impersonal to bear even a remote resemblance to friendship.

The charge here against the communitarian is not that the whole ideal is just impractical – the same might be said of the liberal ideal of a just society. It is rather that it is unintelligible. Friendship, however circumscribed by context, is still a *personal* relationship, and as such it just cannot fit into many of the transactions and dealings which we have with others. This the communitarian may concede; it does not follow, though, that these more impersonal relationships cannot be accounted for by an extension of the ideal. I may not be able to claim the check-out person, or the income tax inspector, as a friend; but the values of friendship, a concern for the 'weal and woe' of these others, can still be a central part of my dealings with them. We may each conduct ourselves in the spirit of *friendliness* towards one another. What this comes to will be shown in my attitude and behaviour towards the others but its the form will be structured by those values of commitment, mutuality and equality which are central to friendship. Part of that might even be a matter of being concerned that he be treated justly. This is a concern for the 'weal and woe' of another without which the claim of justice will make no sense. The point of Aristotle's remark with which I began is that friendship and friendliness are prior to justice.

All the same, we might wonder whether friendliness, this concern for the 'weal and woe' of another, amounts to anything more than that disinterested regard for the rights of others which, the liberal might argue, is part of her ideal too. The best way to answer this question would be with an extensive case by case consideration of a wide range of examples (a task I do not have space to embark on here).

However, it still may be objected that this communitarian ideal has at its foundation affections, emotions, likings which are transient and which thus render the relationships unstable. The idea that affective relations are unstable has been the stuff of philosophy ever since Plato, and reached its apotheosis in Kant. Others have argued consistently against this characterization (e.g. Blum, 1980). In any case, the communitarian ideal is not of a regard for the 'weal and woe' of others which merely consists in having feelings of affection. A group of philosophical friends, need not regard their concern for one another as affection at all. Their concern is given in what they do and how they respond to one another. There is no reason why this should be particularly unstable.

Aristotle claims that where there is friendship, there is no need for justice. I have tried to sketch an account of an ideal community based on the ideal of friendship and friendliness which if extended would fill out a way in which equality and fraternity can be linked to one another. What of liberty? If we think of liberty as freedom from oppression and the possibility of flourishing as a human being should, we can see that friendship encompasses this value too: friends do not oppress one another, and friendship is a part of our human flourishing. Friends do not see their relation to *one another* in terms of justice and rights, but they may need to see each others' 'weal and woe', with respect to *others* in this way, in particular in relation to the state. Where friendship breaks down, or where it never existed, then justice and rights will come in. In other words we may see these values not as part of the ideal, but as a fall-back where the ideal fails. This is the position offered by Waldron. It is important, however, to be clear, as I think Waldron is not, that friendship and justice are not just part of the same neutral conception of the ideal. It is not that where friendship fails then justice is a different way of achieving the same thing. Where friendship fails then something lost, it is replaced by justice. Simone Weil's example of the father playing with his child 'not out of a sense of duty but out of pure joy and pleasure' (Winch, 1972, p. 181) will serve to illustrate this point. If a parent simply does not regard their child with affection but acts only from a sense of duty (some parents, of course, are able to do neither of these), then we surely regard this relationship between parent and child as lacking, indeed we may regard it with horror. Duty may be the best the parent can offer: but it is not the best there is; nor is it just a different path to the same end. A similar argument applies to friendship.

Friendships of both the individual and the communal kind survive and endure, even unto death. Sustaining a community of friends may not be easy, but one should resist the temptation to move from the claim that something is difficult to the claim that it somehow makes no sense. Still, although friendship unto death may not be absurd, it is probably not the sort of thing one would be wise to bet on. However, ideals are not what one bets on, but what one tries to live up to. My suggestion is that the ideal of a community of friends is an ideal which makes sense, and an aspiration which the communitarian can claim is worth the candle.

Notes

1   Attributed to Margaret Thatcher in an interview in *Woman's Own* magazine, September 1987.
2   I do not here suppose that any such complex thought is actually attributable to Margaret Thatcher as an aspect of her conscious processes. My points will hold even on the assumption that she entertained no thoughts at all.
3   Since a great deal of the initial communitarian arguments were directed at Rawls' version of liberalism I shall continue to take Rawls as a suitable representative of what is in fact a broad church. Just as there are several different views collectively dubbed 'communitarian' so too are there varieties of liberalism. As far as my argument goes here the differences are less significant than the similarities.
4   An important discussion of this distinction as it figures in communitarian thinking is to be found in Taylor, 1989b.
5   The argument that liberal rights are a fall-back when affective relations break down illustrates this point, cf. Waldron, 1988.
6   I say this because it appears that the Rawlsian self has no gender and that, as every feminist knows, is a hard trick to pull off if you are an embodied human being
7   Lady Bracknell: 'I would strongly advise you, Mr Worthing, to try and acquire some relations as soon as possible, and a definite effort to produce at any rate at least one parent of either sex, before the season is quite over ... You can hardly imagine that I and Lord Bracknell

would dream of allowing our daughter – a girl brought up with the utmost care – to marry into a cloakroom and form an alliance with a parcel ...' (Wilde, 1948, p. 333)

8 E.g. Sandel, 1982 seems, at any rate, to take such a position.

9 Being a neighbour is another kind of relation which communitarians might make more use of, but that too would need further exploration. My discussion of friendship below will be connected to this issue.

10 One might wish to go further and say that where the bond between parents and children does not develop in this way this is a kind of failure.

Bibliography

Aristotle (1984), *Nicomachean Ethics*, revised Oxford translation, Barnes, J (ed.), Bollingen Series LXXXI, Princeton University Press: New Jersey.

Blum, L. (1980), *Friendship, Altruism and Morality*, Routledge and Kegan Paul: London.

Cooper, J.M. (1980), 'Aristotle on Friendship' in Rorty, A.O. (ed.), *Essays on Aristotle's Ethics*, University of California Press: California.

MacIntyre, A. (1981), *After Virtue*, Duckworth: London.

Sandel, M. (1982), *Liberalism and the Limits of Justice*, Cambridge University Press: Cambridge.

Taylor, C. (1989a), *Sources of the Self*, Cambridge University Press: Cambridge.

Taylor, C. (1989b), 'Cross Purposes: The Liberal-Communitarian Debate' in Rosenblum, N.L. (ed.), *Liberalism and the Moral Life*, Harvard University Press: Boston.

Waldron, J. (1988), 'When Justice Replaces Affection : The Need for Rights', *Harvard Journal of Law and Policy*, 11, pp. 625–47.

Wilde, O. (1948), 'The Importance of Being Earnest' in *The Works of Oscar Wilde*, Collins: London.

Winch, P. (1972), *Ethics and Action*, Routledge and Kegan Paul: London.

13 Doing Justice to Particulars
SCOTT VEITCH

There is a complex relation and important difference between ignorance and injustice. Contrarily, there is an important difference between knowing the truth and being just. That we cannot know everything does not mean we give up on justice. Neither does it mean there is something unknowable about the core of being just. To assert otherwise is to confuse questions of epistemology with those of justice. When contemporary theorists, reacting against the perceived failure of the universalisms of modern justice, display the temptation to see the moment of decision – originary, or right now – as the key to an analysis of justice, they arguably fall into this error. Whether through the form of a particularity void or an aporia, the question of doing justice to the particular (or to the other, or to difference) has emerged as the key focus of much postmodern critical theory. Yet concentrating on this as a matter of knowledge fails to make enough of the distinction between epistemology and justice.

The argument of this paper is that such theorizing loses sight of the *locations* of decisions, shifting its gaze mistakenly away from these locations – and the contestations surrounding their construction – to the detriment of an analysis of justice. In doing so it exalts the issue of ignorance to the level of the mystical, confusing aspects of time, perspective, and theory. The problem identified here is with treating the link between the universal and the particular from within as the central concern of analysis. This view cannot be correct, it will be argued, since the justice of *that* connection can only be gauged from a position *external* to it. And to accept this requires that questions of justice be concerned with contexts and criteria rather than exclusively with the particular and the decision. In the end, it may be that the singularity of the particular is not the prime concern. In a sense that will emerge it may not even exist. It may be, as Simmonds (1993, p. 65) carefully suggests, that 'the absolute particular is itself an abstraction, indeed it is the most abstract of all abstractions'. As questions of justice, the more important issues then are the level of abstraction and degree of closeness of supervision of the application of the rule, as well as the justness of the context of the decision: the need to focus not merely on the decision itself, but its setting. In the matter of doing justice to particulars, it is, it will be argued, the process and context, which count.

The paper begins by introducing Derrida's reading of justice and raising some problems with it along the lines just suggested. It then turns to an example – mercy – to explore further the difficulties with theorizing of this type. Here the work of Michael Detmold and N.E. Simmonds will be drawn on insofar as they have both considered mercy in terms of the issue of particularity.

Justice and Alterity

If justice is concerned with or involved in the relation to the other, then the perceived difficulty here is, as I have suggested, not one that is a result of an impossible duty to the particularity of the other; *not* a failure to perform the impossibility of a justice which 'always addresses itself to singularity, to the singularity of the other, despite or even because it pretends to universality' (Derrida, 1992, p. 20).[1]

The singularity is the postulate of the Derridean analysis of justice. It is that which, in a sense, cannot be done justice to since the singularity (or the other or the event) can only be grasped and known by a law or language in and through which it is reclassified as other than it was. Justice, for Derrida, is the impossible but irresistible attempt to treat or address that event on its own terms. The event is not in itself justice: '[t]his undecidability "before the law" is not *necessarily* (necessary) justice. It is an absolute alterity which is, precisely, undecidable, unknowable before the application of a rule, a norm, a value or a decision which would determine it as justice, or otherwise' (Perrin, 1996, p. 82).

It is this opening application which grasps the other and which, from the need initially to have decided or understood, carries with it a trace of the undecidable. 'The undecidable remains caught, lodged, at least as a ghost – but an essential ghost – in every decision, in every event of decision' (p. 24). The justice of this decision or founding moment exists as an impossibility, as an event neither with nor without justice, but only perceivable as justice when it is too late; when it is no longer at that moment since the 'proper moment if there is one [is] both regulated and without regulation' (p. 23). It exists as or in the incommunicable gap between being and being known, between the being of alterity and the being now known of that once other. It is this impossibility that is carried as a trace from the ultimate unfoundability of the founding moment or the decision onwards: '[e]ach case is other, each decision is different and requires an absolutely unique interpretation, which no existing, coded rule can or ought to guarantee absolutely' (p. 23).

Yet 'justice' – 'infinite, incalculable, rebellious to rule and foreign to symmetry, heterogenous and heterotropic' (p. 22) – also requires law. A decision must be regulated too, Derrida says, in order that it be 'just and responsible ... [This] freedom or this decision of the just, if it is one, must follow a law or a prescription or a rule' (p. 23). While the statement that each decision requires the creation of a new norm – a 'fresh judgment' – has an antecedent in Kelsen, this last sentence shows its antecedents in Kant: freedom is required for responsibility, though freedom is not unconstrained activity. Derrida is arguing against machine-like rule application, against a justice as arithmetic. This has no exercise of discretion, no freedom, no responsibility. Similarly, he is saying, an unfettered decision is arbitrary, follows no rule and is, potentially, mindless.[2] Thus justice requires law, but law cannot simply 'be just': 'justice exceeds law and calculation ... the unpresentable exceeds the determinable' (p. 28).

Let us accept this. Consider, however an example that makes – literally – a mockery of the implications of this position. It comes from Rabelais' imagining a discussion about his character Bridlegoose analysing the benefits of dice-throwing as a way of deciding a law case.

Epistemon gives a story of a hard case:

> [o]n the one side it was an execrable crime. A woman had killed her second husband and her second son. On the other hand, the reasons for the murder seemed to him so natural and to be, as it were, founded on natural law, seeing that together they had murdered her elder son ....

Now, says Epistemon,

> [i]f a man had settled that case by a throw of the dice he wouldn't have been far wrong whichever way they had fallen; if it had gone against the woman, she would have deserved her punishment since she had herself taken the revenge which by right belonged to justice; if it had gone in the woman's favour, the terrible grief would have seemed an excuse for her deed (Rabelais, 1955, Bk 3, ch. 44).

Rabelais' Pantagruel says of this method that,

> Bridlegoose would commend himself to God, the just Judge, invoke the aid of the divine grace, and put himself under the guidance of the most Holy Spirit.

Thus, avoiding the dangers and perplexities of a definite decision, he would by throwing of the dice discover the divine will and pleasure, which we call the final judgement. The said intelligences would then move and turn the dice to fall in favour of the party who, having a just case, would have a fair claim to seeing his rights maintained ... when human beings are anxious and in doubt, only this way can the divine will be manifested (ibid.)

Here, I suggest, the 'divine will' marks the gap, is the name of the gap; in Derrida's terms, the aporia. For Bridlegoose each unique interpretation is one 'no existing code or rule can or ought to guarantee absolutely' (*supra*). Yet the interpretation is not random; it is guaranteed by that which escapes human cognition: in Rabelais' terms, 'God, the just Judge'; in Derrida's, the 'unpresentable', (tellingly) 'another sort of mystique', (imperially) 'the very movement of deconstruction at work[!]' (p. 25). If the 'mystique' for Derrida is not necessarily Augustinian – justice is not of this world – it is at least structurally similar to that discernable through Rabelais' dice-throwing judge. For when Derrida says, 'Justice is an experience of the impossible ... it requires us to calculate with the incalculable' (p. 16), then this is no different from playing with dice. The mystical aporia is the other name for God's will. Positive (posited) law cannot guarantee justice, nor – it is said – should it. This would be to assume as much knowledge as the divine, to know God's mind. But this is impossible, for then we would not be dealing with God, would not be dealing with the other. Besides, in its Promethean human impertinence to think one could have such knowledge, this arrogance would destroy the very mystique of life.

But note, in both cases – religious and 'secular' – the postulate has to be there: God, the other, the singularity. The singularity, the event, absolute alterity, cannot – dare not – be known as such. It can only be a postulate. But why does it have to be postulated? And what reasons might exist for postulating it? In the alternative, if it is not a postulate, is it somehow a real existence? Assuming not, and letting these questions run for the moment, consider two by-products of beginning from this point. First, that justice is other, or involved in the other focuses attention on the decision or event to the exclusion of proper consideration of the frameworks within which decisions must be made and within which conflicts become constructed. Ironically the effect of this is the apparent inability to avoid a co-postulate: (disappointed) realism. Second, it misleadingly forces us back to mythic origins as the source of the trace in the undecidable, and thus diverts attention from the ongoing nature of negotiation as well as the disparate locations of power. To see 'origins' as the crux of justice is an unjustified luxury, for much the same reasons that social contract theorists are continually criticized.

To return to the first point. The *context* within which the 'incalculable' is deemed to exist is surely paramount. While tossing a coin may be a good way to decide which team starts a game of football, it is not, we would imagine, and for sound reasons, a good way to decide liability in a court case. The aporia in any given situation will be breached, yet this alone cannot tell us anything of the justice of the matter. When Bridlegoose suggests throwing the dice would make little difference, this is especially so, he suggests, in a close decision. But what makes a decision close – conventionally, what makes something a hard case – cannot be any intrinsic closeness of the decision, nor the inevitable existence of an aporia. It is the construction of the problem. Indeed, often the biggest difficulty for at least one of the parties in a law suit is in getting a case perceived to be close at all. As such, the inevitable existence of the aporia cannot tell us anything further about the justice of the decision. In Derrida's analysis the fact of application of (whatever) law or language to the postulated other will be the same *regardless* of what we may think about the justice of the norms applied. For the former is a point about knowing or grasping the other, yet the question of justice is not answered without due consideration of *criteria*, and this is ignored by the Derridean analysis insofar as the interplay of law and the other in the decision becomes the central concern. (We get a hint of the truth of this in the fact that the relation to the singularity must come from 'the application of a rule, a norm, a value or a decision' (*supra*). But what is the justice of *these* rules, norms, etc.?) So we might get to the stage of a hard case for reasons, but we get there for reasons all the same and what these reasons are is of the utmost importance as a matter of justificatory practice. Moreover, that they are reasons at all, means the process comes with claims to criteria, to argument, to reasoning, not the lack of it (the gap). ·

Focus on the ultimate undecidability or unfoundability of the decision will tend to the overstated or the spurious. We do not need to postulate the God or the gap or the gap as God just because we are ultimately in all details ignorant. *A fortiori*, we do not need to postulate this at the centre of a theory of justice. If calculating with the incalculable is the demand of justice, so much more important to know *why* calculations are going on *at all*, what they mean, and to whom, rather than focusing on the problems of the mystical or infinite, which are – no doubt – fine and well but fail to address the present political conditions for the exercise of a more secularized justice, a justice that has to concentrate on far more than the single event.

Consider a little closer now the issue of the justice of the judgment. While doing justice to the postulated singularity inevitably involves the application of the law, there are different degrees of closeness of application in any given situation; moreover, a rule can be more or less precise in its demands or expectations. Importantly, the justice or injustice of the rule's application cannot be ascertained from a study of the relation between the universal (law) and the singularity (other). In a sense, the *relation* is the same for any rule, just or unjust. What would make the application unjust, therefore, must be perceivable only from a point of view *external* to this relation itself. For example: if we take the rule 'Kill no living being' we might subsume any amount of 'particulars' under this; adults, children, sheep, cows, trees, etc. To determine whether or not it is just to subsume one group (humans, say) rather than another (cows, trees) cannot be ascertained from the process of subsumption alone. We could easily subsume any group. What makes the application just therefore is a matter of the strength of the 'interpretive commitment' within which we make sense of the rule in its setting. And this commitment comes less from doing justice to the singularity (in fact as a historical matter in post-privilege [*prive lege*] legal reasoning it is usually a group anyway) than the justice of the (contested) narratives within which that commitment is understood.[3] That is, in the very construction of the issues at stake, their possible consequences, and the ideals which inform an understanding of all these. Besides, this cannot be separated from a point I made a moment ago about the justice of the norm itself. A judge in Apartheid South Africa, for example, may have conscientiously applied a discriminatory rule but the 'justice' of the judgment cannot be ascertained from the process of subsumption alone; that is, from the application which produces the decision. We assume here that the injustice of the Apartheid régime lay less in the problematic of rule-application than in the fact that commonality (not singularity) was drawn at the wrong level in the creation of the rule itself: common humanity rather than colour of skin should count as the relevant commonality, we might think. Once again, in other words, the elusive, mystical, nature of justice may have more humble lodgings in the light of injustices than Derrida's analysis suggests.

Despite this we are told that deconstruction seeks not to shirk from political activity:

> that justice exceeds law and calculation, that the unpresentable exceeds the determinable cannot and should not serve as an alibi for staying out of juridico-political battles, within an institution or a state or between institutions or states and others ... incalculable justice *requires* us to calculate (p. 28).

But this in itself says no more than what Stanley Fish says over and over again: do what comes naturally, there's nothing else to do. When Derrida does push the argument further, it sees him return futilely to the mythic violence of origins in the social contract sense, an analysis so finely demolished by David Hume in the eighteenth century.

Hume's two main criticisms of social contract were the following. First, how do we create from scratch social obligations through a contract when the institution of promising requires the idea of social obligations in the first place? Second, if there are good reasons for creating social obligations then these will hold regardless of whether there is a contract or not. Hume rightly draws attention away from origins to a historically situated – albeit for Hume conservative – justice of the ongoing. For there is no real beginning; the violence of the injustice cannot begin, but is always already there. Beginnings-talk begs the question. Of course Derrida agrees. But what are we to make of it? I suggest that thoughts must be not of origins, mythical or otherwise, but of the ongoing negotiations around the *construction of commonality*.

But significantly, such construction depends on access to the control of the mediums of communication, as much as directly being able to speak in this idiom. It is not so much the speech, as the *speaking*. The question of justice cannot be addressed without attention to this dimension. As far as the singularity goes, we might come to think that the crucial question concerns this: how to agree to disagree. But then this is a question about agreement, about criteria, and about commitment to commonalities, at least at some level. And the issues of importance lie less in repeating this than in acting; acting that is, with a view to doing justice to commonalities, not postulated singularities. As such an impossible but irresistible attempt to know the other mis-locates the prime concerns of justice, even though – and this is the irony as well as the perceived conservatism of deconstruction – they will be being addressed elsewhere.

One other point should be made in passing. The tradition of universal-particular as the dilemma-producing dualism is effectively repeated here. It itself is not problematized. Different senses of the concrete or particular are not explored, merely made uniform. The inductive method of reasoning is neglected, as is the context of reasonings. The Kantian universalism-hangover from which – by association of critique – the deconstructionist dare not escape, remains. In the understated theory-building going on language and law are conflated in their manifestations and presuppositions, the other is postulated and the mystical fetishized. Such an analysis leaves aside gradations of power and comparative locations of injustice; for it looks in the wrong places.

The Place of Criteria: An Example – Mercy

Nigel Simmonds (1993) argues the inadequacy of treating the exercise of mercy as taking place in the gap between particular and general.[4] The most significant feature of his analysis is the prominence he gives to the context of judgment, and, through this, the important insight into the problematic nature of postulating the exercise of mercy as fidelity to the unique particular. On such a view, he says, mercy asserts the importance of particularity over and against the abstract universality of justice and law (ibid., p. 59). This latter notion he finds improbable in one sense, although, significantly, not in another. The flaw in the setting of the problem in the commonly-suggested way is the wrong postulating of the unique particular at all. How could we know the unique particular, he asks, except through 'the mediation of concepts. There is therefore no unique particularity which could escape the general categories of thought' (ibid., p. 64).[5]

Simmonds thus appears strongly to reject the postulation of the particular or singularity as existing in itself. In order to do so he makes an important point, albeit one not usually drawn out and one which introduces, for us, the relevance of perspective in the current context. For, he continues, '[s]ince a "total" description of any concrete situation is impossible and inconceivable, *all descriptions must be more or less abstract*' (ibid., p. 61, emphasis added). This is a different point from the one Derrida has made. In refusing to endorse the existence of the particular as such he sees the construction of it as a matter of relations between relative ('more or less') abstracts. The important point here is that there are *degrees* of abstraction, rather than *the* abstract (as opposed to *the* particular or *the* concrete). The particular does not have to be postulated here since any particular can exist only within a context of *relative* abstracts, and it is particular only for a specified context rather than particular in itself. There is thus no possibility of an unknowable 'before the law'. Particulars are constructed within contexts and what changes as regards the description of particulars is the context. It is in this sense that one cannot be faithful to the particular (or 'do justice to the particular' or, in Derrida's terms to 'the singularity of the other') in itself because the particular as such does not exist.[6]

What then does Simmonds mean when he says 'a "total" description of any concrete situation is impossible and inconceivable'? The impossibility lies not in the adequacy of an understanding of any particular (*adequate to what?*, we could ask), but that the amount of possible descriptions can never be finalized. And here is the crux of the matter: there is a difference between the inevitable ignorance of all possible descriptions, and the adequacy of doing justice to a particular *according to* the values or rules or standards involved. The former is a point about descriptive possibilities; the latter concerns the attempt at justice. There may be a confusion sometimes made here between the two in what may seem an intermediate or more involved ignorance. For example, one can, say, be a good friend or a poor friend (or spouse or lawyer or whatever). But this state does not rely whatsoever on the relevance of the fact that we do not know what being that good friend means in any or all possible situations. Our ignorance of this tells us nothing about what it means to be a good friend. (We might suggest here that this can only be a matter of intersubjective evaluation. For as Wittgenstein put it in another context (1989, s.202, on rule-following)– *thinking* one was a good friend is not the same as *being* a good friend (or spouse or lawyer or whatever). Being that good 'whatever', or, I suggest, being *just*, concerns the validity of the criteria of evaluation involved, and does not emerge either from the existence of the other as other, nor from the existence of descriptive ignorances.[7] Yet the postulated relation between universal and particular cannot fully grasp the degrees of norms and normative contestation which exist across the spectrum of activities (friendship, marriage, lawyering) within which it is possible to be just or unjust. For as I have said before, that *relation*, when put in terms of universal-particular, is the same, and so cannot develop our analysis of justice in the matter.

Let us come to our example and consider two interpretations. The first is given by Professor Detmold in his discussion of the particularity void. There exist, he says, particular situations, 'practical problem[s], which universal hypothetical (theoretical) reasoning does not solve. And the whole problem is that no reasoning can solve it. It is particular, about which nothing *c*an be said (anything I *say* will be universal)' (Detmold, 1989, p. 456). The example he gives of this 'moment of indecision' as he calls it, is a point in *War and Peace* where Pierre is brought before Davoût (suspected of being a spy) and is quoted as follows:

> Davoût looked up and gazed intently at him. For some seconds they looked at one another, and that look saved Pierre. Apart from conditions of law and war that look established human relations between the two men. At that moment an immense number of things passed dimly through their minds, and they realised they were both children of humanity and were brothers (ibid., p. 457).[8]

Now, of this, Detmold assesses 'I, the judge, and Davoût, at the moment of practicality entered the unanswering void of particularity, the realm of love, about which only mystical things can be said ...; or nothing' (ibid.).[9] Arguably, however, nothing could be further from the truth. In this case, the two know only minimally of each other. The silence – which is not of course silence but something that says so much, as a part of the language of *speaking* – in which the particularity void is thought to consist has its roots not in any particularity, or event or singularity, but on the contrary exists in the perceived possibility of one of the most abstract, if rarely felt, commonalities. For as Tolstoy (ibid.) continued, up till that point, 'Pierre had only been a case, and Davoût could have had him shot without burdening his conscience with an evil deed; but now he saw in him a human being. He reflected for a moment'. This is not, it would seem, 'the particular about which nothing can be said': mystical it may be, in a sense, but not at the level of the singularity. The striking aspect of this interchange is its sudden, unexpected (given the circumstances) flowering of a known commonality. It could be *anyone* there: friend or enemy, it does not matter; it is the similarity ('they realised they were both children of humanity') that counts, not the singularity.

Yet Detmold's response in nevertheless instructive. By his account, '... the void of reason (the *particularity* void as we called it) stood between this norm [execute Russian spies] and the particular Pierre' (ibid., p. 464, emphasis added) The issue this raises concentrates on the limits of reason, but, I suggest, not the limits of criteria for action, a point I will return to in a moment. For what is being exposed here is not a gap in reasoning as such but a shift in contexts within which Pierre's being there is understood. That is, a shift from the norms of war – where indeed Pierre was 'only a case' – to one of shared humanity – 'and now he saw in him a human being'; different conditions or contexts, in other words within which 'the particular Pierre' is being understood.[10] Again this is only perceivable when we see beyond the relation (universal-particular, norm-singularity) itself to the context within which the relation occurs.

The second example shows a progression from this apparent misreading, though one which does not in the end make enough of its own premises. N.E. Simmonds notes Detmold's comments from the above quoted article but says, however, that his (Detmold's) 'radical antithesis between generality and particularity is false and misconceived ... [It] fails to grasp the *dependence* of unique particularity on upon abstraction ...' (Simmonds, 1993, p. 62, fn. 28.) By this Simmonds is expanding on the argument we have already encountered. Since the very notion – the very expressibility – of the particular is in language, and since this works at the level of certain categorizations, the particular must be dependent on processes of abstraction. That is, it is always constructed to some varying degree. This does not, however, mean the same thing as what

Detmold just said as quoted above: 'anything I *say* will be universal'. For this is not true, in an important way. It is one thing to note that the world is mediated by the concepts and categories of language and thought; another that what is said is thereby universal. Language and thought clearly work at varyingly different levels of abstraction. When I refer to 'cats' I do refer to something very general (many, all cats). When I refer to 'my cat Donald' I do not. All naming does not work at the same level of abstraction. It is not therefore 'universals' of which language always talks. Indeed if it was, we would have very little need for interpretation as an activity.

Naming is in some ways similar to concepts and categories once the dynamic between particular and abstract is brought out. That dynamic, that *dependence*, as Simmonds rightly notes, is in the hinge between the most abstract and the most particular, and the linguistic referent changes place as, so to speak, this hinge opens and closes. Acts of interpretation are contested here as problems of inclusion, difference, analogy, specificity, subsumption, etc. In other words, the whole range of interpretative contestations informed by a variety of attributes and disparately located struggles.

Consider another example, which, interestingly, Simmonds also takes from the literature of war, this time from the work of George Orwell. Orwell had been a sniper in the Spanish Civil War when he saw an opposing soldier running along, trying to hold his trousers up with both hands. Orwell's description follows: 'I did not shoot because of that detail about the trousers. I had come here to shoot at "Fascists"; but a man holding up his trousers isn't a "Fascist"; he is visibly a fellow-creature, similar to yourself, and you don't feel like shooting him' (quoted ibid., p. 62). Here again, as with Tolstoy's scenario, we seem to be confronted not with an appeal to the particular, but to the level of generality: 'a fellow creature, *similar* to yourself'; a commonality, in other words, not a singularity. To the extent that Simmonds refuses to see the pure opposition between general and particular, it might be possible for him to agree with this. Yet in an important sense he does not. According to his interpretation, '[w]hat struck Orwell as relevant to his act of mercy could not have been some general fact about the situation ... Rather, what is important here is the extent to which *no* description of the situation seems fully to exhaust its reality' (ibid.).

This statement gets to the heart of our confusion. For Simmonds, there exists a gap between what one can know and say: 'between the project and the execution falls the realization that one's descriptive grasp of the situation approaches it from one aspect only, and therefore leaves an infinite amount unsaid' (ibid.). This seems true, no doubt. But, it would seem, precisely in the ambivalence between the detail and the generality in Orwell's situation lies the interesting facet of the dependency of the general and particular. As I have said, Simmonds points this out well. But, is this relation interesting in *its* so-called 'infinite' aspect vis-à-vis the *exercise* of mercy? 'You don't feel like shooting him,' says Orwell, astonishingly plainly (even for him). This thought and (in)action is as important a thought and action as is possible, both for Orwell and for the 'exposed Fascist' in their real lives. But as Orwell lowers his sights from the 'Fascist's' body, the decision has been made. And it has been made with criteria – this is a fellow creature, no less. It is not 'a moment of madness', but the appraisal of a situation in which the other is unknown as the other, yet is perceived as the same and his life is saved.[11] In this sense something can be said of it, though of course not everything (if even such transparency were desirable). Maybe then the problem is an aesthetic point; our description is more or less adequate not to 'the reality' of Orwell's actual exercise of mercy, but to the situation as it strikes us reading or writing it. If anything, what carries the artistic imagery in Orwell's description is the detail of the trousers. Its interpretation in prose and Orwell's action are separate matters. In good writing or in art there is the element of the mysterious, exposing us to something never fully to be grasped, yet something of which we might yet say 'Yes, that's it, that's exactly it!'. But to say that this mystery is at the heart of decision-making is to confuse positions of time and perspective. It is to confuse the position of writer or theorist with that of the actor deciding in a given situation.

Are there criteria for being merciful? Consider this: might it be 'out of place' to be merciful? One could read Douglas Hay's (1975) critique of the workings of the eighteenth century criminal law precisely as a critique of mercy misplaced. Mercy was used, he says, as one of a number of more or less deliberate strategies to keep the lower orders in their place. What greater power could a ruling class have than the power to sentence to and then reprieve from death, an 'attribute to God himself'? But it is important why this is out of place from our point of view. Our main reason perhaps would be that this is no way to run a criminal justice system. It ought, we would expect, to be based on sound procedure, reasonable methods of proof and clear findings of guilt. Here then the context of the exercise of mercy is significant. It suggests that mercy may be used instrumentally.[12] It may also hint, however, at the possibility of there existing criteria for the exercise of mercy, some with which we would agree, and some disagree. But again the context is the thing. The fact that we might think that 'keeping people in their place' was not a reasonable exercise of mercy, would suggest we think there *do* exist times and situations where mercy would be justifiable. (Again, not everything may be known entirely, but then that point is becoming trite.)

To suggest that the gap – the particularity void or aporia – is the key to understanding (or failing to understand) the exercise of mercy neglects to take these points into account. The *justifiable* use of mercy depends less on the particular decision, but on the criteria that are used. There are different perspectives from which to see this. One comes from the point of view of the person who seeks mercy. To what are they appealing if not something: an argument, strategy, emotion, state of mind, situation, etc.? That is, there may be reasons why mercy should be granted, and the fact that we (from a descriptive perspective) cannot predict or table them in a formulaic sense does not mean that they exist as non-criteria. Likewise from the perspective of the person who grants mercy. They may not have to produce their reasons in the form we would expect of a legal judgment, say, but to suggest there are no reasons at all (that their grant of mercy is no more than whim) fails to capture the subtlety of conditions in which mercy might be thought appropriate. (In fact we could see the use of immunity from prosecution in the Truth and Reconciliation Commission in South Africa as merely one such instance.) Here again the context of judgment in the particular case is crucial.

What then does this say about our broader concerns? Here are three related conclusions. First, and ironically from the deconstructionists' position, there is a curious privileging of reason. For the aporia to be exalted to the place of the mystical – as both Derrida and Detmold seem to do – -suggests that where strict reason cannot be found at work, all criteria for judgment go. This seems dangerously wrong, as the example from mercy shows. Such a position confuses, I suggest, the perspectives of theoretician and actors involved in the practice. Moreover, the response that decisions still need to be made under imperfect knowledge conditions is neither insightful nor original; as an issue of justice it tends if anything to the conservative. Second, treating law as universal and the other as particular or singularity endorses a positivist approach to law and legal reasoning and neglects to see that the legal form may justifiably be seen to be 'another other' rather than *the* universal.[13] In repeating this error, and in conflating law with language, such theorizing flattens or narrows the diverse range of linguistic, legal, and political practices within which both the meaning of law and language and the construction of 'particulars' takes place. Consequently, and finally, doing this leaves in place the postulated other as a real existence outside language rather than treating it as an already located within a set of practices. In singularizing the event it conflates the position of theorist with the position from which justice is sought or applied. But how the other is known is, as I have said, separable from the question of justice from the point of view of those involved in any activity. Indeed, insofar as there is seen to be only one way to know the other (the way in which Derrida describes the grasping the other through language) – to the extent, that is, that there is seen to be only *one way of knowing* – it has to be the case that this cannot tell us anything about the questions of justice.[14]

Notes

1 Page references in brackets in the text are to this article.
2 Cf. Harry Frankfurt on identity and the impossibility of the wholly unconstrained self, 1982, pp. 319–21.
3 The language here is borrowed from Cover, 1983.
4 The paradox of mercy is commonly in the form: 'Mercy seems to require a *departure* from justice, and therefore to require *injustice* … [As such] Mercy seems either to be reducible to justice or not to be a virtue (as itself being unjust)' (p. 53, original emphasis).
5 Referring in this instance to the notion of 'the concrete person', though the point being made is a general one.
6 Arguably the Derridean position is similar to Kant's dualism on this point. See *Critique of Pure Reason* (passim); also Kant acknowledges, in the realm of empirical knowledge, the existence of 'comparative universality' in much the same sense as I am using the notion of 'relative abstracts' in this paragraph (see ibid., p. 125).
7 One set of theories of justice does take ignorance as central to its mode of justification, that inspired by the libertarian economics of Hayek. It would be surprising if this was the line being pushed here by Derrida and others, although clarifying their differences would prove insightful.
8 Quoted from Leo Tolstoy, *War and Peace*, Book XII, Ch. X. (Cf. Rosemary Edmonds' (1982) translation: '… It went beyond the circumstances of war and the court-room, and established human relations between the two men. Both of them in that one instant were dimly aware of an infinite number of things …'.)
9 'Judges enter that realm every day (if only they knew)', Detmold adds. Note here the similarities with Derrida's analysis.
10 A point perhaps clearer in the Edmonds translation.
11 One is reminded here of one of the central tenets of the moral philosophy of Adam Smith (1976, I.i.I.10): 'Sympathy … does not arise so much from the view of the passion, as from that of the situation which excites it'.
12 For a reading of this in a contemporary context, see Kalt, 1996.
13 For further treatment of this point see my 'Law and "Other" Problems', 1997.
14 My thanks to Valerie Kerruish and Colin Perrin for all their discussions and their comments. Earlier versions of this chapter were delivered at the 1997 Annual Meeting of the UK Association for Legal and Social Philosophy in Edinburgh, and at the Faculty of Law, University of Adelaide; I would like to thank participants at both for their constructive criticisms. Thanks also to Emilios Christodoulidis and John Touchie for ongoing debate. Responsibility for the views expressed is mine alone.

Bibliography

Cover, R. (1983), 'Foreword: Nomos and Narrative', *Harvard Law Review*, 97, p. 7.

Derrida, J. (1992), 'Force of Law: The "Mystical Foundations of Authority"' in Cornell, D., Rosenfeld, M. and Gray Carson, D. (eds), *Deconstruction and the Possibility of Justice*, Routledge: New York.

Detmold, M.J. (1989), 'Law as Practical Reason', *Cambridge Law Journal*, 48, pp. 436–71.

Frankfurt, H. (1982), 'Comments on MacIntyre', *Synthese*, 53, pp. 319–21

Hay, D. (1975), 'Property, Authority and the Criminal Law' in Hay et al., *Albion's Fatal Tree*, Allen Lane: London.

Kalt, B.C. (1996), 'Pardon Me?: The Constitutional Case Against Presidential Self-Pardons', *Yale Law Journal*, 106, pp. 779–809.

Perrin, C. (1996), 'Breath from Nowhere: Justice and Community in the Event of Human Rights', PhD thesis, University of Kent.

Rabelais, F. (1955), *Gargantua and Pantagruel*, Penguin: London.

Simmonds, N.E. (1993), 'Judgment and Mercy', *Oxford Journal of Legal Studies*, pp. 52–68.

Smith, A. (1976), *Theory of Moral Sentiments*, Clarendon: Oxford.

Tolstoy, R. (1982), *War and Peace*, tr. R. Edmonds, Penguin: London.

Veitch, S. (1997), 'Law and "Other" Problems', *Law and Critique*, VIII/1, pp. 97–109.

Wittgenstein, L. (1989), *Philosophical Investigations* (2nd edn 1958), Basil Blackwell: Oxford.

Contributors

Mark Bovens is Professor of Legal Philosophy in the Faculty of Law at Utrecht University. He is author of *The Quest for Responsibility: Accountability and citizenship in complex organisations* (Cambridge University Press, 1998), co-author, with Paul 't Hart, of *Understanding Policy Fiascos* (Transaction, 1995) and has written and edited a number of books in Dutch in the fields of law, political theory and public administration.

Emilios A. Christodoulidis is a lecturer at the Centre for Law and Society of the Faculty of Law, University of Edinburgh and Visiting Professor of the European Academy of Legal Theory in Brussels. He teaches jurisprudence and sociology of Law. He is author of 'Law and Reflexive Politics' (Kluwer, 1998) and has written articles on legal reasoning, constitutionalism, systems theory, critical legal theory and the sociology of law.

Gerard Delanty is Senior Lecturer in sociology at the University of Liverpool, Visiting Professor of Sociology, York University, Ontario (1998) and editor of the new Sage journal, the European Journal of Social Theory. He is author of *Inventing Europe: Idea, Identity, Reality* (Macmillan, 1995), (with Patrick O'Mahoney) *Rethinking Irish History: Nationalism, Identity, Ideology* (Macmillan, 1998) and *Social Science: Beyond Constructivism and Realism* (Open University, 1997). His research interests are in social theory, the philosophy and sociology of science and political sociology. He is currently completing a book entitled *Conceptions of Modernity: Understanding Social Change* (Polity Press).

Avner de-Shalit was awarded a BA at the The Hebrew University and DPhil at Oxford University. He is Senior Lecturer at the Hebrew University of Jerusalem. He is the author of *Why Posterity Matters* (Routledge, 1995), co-editor of *Communitarianism and Individualism* (Oxford, 1992) and of *Liberalism and its Practice* (Routledge, 1998). He has now finished writing a book called The Environment: Between Theory and Practice.

Cecile Fabre completed her doctoral thesis at Oxford on the topic of constitutional social rights. As well as preparing her thesis for publication, she is currently working on theories of international distributive justice. Her publications include books reviews as well as an article on constitutional social rights for the *Journal of Political Philosophy* (forthcoming).

Paul Havemann is Professor of Law at the University of Waikato in New Zealand and has taught in the UK, Canada and Australia. His interests include criminology, human rights, comparative political jurisprudence, the rights of indigenous peoples and legal, social and political theory. His current research is focused on the question of life chances in the North and South, the limits of the law and scope for citizenship and social rights discourse to enhance life chances, in the context threats posed by dimensions of late modernity, globalization and the 'risk' society.

Elizabeth Kingdom is Senior Lecturer in the Department of Sociology, Social Policy and Social Work Studies at the University of Liverpool. Her research is on, first, the politics of rights discourse and, secondly, the legal recognition of cohabitation contracts. Her publications include 'Transforming Rights: feminist politics heuristics' in *Res Publica* (1996) and 'Cohabitation contracts and the private regulation of time' in *Time and Society* (1996).

Arto Laitinen was awarded an MA in Philosophy from the University of Kent at Canterbury in 1995. He is currently researching a project entitled 'Liberalism, Communitarianism and Democracy' at the University of Jyvaskylä, Finland. His publications include articles in Finnish on the moral philosophy of Charles Taylor and Paul Ricoeur: in addition he is editor of *Normatiivisuuden Lähteet*, a collection of articles concentrating on the sources of normativity and co-editor of *Yhteisö. Filosofian näkökulmia hyteisöllisyyteen*, a collection of articles focusing on the concept of community from a variety of philosophical perspectives.

Sandra E. Marshall is Head of the Philosophy Department, University of Stirling. She works in the overlapping areas of legal, social and moral philosophy. She is currently President of the UK Association for Legal and Social Philosophy.

Maurizio Passerin d'Entrèves is Senior Lecturer in Political Theory at the University of Manchester. He has published widely in the fields of critical social theory and political philosophy. He is the author of *Modernity, Justice, and Community* (1990), *The Political Philosophy of Hannah Arendt* (1994), co-editor of *Habermas and the Unfinished Project of Modernity* (1996) and *Public and Private: Legal, Political and Philosophical Perspectives* (1998) and is currently working on a book entitled *Democratic Deliberation*.

Burkhard Schäfer has studied logic, theoretical linguistics and law at the Universities of Mainz, Munich, Florence and Lancaster. He is currently Lecturer at the Centre for Law and Society, University of Edinburgh, and associate member of the Archelogos research project on philosophical expert systems. His main research interests are the use of formal methods in comparative law, mereology and formal ontology, and artificial societies and socio-legal simulation in the context of European integration. His publications include 'Inheritance Principles and the Community of Heirs' in N. Guarini (ed.), *Frontiers in Artificial Intelligence* (IOS Press, 1998) and 'Lesniewski-Quantifiers and Multi-Modal Arguments in Legal Discourse', *Logic and Logical Philosophy* (forthcoming).

Philip Selznick is Professor Emeritus of Law and Sociology, School of Law, University of California at Berkeley. Born in 1919 in Newark, New Jersey, USA, he received a PhD in sociology from Columbia University in 1947. Following military service during 1943–46 he taught at University of Minnesota and University of California at Los Angeles, joining the Berkeley faculty in 1952. He was chair of the Department of Sociology, 1964–68, and was founding chair of the Center for the Study of Law and Society, and of the Jurisprudence and Social Policy Program in the School of Law. His books include *TVA and the Grass Roots*, *Leadership in Administration, Law, Society, and Industrial Justice*, and *The Moral Commonwealth*. He was elected to the American Academy of Arts and Sciences in 1961, and received an honorary degree of Doctor of Jurisprudence from the University of Utrecht in 1986.

John Varty teaches sociology and school courses in the social sciences at the University of Sussex, where he is also undertaking doctoral research on Adam Ferguson and the idea of civil society in the Social and Political Thought graduate Programme.

Scott Veitch teaches jurisprudence and torts/legal history at Macquarie University in Sydney. He has published in the area of legal philosophy and is currently working on legal issues relating to mercy and reconciliation.